Harlem U.S.A.

Edited and with a new foreword
by

JOHN HENRIK CLARKE

A&B BOOKS PUBLISHERS
Brooklyn, New York
11201

The Macmillan Company
866 Third Avenue, New York, N.Y. 10022
Collier-Macmillan Canada Ltd., Toronto, Ontario

Harlem, U.S.A. was originally published by Seven
Seas Books, Berlin, D.D.R. This revised edition is
reprinted by arrangement.

Library of Congress Catalog Card Number:
72-151162

First Collier Books Edition 1971

Printed in the United States of America

> *To all the people in all the Harlems (black communities) of the world, this book about life, literature, and transition in the world's most famous ethnic ghetto.*

To the Bradley Library from John H. Clarke A product of the Columbus, Georgia Public Schools who grew to early manhood in this city.

Nov. 16, 1995

Blackmen say Goodbye to Misery	10.00
Education of the Negro	9.95
Heal Thyself	9.95
Heal Thyself Cookbook	9.95
Vaccines are Dangerous	9.95
Columbus and the African Holocaust	10.00
Columbus conspiracy	11.95
Dawn Voyage	11.95
Aids the End of Civilization	9.95
Gospel of Barnabas	8.95
African Discovery of America	10.00
Gerald Massey's Lectures	9.95
Historical Jesus and the Mythical Christ	9.95
First Council of Nice	9.95
Arab Invasion of Egypt	14.95
Anacalypsis (set)	40.00
Anacalypsis Vol. 1	25.00
Anacalypsis Vol. 11	20.00
Harlem Voices	11.95
Harlem U.S.A.	11.95
Lost Books of the Bible	9.95

Acknowledgments

The idea for *Harlem, U.S.A.* was developed from a special issue of *Freedomways*, a Quarterly Review of the Negro Freedom Movement in the United States published in New York City.

The contents of this book, in part, have been taken from various issues of *Freedomways* and appear with the permission of that publication.

Permission to use the following materials has been granted by the authors:

The articles and poems of John Henrik Clarke.

"Aspects of the Economic Structure of the Harlem Community" by Hope R. Stevens.

The poems "Ballad of Joe Meek," "An Old Woman Remembers," and "Southern Cop" by Sterling A. Brown.

"The Music of Harlem" by William R. Dixon.

"Bedford-Stuyvesant—Harlem Across the River" by Milton Galamison.

"And Then Came Baldwin" by Julian Mayfield.

"The Negro Theatre and the Harlem Community" by Loften Mitchell.

"Purlie Told Me!" by Ossie Davis.

The cartoon "Go Back to the Jungle" by Brumsic Brandon, Jr.

"Africa-Conscious Harlem" by Richard Moore.

"Harlem, the Making of a Ghetto" by Gilbert Osofsky.

viii ACKNOWLEDGMENTS

"Four Rebels in Art" by Elton Fax.
"The Negro in American Films" by Carlton Moss.
The poems "Sugar Hill Preacher," "Harlem Junk Man,"
"Billy the Kid in Harlem," and "Black John Henry" by
Ricardo Weeks, from his book *Freedom's Soldier.*
"Winds of Change" by Loyle Hairston.
"Talking About Harlem" by Sylvester Leaks.
"The Harlem Rat" by John H. Jones.
"Some Get Wasted" by Paule Marshall.
"Birmingham's Harlem" by Leonard W. Holt.
"The Health Card" and "I Go to a Funeral" by Alice
Childress, originally published by Independence Pub-
lishers, 1956.
"The Legacy of Alain Locke" by Eugene C. Holmes.
"The Nationalist Movements of Harlem" by E. U. Es-
sien-Udom.
The Bootsie cartoons and "How Bootsie was Born" by
Oliver Harrington. The cartoons originally appeared in
The Pittsburgh Courier and were subsequently published
in book form by Dodd Mead under the title *Bootsie and
Others,* copyright © 1958 by Oliver Harrington.
"Growth and Survival in Harlem" is reprinted with
permission of The Macmillan Company from *Manchild in
the Promised Land* by Claude Brown, Copyright © 1965
by Claude Brown.
"HARYOU-ACT in Harlem; The Dream that Went
Astray" is reprinted by permission of Harper & Row, Pub-
lishers, Inc. from pp. 1–5, 218–222 in *A Relevant War
Against Poverty* by Kenneth B. Clark and Jeannette Hop-
kins, copyright © 1968, 1969 by Metropolitan Applied
Research Center, Inc.
"A Talk to Harlem Teachers" by James Baldwin, copy-
right © 1963, is used with the permission of Robert Lantz
—Candida Donadio Literary Agency, Inc.
"Education in Harlem; I. S. 201 in Perspective" by
Charles E. Wilson was written especially for this book
and is used with the author's permission.
"A Challenge to Artists," copyright © 1963 by Robert
Nemiroff as Executor of the Estate of Lorraine Hans-
berry, is reprinted with his permission. First published in
Freedomways.

ACKNOWLEDGMENTS

The poems "My People" and "I, Too," copyright ©
1926 by Alfred A. Knopf, Inc. and renewed 1954 by
Langston Hughes, by permission of the publisher.

"Who is Simple" from *The Best of Simple* by Langston
Hughes, copyright © 1961 by Langston Hughes is reprinted by permission of Hill and Wang, Inc.

"Yet Do I Marvel" and "Incident" from *On These I
Stand*, by Countee Cullen, copyright © 1925 by Harper
& Row, Publishers, Inc. and renewed 1953 by Ida M.
Cullen, Reprinted by permission of the publishers.

The poems "The Harlem Dancer," "Harlem Shadows"
and "If We Must Die" by Claude McKay are used with
Inc., Twayne Publishers, Inc.

Reprinted by permission of Harold Ober Associates Incorporated are:

Sketches—"My Early Days in Harlem," copyright ©
1963 by Freedomways Association Inc., and "Banquet
Hughes.

"Dear Dr. Butts," copyright © 1953 by Langston
Hughes.

Poems—"Juke Box Love Song," copyright © 1951

The following photographers have granted permission

Acknowledgment of the painters and sculptors and their
work is to be found in the *Harlem: Her Artists and Sculptors* pages at the end of this book.

Note: Some of the articles quote statistics and other

JOHN HENRIK CLARKE

Contents

FOREWORD
INTRODUCTION
HARLEM, CITY WITHIN A CITY

HARLEM AND THE ARTS, SCIENCES, AND PROFESSIONS

Foreword

"FEDERAL AUTHORITIES finally have agreed to honor what a recently formed watchdog group had been demanding ever since a major historic find literally was unearthed when construction began on a federal construction project in Lower Manhattan last October. At least for now, there is a promise that a concerted effort would be made to ensure that none of close to 200 grave sites so far uncovered during excavation for the buildings' foundation would be destroyed by construction crews.

But that is not nearly enough. For these are sacred bones. And, after more than two centuries, it is time they get the respect they deserve.

Much of what we know today as the City Hall area and the financial district, in the 1700's was the only place Black people could bury their dead. It is said that as many as 20,000 people of African descent may be buried in the area, too many of them, the victims of enslavement, lynchings, torture and the abject poverty that eventually consumed them. The courthouses, city administration buildings, banking and investment firms, the so-called 'heartbeat of New York'—they now cover the precious bones of a people who could tell America a thing or two about 'equal opportunity' and 'freedom' and "the pursuit of happiness." *

The above quote refers to a recently-discovered grave-yard in Manhattan that was the early burial ground for the Africans in what was later to become New York City. This was their troubled beginnings.

Early in the 1600's, twenty or more African indentures were brought to the Dutch colony called New Amsterdam. They were settled in an area in New York City around Chatham Square, now Chinatown. What is now Greenwich Village was a swamp difficult to drain, so the Blacks were given this land as their first farms and an extension of their homes in lower Manhattan. The arrival of other immigrant groups impinged on the territory of those indentured Africans who were later moved to an area that is now around 29th Streeet and 30th Street. This community was torn down to build the Post Office and Pennsylvania Station. This is the first urban renewal and Black removal project on record.

On the eve of the Civil War, many Irish and other immigrants were being drafted. When these men noted that Black men were not being drafted, they resented this fact, assuming that they would go to war and leave their women at the mercy of these Black men. This was part of what started the New York riots of that day.

The troubled beginnings of Blacks on their way to Harlem had started. At this time the area of the city that would much later become the world's most famous ethnic community was partly a Dutch farm and partly a middle-class Dutch residential area.

* The City Sun, editorial, Feb. 26-Mar. 3, 1992, Brooklyn, NY

More pressure from immigrant groups seeking space, mostly Irish, pushed the Black population to the area of 59th Street on the west side, what is now 8th and 9th Avenues. Many Black soldiers coming back from the Spanish-American war settled in this area rather than return to the South. They had to fight these immigrant groups in order to hold on to the space. This is part of the folklore of New York City explaining that this is why this part of New York was later called "Hell's Kitchen." Major Black church institutions, such as Abyssinia and Mother Zion, were downtown in New York.

In the closing years of the 19th century, Blacks began to be hired as entertainers with some Broadway shows and in vaudeville in general.

Early in the 20th century, real estate developers had overbuilt the community of Harlem in that they had more apartments available in the community than apartment seekers. The realtors began to rent some apartments to Blacks on 133rd Street and gradually they began to expand into other areas. Several Black real estate firms were established and became rich finding apartments for Blacks in this community originally built for middle-class whites.

Some of the better paid Black entertainers, musicians and more regularly employed craftsmen and caterers began to buy houses in an exclusive area of Harlem, 139th Street and 138th Street. They bought these homes for exaggerated prices for that day and had to strive consistently to keep up the payments.

They did keep up the payments and made this section of Harlem a special kind of middle-class community called Strivers Row. Today it is one of the better kept areas of Harlem, still with a large number of beautifully designed town houses and quiet and well-kept streets in most cases. The next middle-class Black community was further uptown on Edgecombe Avenue. It is still referred to as Sugar Hill.

Before the emergence of the late Adam Clayton Powell, Jr., the two most outstanding Harlem politicians were Charles Anderson and Ferdinand Q. Morton. They were as colorful as Adam Powell in a different way.

✓ The period from 1920 to 1930 is called the era of the Harlem Literary Renaissance. It was a Renaissance in the true sense only if you stretch the dictionary definition of the word. To some extent it was a fad, partly created in Harlem, partly imposed on Harlem. Many of the writers of this period, such as Langston Hughes, Claude McKay, W.E.B. DuBois and James Weldon Johnson would have written just as well had there been no period called the Harlem Renaissance. A lot of Black residents of the community lived and died during this period without hearing the word or knowing its meaning.

From the beginning of his active public career after the Harlem Riot of 1935 until his death in 1972, the political life of the Harlem community can be written to a great extent around the life and activity of Adam Powell. His influence in the church and in community activities during this period was so persuasive, that a great deal of the radical political history of the community can be written around the fact that he and the church that he pastored had a lasting influence on Harlem in transition and may shape the Harlem still to be.

Harlem is now a community under siege, because of urban renewal, gentrification and other designs to push the poor out of Manhattan Island. It will be difficult in the future for Blacks to hold on to this valuable piece of real estate called Harlem. Before the battle on this issue is joined, it might be in order to mention that Harlem has been the proving ground and the window on the world for all of the major movements existing in Black America.

The George Wilson Becton Movement, that was the forerunner of the Father Divine Movement, had its greatest day in Harlem. From Harlem, Marcus Garvey's Back-to-Africa Movement attracted world attention. It was only in Harlem that a Black man, Father Divine, whom others called God, built a kingdom with thousands of followers, black and white. Malcolm X, under the influence of Elijah Muhammad, gave nation-wide projection to the movement called the Lost Nation of Islam in Harlem.

Harlem has been called the culture capital of Black America. It is now under siege, the same as all Black communities in America. Whether it can be saved will depend on the collective efforts of the African people in the United States and not only those who live in Harlem. Intellectually, I grew up in Harlem. I came to New York City in 1933 as a teenager and, except for foreign travel, I have lived in Harlem since this time. The fight to save Harlem has already started. I am in this fight with a whole lot of people, some younger than I am, some older and a lot stronger than I am. I am of the belief that the generation that follows me deserves to see and live in a Harlem community that is intact.

John Henrik Clarke
June   1993

Introduction

IN THE years before the Montgomery Bus Boycott
and the rise of the Southern Freedom Movements that
initiated the prevailing phase of history known as "The
Negro Revolution," Harlem was the nerve center of advancing black America. Harlem is more than a com-
munty; it is a city within a city—the foremost ethnic
city in the world. Among black communities in the
United States, Harlem is unique. It is the only large
community of this nature that is not on the "other
side" of town. Harlem is located in the heart of Manhattan Island. It is probably the most written about and
the least understood community in the world.

In many ways it is more than a community. It is a
frame of mind with international implications. It is the
headquarters of cults, self-proclaimed kings and pre-
tenders. It is the intellectual and spiritual home of the
African people in the Western World. Some of the most
important men and movements in America's black
urban ghettos have developed in Harlem.

When the spread of lynching, the lack of job opportunities and the lure of two world wars started a
vast black migration from the South, Harlem was the

most desirable community for the new settlers looking for a better way of life for themselves and their children. Some failed to improve their condition, yet refused, out of pride, to return to the South. Others rejected the South out of preference, saying philosophically, "I would rather be a lamppost in Harlem than the mayor of the biggest city in the South," or, "I left nothing in the South but my chinches."

In spite of these attitudes, much of what they knew in the South, and sometimes treasured, was transferred to the Northern ghettoes, such as the store-front church and restaurants specializing in "soul food" long before the term became popular.

Roi Ottley, writing about Harlem in 1943, said: "It is the fountainhead of mass movements. From it flows the progressive vitality of Negro life. Harlem is, as well, a cross section of life in black America—a little from here, there and everywhere. It is at once the capital of clowns, cults and cabarets, and the cultural and intellectual hub of the Negro world. By turns Harlem is provincial, worldly, cosmopolitan and naive—sometimes cynical. From here, though, the Negro looks upon the world with audacious eyes. . . . To grasp the inner meanings of life in black America, one must put his finger on the pulse of Harlem."

Claude McKay, writing about Harlem in 1940, called it a "Negro Metropolis" and added: "Harlem is the most interesting sample of black humanity marching along with white humanity."

James Weldon Johnson, in the 1930's, found it different from any other black settlement in the northern United States cities. He found it an extremely healthy and attractive community and worried whether Negroes would be able to "always hold it as a residential section." Johnson's optimistic view continued: "Harlem is indeed the great mecca for the sightseer, the pleasure-seeker, the curious, the adventurous, the enterprising, the ambitious and the talented of the whole Negro world; for the lure of it has reached down to every island of the Carib Sea and has penetrated into Africa." Harlem has been called, and may well be, the cultural and intellectual capital of the black race in the Western world. It has also been called other names less complimentary—names like "a cancer in the heart of a city" and "a large-scale laboratory experiment in the race problem." Some of the most colorful and dynamic personalities in the black world have used Harlem as a vantage point, a platform and proving ground for their ideas and ambitions. The "Back to Africa" movement and the more vocal aspects of black nationalism found a greater acceptance in Harlem than in any other place. This cannot be understood without some knowledge of how and why Harlem came into being in the first place.

Some time in 1626, when what is now New York City was a Dutch outpost called New Amsterdam, eleven Africans were imported and assigned quarters on the fringe of what is now the Bowery. These black laborers eventually built a wagon road to a place in the upper part of the settlement that the Dutch called "Haarlem." About 274 years passed before Harlem (now spelled with one "a") was changed into a black metropolis.

Eighteen years after their arrival, the eleven Africans petitioned the Dutch authorities, with the support of the rank and file colonists, and were finally granted their freedom. The liberated men, who now had wives, settled in a swamp, known today as Greenwich Village. They built this swamp into a prosperous community and attracted other settlers.

The peaceful relations between the Africans and the white settlers came to an end when the British gained control of New Amsterdam in 1664, and introduced chattel slavery.

In 1741, an African named Caesar led the first slave uprising in New York. In 1799, more than half a century before Lincoln's proclamation, a bill was passed in New York beginning the gradual emancipation of slaves.

Black slaves fought in the American Revolution in large numbers; some of them fought as replacements for their white masters who did not choose to fight. The first independent act of these slaves after the end of slavery in the North was to break away from the Methodist Episcopal Church and start the African Methodist Episcopal Zion Church.

After the Civil War, Negroes moved further uptown, but they were still a long way from Harlem.

The mass exodus and settlement of black Americans in Harlem started in 1900, after New York's disastrous race riot. One of the spiritual leaders of the movement to Harlem was the Reverend Adam Clayton Powell, Sr., father of the congressman. The Harlem they came to around 1900 was a cheerful neighborhood of broad streets, brownstone dwellings and large apartment houses. Thoroughbred horses were seen on Lenox Avenue and polo was actually being played at the Polo Grounds.

Bert Williams, the famous actor and comedian, and Harry T. Burleigh, the composer, had moved to Harlem ahead of the mass movement. By 1910, the white residents of Harlem were in full flight.

The early twenties was a time of great change and accomplishment in the Harlem community. It was a period when Harlem was literally "put on the map." Two events made this possible— a literary movement known as the Harlem Renaissance, and the arrival in Harlem of the magnetic and compelling personality, Marcus Garvey.

Of the numerous black Manassehs who presented themselves and their grandiose programs to the people of Harlem, Marcus Garvey was the most tempestuous and flamboyant. Garvey came to the United States from Jamaica, British West Indies, where he was born. He had grown up under a three-way color system—white, mulatto and black. Garvey's reaction to color prejudice and his search for a way to rise above it and lead his people back to Africa, spiritually if not physically, was the all-consuming passion of his existence.

Marcus Garvey's glorious, romantic and riotous movement exhorted black men to reclaim and rebuild their African homeland and heritage. Garvey came to the United States as a disciple of Booker T. Washington, founder of Tuskegee Institute. Unfortunately, Booker T. Washington died before Marcus Garvey reached this country. Garvey had planned to raise funds and return to Jamaica to establish an institution similar to Tuskegee. In 1914 he had organized the Universal Negro Improvement Association in Jamaica. After the failure of this organization, he looked to the United States, where he found a loyal group of followers willing to listen to his message.

Garvey succeeded in building a mass movement among American blacks while other leaders were attempting it and doubting that it could be done. He advocated the return to Africa of all people of African descent. To transport them from the United States, he organized, very rashly and incompetently, a steamship company called, the Black Star Line. Garvey and his movement had a short and spectacular life span in the United States. His movement took really effective form around 1921, but by 1926 he was in a federal prison, charged with misusing the mails. From prison he was deported home to Jamaica. This is, briefly, the essence of the Garvey saga.

The self-proclaimed Provisional President of Africa never set foot on African soil. He spoke no African language. But Garvey managed to convey to members of the black race everywhere (and to the rest of the world) his passionate belief that Africa was the home of a civilization which had once been great and would be great again. When one takes into consideration the slenderness of Garvey's resources and the vast material forces, social conceptions and imperial interests which automatically sought to destroy him, his achievement remains one of the great propaganda miracles of this century.

Garvey's voice reverberated inside Africa itself. The King of Swaziland later told Mrs. Marcus Garvey that he knew the names of only two black men in the Western world: Jack Johnson, the boxer who defeated the white man Jim Jeffries, and Marcus Garvey. From his narrow vantage point in Harlem, Marcus Garvey became a world figure.

While the drama of Marcus Garvey's rise and fall was unfolding in Harlem, another event, less colorful, but equally important, was contributing toward making Harlem the center of racial awakening and literary activity. The period called "The Negro Renaissance" was reaching its zenith. This was the richest and most productive period of Afro-American writing in the United States. The cultural emancipation of black Americans that had begun before World War I was now in full flower, and the community of Harlem was its center, spiritual godfather, and midwife. The black writers discovered a new voice within themselves and liked the sound of it. The white writers who had been interpreting black American life with an air of authority and a preponderance of error looked at last to the black writer with a degree of respect.

Migration to the North and World War I had reoriented the black man's thinking. Black soldiers had fought in large numbers "to make the world safe for democracy." They now wondered, out loud, why the world was not safe for them. In Harlem this wondering helped to develop a political renaissance that had started much earlier. This was Harlem's first use of its political strength to gain control of the institutions that wield power in the community. This movement had its genesis in the early development of the Harlem community. It would later create the political atmosphere that prevailed in Harlem during the Literary Renaissance.

Writers like Jean Toomer, Langston Hughes, Zora Neal Hurston, Rudolph Fisher and Countee Cullen produced a pyramid of imaginative and arresting literature. Strong voices from the West Indian community were heard. The Jamaican writer Claude McKay finished a group of novels and short stories about his homeland before writing *Home to Harlem*, still the most famous novel ever written about this community.

Early in the Harlem literary renaissance period, the black ghetto became an attraction for a varied assortment of white celebrities and thrill-seekers. Some were attempting to rebel against their upbringing by associating on equal terms with blacks. Some were too rich to work, not educated enough to teach and not holy enough to preach. Others were searching for the "noble savage," the "exotic Negro." Some sophisticated but untalented would-be black writers took advantage of the white visitors' gullibility and became professional "exotic Negroes."

These professional exotics were generally college-educated blacks who had become estranged from their families and the environment of their upbringing. They talked at length about the great books within them waiting to be written. The white sponsors continued to subsidize them while they "developed their latent talent." Of course, the "great books" of these camp followers never got written and eventually their white sponsors realized that they were never going to write—not even a good letter.

Concurrently with the unfolding of this mildly funny comedy, the greatest productive period in Afro-American literature continued. The most serious and talented black writers were actually writing their books and getting them published.

The stock market collapse of 1929 marked the beginning of the Depression and the end of the period known as the Negro Renaissance. The "exotic Negro," professional and otherwise, became less exotic now that a hungry look was on his face. The numerous white sponsors and well-wishers who had begun to flock to Harlem ten years before no longer had the time or the money to marvel over black ghetto life. Many Harlemites lived and died in the community during this period without once hearing of the famous literary movement that had flourished and declined within their midst. It was not a mass movement. It was a fad, partly produced in Harlem and partly imposed on Harlem. Most of the writers associated with it would have written just as well at any other time.

In the years following the Harlem Literary Renaissance period, the Harlem community became a land of opportunity for new cultists and their leaders. George Wilson Becton, first of the famous cult leaders to excite the imagination and stir the enthusiasm of the entire Harlem community, died and left the field open to Father Divine, who expanded the domain of his Kingdom of Peace and found a way to feed Harlem's hungry people at a price they could pay.

The insecurity of the Depression years had produced widespread discouragement and apathy in Harlem. The mood of the people called for new leaders, and new leaders appeared—some false and some true. In the midst of this era, a young man born of poverty-stricken parents in the cotton fields of Alabama entered the prize-fighting ring of this nation and made poetry with his gloved fists. He was soon to be hailed as the greatest prize fighter of this century. His name was Joe Louis. In Harlem and in other black communities, he was the great symbol and the new hope. He lifted the spirit of an entire people and gave them a sense of self-importance.

Many aspects of Afro-American life totally removed from the boxing profession were influenced by the rise of Joe Louis. Dr. Alain Locke, a professor at Howard University, had recorded what he called "the dramatic flowering of a new race-spirit" in his book *The New Negro* (1925). Black scholars rewrote those chapters of history which ignored or minimized the part played by their people. "The American Negro must remake his past in order to make his future," said Arthur A. Schomburg, founder of the famous collection of literature that bears his name.

The economic dislocation of the Harlem community during the depression years motivated in Harlem, and in other black communities, the growth and development of a "Don't Buy Where You Can't Work" movement. The boycott and the picket line became the main weapons in a war against job discrimination. Some groups picketed City Hall and demanded that city agencies change their hiring policies.

In Harlem, and in other Northern ghettos, most of the stores servicing the community were owned by whites who did not readily employ people from the community. The campaigns for jobs in these stores brought forth a number of remarkable and often colorful new leaders. Sufi Abdule Hamid, who had been known in Chicago as Bishop Conshankin, started a new movement for jobs in Harlem. Also in Harlem the Citizens Committee for Fair Play and the Greater New York Coordinating Committee projected new ideas and methods into the fight for jobs. The political career of Adam Clayton Powell had its early development in these campaigns.

J. A. Rogers, lecturer and traveler and once a member of Marcus Garvey's staff of advisors, became the most widely read pamphleteer in black America. During the Italian-Ethiopian War, J. A. Rogers and another Harlem resident, Dr. Willis N. Huggins, author of a remarkable book, *Introduction to African Civilizations*, were assigned to report and explain this war to the people of African descent in the United States. Dr. Huggins went to Geneva and reported to the League of Nations meetings concerning the Italian-Ethiopian War. J. A. Rogers went to the battlefront in Ethiopia. Both Rogers and Huggins saw behind and beyond the headlines and foretold the future repercussions of Ethiopia's betrayal. Their reports were a highwater mark in Afro-American journalism.

In Harlem and in other communities throughout the nation, the search for the lost African heritage continued.

Politically, the world's largest black community resembles an underdeveloped nation dominated by leaders who are no more than messenger boys for the neocolonial powers—in this case the larger and richer political machine bosses in downtown New York City. There are two outstanding exceptions: Benjamin J. Davis, Jr. and Reverend Adam Clayton Powell, Jr.

The political career of Ben Davis started a long way from Harlem, where Adam Clayton Powell grew up. In 1943, under proportional representation, a progressive and democratic form of election, Benjamin J. Davis, Jr. was elected to the New York City Council to fill the seat vacated by Adam Clayton Powell, Jr., who had been elected to Congress. In the City Council, Ben Davis was a thorn in the side of machine politicians who were determined to get him out of the City Council and out of Harlem. Finally, these forces succeeded in bringing down their prey. First, proportional representation was abolished. Before his last term had expired, Davis was barred from the City Council because he had been convicted under the Smith Act.

Then in 1951, the Supreme Court upheld the Smith Act, and Ben Davis and his comrades were sent to prison. In prison, Ben Davis continued his lifelong fight against Jim Crow and second-class citizenship. The long prison term diminished his effectiveness but not his popularity in the Harlem community.

Adam Clayton Powell, Jr. was born into controversy and comfort. For more than thirty years, this self-proclaimed "Disciple of Protest" had been the most colorful and sometimes the most effective politician in black America. He has always been a man who provokes extreme reactions in most people. In Washington, reporters and legislators compete in denouncing him. In Harlem and in other black communities, he is the deliverer of the word—spokesman of the black oppressed. As the Congressman from the 18th District in Harlem, he has been the creator of a political mystique and a dramatic enigma. This mystique and this enigma stand in the way of every attempt at making an objective appraisal of the adventurous career of Reverend Adam Clayton Powell.

In the years after the second World War, Harlem became a community in decline. Many old residents, now successful enough to afford a better neighborhood, moved to Westchester, Long Island, or Connecticut. The community leaders who had helped to make Harlem the cultural center of black America had either died or moved away. Only one black writer of note, Langston Hughes, and two musicians of distinction, Duke Ellington and Lionel Hampton, still lived in Harlem.

Harlem is not a self-contained community. It is owned and controlled by outsiders. It is a black community with a white economic heartbeat. Of the major retail outlets, national chains and local merchants, only a handful are black-owned. In the raging battle for integration and equal job opportunities for blacks, little is heard about the blacks' long fight to gain control of their community. A system of pure economic colonialism exists in the Harlem community. This colonialism extends into politics, religion and every money-making endeavor that touches the life of a Harlem resident.

This kind of exploitation in Harlem and in other black communities has helped to produce a phenomenon called black nationalism. This phenomenon brings into focus the conflicts, frustrations and crises encountered by Harlem's inhabitants, both outside their immediate environment and among themselves.

For over half a century of Harlem's existence, various

local groups within the community have been planning and fighting to free the people in the world's most famous ghetto from outside control. The creation of HARYOU-ACT in 1964 made some people of the community believe that this was possible.

The announced objective of the HARYOU-ACT programs was to place persistent emphasis and insistence upon social action rather than dependence upon mere social service. The ultimate goal was to develop in Central Harlem a community of excellence through the concern and initiative of the people of the community.

The basic guide for the project was a momumental document called, "Youth in the Ghetto—A Study of the Consequences of Powerlessness and a Blueprint for Change." The proposed "blueprint for change" was a landmark in creative research and astute planning.

In the preface to this document, the Board of Directors and the Executive Committee of HARYOU made the following collective statement:

This study is completed at an historic moment in American life. A century after Emancipation and a decade after the *Brown* Decision, Negro Americans still wait on the fulfillment of great hopes.

Meanwhile, the flags of newly sovereign people flying before the United Nations buildings symbolize the fact that freedom and equality have come to twice as many peoples as were in the family of nations only two decades ago. The glacial slowness with which freedom and equality come to the minorities within our own nation heightens the contrast, converts hopes into expectations, and expectations into demands. The American Revolution waits to be completed.

It is in this context that the present study of Central Harlem is to be understood and interpreted. Massive deterioration of the fabric of society and its institutions is indicated by the findings of this study. Such massive deterioration calls for corrective action on a scale to match the magnitude of the problem.

As America moves forward, the heart and core of the

largest Negro community in the world will be able to play its part in this forward movement only as the debilitating and degrading effects of a deteriorating ghetto are effectively countered.

To enable Central Harlem to play its part in the realization of the American Dream will be to bring the full realization of that dream a little closer.

The document, like HARYOU itself, was long on promise and short on fullfillment.

Three major components of HARYOU-ACT were developed as the vehicles for dynamic social change: The Community Action Institute, The Neighborhood Boards and Harlem Youth Unlimited. The main functions of these components are to suggest, select and refine the types of services which particular families and individuals might require; and at the same time to provide the training, orientation and specific skills necessary for sustained and successful community action.

In the area of political action, the intent of HAR-YOU-ACT was to show the people of Harlem how they could force governmental agencies to respond to their needs. The intent was also to show that this involves knowledge both of the formal political institutions and of the groups and individuals who, for one reason or another, actually—or might potentially—determine and influence what occurs within the political structure. For Harlem this was meant to be a way of discovering its political self and how to make the most of it.

Unfortunately, the bright dreams of HARYOU-ACT faded before community support could be marshalled behind them. A number of times the agency was harassed by lengthy investigations that proved nothing of consequence. By the end of 1968, HARYOU-ACT was only a shell of its former self. The community of Harlem was involved in a fight to control its schools and to restore some of its lost political prestige.

Harlem, the six-square-mile area in Manhattan's geographical center, containing over half of New York's million-plus black people, continues to grow and grapple with its problems. It continues to be a community in transition, searching for its proper place in the black revolution.

JOHN HENRIK CLARKE

New York, N.Y.
October, 1970

HARLEM: CITY WITHIN A CITY

Sylvester Leaks

TALKING ABOUT HARLEM

I'M TALKING now about Harlem: A six square mile festering black scar on the alabaster underbelly of the white man's indifference.

HARLEM: A bastard child, born out of wedlock, baptized in the gut bucket of life, midwifed by oppression and fathered by racial hate, circumscribed by fear and guilt-ridden detractors.

HARLEM: A hot-hearted, generously kind, and jovial black woman, whose blood-sucked veins are a playground, whose skinned and scarred, bruised and battered, used and tattered, seduced and raped body is a privileged sanctuary for that unholy trinity of rent gouging landlords, graft grabbing cops, and usurious loan sharks; for silver tongued pimps and phony prophets, thieving politicians and vendors of sex and religion, fake healers and fortune tellers and atrocious peddlers of narcotics and death.

HARLEM: Whose expansive bosom is nestling place, hiding place, haven and hell, for her three hundred thirty-six thousand, three hundred sixty-four black and brown, tan and yellow children—thirty-one per cent of whom are either separated, widowed or divorced. And no matter how full her house gets she never refuses them a helping hand, she never scorns, she never complains, she is always understanding.

HARLEM: Here slum life is the total sum of life for so many thousands of her children, with only fifty per cent of the children under eighteen years old living with both parents; here forty-nine per cent of the dwelling units is dilapidated, twenty-five per cent is overcrowded; here the average *family* income approximates $3,723, whereas statistics show the average family needs $6,000 just to make ends meet.

HARLEM: Here nine thousand eight hundred and eighty jobless souls exist, with no State Unemployment Office in the community to serve them; here twelve thousand, four hundred and fifty-four receive public assistance; here women constitute forty-eight per cent of the labor force, twenty-five per cent of them married; four and a half per cent have children under six years of age.

HARLEM: A dingy-dirty cluster of roach-crawling, rat-infested brownstones and tenement flats, interspersed here and there with housing projects, creating a bizarre effect; here the birth rate is twenty-six per thousand, the death rate thirteen per thousand; here juvenile delinquency has escalated to one hundred thirty-five per thousand; from here came fifteen per cent of admissions to mental hospitals in 1957.

HARLEM: Here one hundred twenty-five thousand church members raise their voices in prayers and songs in two hundred fifty-six churches, imploring unknown gods for surcease to their man-made plights; while some of their ministers drive flashy cars and live in fancy homes, misery stalks the street and the blues are the only antidote to atavistic pain.

HARLEM: A lucrative colony for white retail merchants, whose three thousand eight hundred ninety-eight retail stores produce an annual gross sale of $345,-871,000—exclusive of doctors, lawyers, undertakers, insurance, rent, utilities, dry cleaners, etc. While little, if any, of this wealth is left in the community for improvement. Most, if not all, of these merchants live in neighborhoods where black folks can't live, even if they could afford it.

HARLEM: Here the lust for life is infectious; one feels its accelerating rhythm and demoniacal beat of life the moment he enters the enfolding confines of her streets; here $34,368,000 worth of liquor is purchased annually in one hundred sixty-eight liquor stores, exclusive of the untold millions spent in bars. And the unpretentious purchasers thumb their noses at their maligners and shout at the top of their voices. "It ain't nobody's business if I do!"

HARLEM: The home of Sugar Hill[1]—but minus the dollar bills now; of City College and Lewisohn Stadium and its yearly concerts which every man can afford; The Grange (Alexander Hamilton's home); Schomburg Library,[2] with its more than thirty-seven thousand volumes of material by and about black folks—the largest in the world; of Jumel Mansion (George Washington's Revolutionary War head-quarters); of Delano Village, Lenox Terrace, Morningside Garden Cooperative, Bowery Savings Bank apartments,[3] with their high rents which most of Harlem can't afford. Here one sees black knots of humanity on the street corners every day around five in the evening, waiting breathlessly and hopefully for the last number. And when the news is learned one hears subdued and oftentimes explosive imprecations from the unfortunate, as they dejectedly walk away.

Although I'm talking about you, dear Harlem, I love you just the same—with your woes and all, ills and all, laughter and all, your troubles and all. For I see in you a profound beauty, manisfested by your ceaseless struggles to mold and fashion something good and meaningful out of it all, in spite of it all; in your Senior Choirs competing with the Usher Boards[4] to see which will raise

the most money for "the building fund"; in your picket
lines, protesting this and demanding that; in your fifty-
four social agencies, serving fifty-five thousand souls;
in your poring over books in libraries, unlocking the
portals of knowledge; in NAACP meetings, planning
legal assaults on the ramparts of jim crow; in the Black
Muslim Temple, demanding some of this good earth
for ourselves; in the African Nationalist street meetings
on Seventh Avenue and 125th Street, with the speaker
exhorting his listeners to "buy black" and reminding
them that "when you mess with the dollar, the white
man will holler"; in the Negro American Labor Council,
struggling to get us some jobs.[5]

And, yes, I love the way you relax and enjoy life;
twisting at Smalls on Wednesday nights, dancing at
Rockland Palace and the Audubon Ballroom, the
Renaissance and Connie's[6] on Fridays, Saturdays, and
Sunday nights; giving cocktail sips, teas, readings,
fashion shows, beaux arts balls; forming a line a block
long to see Jackie Wilson "work out" at the Apollo[7]
and to hear Moms Mabley say, "I got somp'n to tell
ya" and explode in uninhibited laughter. You are a
black wonder, Harlem. You survived.

Gilbert Osofsky

✑

HARLEM:
THE MAKING OF A GHETTO

IN THE last three decades of the nineteenth century
Harlem was a community of great expectations.[8] During
the previous half-century it had been an isolated, poor,
rural village inhabited largely by squatters who lived in
cottages pieced together with any material that could be
found—bits of wood, twigs, barrel staves, old pipes, tin
cans hammered flat. The community was now, however,
being transformed into an upper- and upper-middle-
class suburb—New York's first suburb.

The phenomenal growth of Harlem in the late nineteenth century was a by-product of the general development of New York City. From the 1870's on, the foundations of the modern metropolis were laid. This urban
revolution was characterized by improvements in
methods of transportation, sanitation, water supply,
communication, lighting and building. As the city expanded, so did its population. In 1880, for the first time
in its history (and in the history of any American city),
the population of Manhattan alone passed the one million mark (1,164,673). This increase in population
coincided with an expansion of business and industrial
activity; both made serious inundations on living

8 HARLEM U.S.A.

quarters in formerly staid residential areas of the island.
Many New Yorkers, attempting to avoid the bustle of
the new metropolis and escape contact with its newest
settlers, looked to Harlem as the community of the
future: "In our family, we were careful to explain that
we lived in Harlem, not in New York City," recalled a
man whose family moved uptown in these years. "It was
our way of avoiding contact with such uncouth citizens
as might be found downtown. . . ." Harlem was to be
the city's "choicest residential section," remembered a
man who settled there in the 1880's.

One great barrier to Harlem's development in the
early nineteenth century had been its distance from
lower Manhattan. Between 1878 and 1881, however,
three lines of the elevated railroad reached 129th Street;
by 1886 they had come even further north. From this
point on Harlem's growth was amazing. Rows of brownstones and exclusive apartment houses appeared overnight: "Business grows, blocks and flats go up with
apparently so little effort, that the average Harlemite is
in a continuous swim of development and prosperity,"
editorialized the white *Harlem Local Reporter* in 1890.
Practically all the houses that stand in Harlem today
were built in a spurt of energy that lasted from the
1870's through the first decade of the twentieth century.
The old shanties were doomed by "the wilderness of
brownstone, brick and motar. . . ." A man who had
lived in Harlem since the 1840's saw a "one horse
town . . . turned into a teeming metropolis."

Older and wealthier Manhattanites ("people of taste
and wealth") were attracted to this new "residential
heaven." In a society whose working-class families paid
an average of $10-$18 a month rent, the rents for one
group of apartments in Harlem in the 1890's *started* at
just under $80 a month, and ranged between $900 and
$1700 a year.

The homes of municipal and federal judges, mayors,
local politicos, and prominent businessmen were scat-

tered throughout Harlem. Their children could attend Grammar School 68, "referred to as the 'Silk Stocking School' of the City [because] the pupils were practically all from American families, and . . . more or less prosperous people." Young girls could go to "Mme. De Valencia's Protestant French and English Institute for Young Ladies." Local citizens, after attending a performance at the Harlem Opera House (built in 1889), might dine at the luxurious Pabst Harlem: "where gentlemen and ladies can enjoy good music and a perfect cuisine amid surroundings which have been rendered as attractive to the eye and senses [as] good taste, combined with lavish expenditure, could make them." Late nineteenth century Harlem was able to support a monthly literary magazine, a weekly magazine of local affairs and a bi-weekly newspaper. It certainly promised to be a vital, ever-growing, genteel community. Its future seemed boundless.

To the generation who remembered only this Harlem, who had never known the Harlem of squatters and shanties, its memory remained warm and bright. Few would have disagreed with the editor of *The Harlem Monthly Review* who saw Harlem developing as a "district . . . distinctly devoted to the mansions of the wealthy, the homes of the well-to-do, and the places of business of the tradespeople who minister to their wants . . ." "It is evident to the most superficial observer that the centre of fashion, wealth, culture, and intelligence, must, in the near future, be found in the ancient and honorable village of Harlem. . . ." and "we have no adequate idea of . . . the greatness that lies in store for Harlem," thought another resident in 1890.

A few factors combined to alter Harlem life radically in the first decade of the twentieth century. Underlying them all was a wave of speculation in Harlem land and property that was set off by the construction of new subway routes into the neighborhood in the late 1890's.

Land that had been left unimproved or undeveloped at that time—marshes, garbage dumps, empty lots—were bought up by speculators who intended to make astronomic profits when the subway was completed. Between 1898 and 1904, the year that the Lenox Avenue line was opened at 145th Street, "practically all the vacant land in Harlem [was] built over. . . ." "The growth of . . . Harlem . . . has been truly astonishing during the last half dozen years," commented a leading real estate journal in 1904.

It was taken as business gospel that investments would be doubled and trebled when the "tunnel road" was completed:

Even a five-story single flat in Harlem would net . . . at the end of . . . three to five years . . . at the utmost . . . a very handsome unearned increment." A supposed expert in New York real estate concluded that no "other class of public improvements had such a great, immediate and permanent effect upon land values as rapid transit lines. . . .*

The existing speculation in flats and tenements," wrote another observer," surpasses . . . anything of the kind which has previously taken place in the real estate history of the city.

In West Harlem, along Seventh Avenue and Lenox Avenue in the 130's and 140's ("the best of Harlem," it was called), luxurious apartment houses were built. It was believed, in keeping with the traditions of the neighborhood, that West Harlem would be inhabited by richer people who wanted "high-class flats," "costly dwellings," and who earned enough money to afford them. Many of these buildings were equipped with elevators (then first being installed in better houses), maids' rooms and butlers' pantries. In 1899 William Waldorf Astor erected an apartment house on Seventh Avenue which cost $500,000. Sunday real estate sections of New York

City newspapers at the turn of the century bristled with full-page advertisements and pictures of the elegant homes in this part of Harlem. The building activity of these years created the physical foundations for what became, initially, the loveliest Negro ghetto in the world.

Speculation in West Harlem property at the turn of the century led to phenomenal increases in the price of land and the cost of houses there—increases inflated out of all proportion to their real value. John M. Royall, Negro realtor, recalled that from "1902 to 1905 real estate speculative fever seized all New York City. The great subway proposition . . . permeated the air. Real estate operations and speculators [imagined] becoming millionaires, bought freely in the West Harlem district in and about the proposed subway stations. Men bought property on thirty and sixty day contracts, and sold their contracts . . . and made substantial profits. I have known buyers to pay $38,000 and $75,000 for tenements which showed a gross income of only $2,600 and $5,000 a year. On they went buying, buying. . . . [Houses] had been continually changing hands." Each time a building was sold it brought a higher price. In the urge to get rich quick on Harlem property few persons realized how artificial market values had become.

The inevitable "bust" came in 1904–1905. Speculators sadly realized afterward that too many houses had been constructed at one time. Harlem had been glutted with apartments and "excessive building . . . led to many vacancies." No one knew just how long it would take to construct the subway and many apartment houses had been built four and five years before it was completed. Some of these homes remained largely unoccupied. The first of them to be inhabited by Negroes, for example, had never been rented previously. Rents were too high for the general population ($35-$45 per month) and precluded any great rush to Harlem even after the subway was completed. There was, remembered one man, a widespread "overestimation of rental values" at first.

When the market broke, landlords competed with each other for tenants by cutting rents or by offering a few months rent-free occupancy to them. Some local business groups attempted to get landlords to stabilize rental values, but this movement had little success. The formerly inflated prices asked for land and property in Harlem "solemnly settled beneath a sea of depreciated values."

The individuals and companies that were caught in Harlem's rapidly deflated real estate market were threatened with financial ruin. Rather than face destruction, some landlords and corporations were willing to rent their houses to Negroes and collect the traditionally high rents that colored people paid. Others, instead of accepting their losses, used the threat of bringing in Negro tenants to frighten their neighbors into buying them out at a higher than market price. Shrewder operators (present day realtors call them "blockbusters") hoped to take advantage of the unusual situation by "placing colored people in property so that they might buy other parcels adjoining or in the same block [reduced in price] because of fears on the part of the whites to one-half of the values then obtaining." By using these techniques "a great number" of property owners were able "to dispose of their property or . . . get a . . . more lucrative return from rents paid by colored tenants." Negroes, offered decent living accommodations for the first time in the city's history, "flocked to Harlem and filled houses as fast as they were opened to them."

But not all property owners in the neighborhood were ready to open their houses to Negroes. It seemed unbelievable to some that theirs, one of the most exclusive sections in the entire city, should become the center of New York's most depressed and traditionally worst-housed people. Some owners banded together in associations to repulse what they referred to as the Negro "invasion" or the Negro "influx." The language they used to describe the movement of Negroes into Harlem (the word "invasion," for example, appeared in almost all denunciations of Negroes) was the language of war.

In the 1880's and 1890's Harlemites annually celebrated the historic Revolutionary Battle of Harlem Heights.[9] These patriotic fetes were symbols of community pride, and pamphlets were widely distributed informing the neighborhood of all the organizations and dignitaries that participated in them. In the early twentieth century, however, Harlem's residents gathered, not to preserve the memory of a Revolutionary conflict, but to fight their own battle—to keep their neighborhood white.

The formal opposition to Negro settlement in Harlem centered in a number of local associations of landlords. Some were committees representing individual blocks, others were community-wide in structure. Between 1907 and 1915, the last year in which there was significant organized opposition to Negro settlement, a number of protective associations were founded. Property owners on West 140th, 137th, 136th, 135th, 131st, 130th, 129th Streets (in descending order as the Negro community spread southward), and along the avenues, signed agreements according to which each swore not to rent his apartments to Negroes for ten or fifteen years—till when, it was thought, "this situation . . . referred to . . . will have run its course"; "The premises, land, and building of which we . . . are the owners . . . shall not be used as a . . . Negro tenement, leased to colored . . . tenants, sold to colored . . . tenants . . . or all [other] persons of African descent." "Each of the parties," reads another agreement, "does hereby covenant and agree [not] to . . . hereafter . . . cause to be suffered, either directly or indirectly, the said premises to be used or occupied in whole or in part by any Negro, quadroon, or octoroon of either sex whatsoever. . . ." Some covenants even put a limitation on the number of Negro janitors, bellboys, laundresses and servants that could be employed in a home.

Following a pseudo-legal procedure which was sup-

posed to make these agreements binding, each signer
paid all the others a fee of one dollar. The finished
products were notarized and filed at the County Clerk's
Office in the New York City Hall of Records (where
they can be read today). The streets covered by such
restrictive codes were known in the Negro community
as Covenant Blocks, and Negroes took pride in being
the first colored landlords or tenants to live in them ("to
knock [the covenants] into a cocked hat," said one).

Other community groups led by white realtors tried to
hold back the Negro's "steady effort to invade Harlem."
(One realty company dealing in upper-Manhattan property was called the Anglo-Saxon Realty Corporation.)
These people formed such organizations as the Harlem
Property Owners' Protective Association, the Committee
of Thirty, the Harlem Property Owners' Improvement
Corporation and the West Side Improvement Association. Each group planned to arouse the interest of all
white Harlemites in "the greatest problem that Harlem
has had to face." Meetings were held and programs introduced which proposed the eviction of all Negroes
already in Harlem or, failing this, at least to prevent
the further sale and rental of property to Negroes. A
propaganda war was waged as "White Only" signs were
hung in the windows of Harlem apartment houses.
Advertisements were printed in the white *Harlem
Magazine* asking all property owners to join the movement: "Will you help yourself?"; "Help protect your
property."

Negro realtors were contacted and told they would be
wasting their time trying to find houses on certain
streets: "We herewith resolve that every colored real
estate broker be notified as to the following: That the
owners of this section have unanimously agreed not to
rent their houses for colored tenancy. . . ." Like an
enemy negotiating a line of truce, the Committee of
Thirty called a meeting of Negro real estate men to try
to draw a voluntary boundary line that would perma-

nently separate the white and Negro communities. Four members of Harlem's Church of the Puritans (white) attended meetings of the New York Presbytery to protest the proposed movement of St. James Presbyterian Church (Negro) into the neighborhood. Others called on city fathers to try to prevent the licensing of a Negro-owned movie house on Lenox Avenue. The Lafayette Theatre, on Seventh Avenue, permitted Negroes to sit only in its balcony. People who signed restrictive covenants and subsequently broke them were brought into court.

All these movements failed. That it was necessary to found so many different organizations in a relatively short period of time was a reflection of the general failure of each. Racially restrictive housing covenants were unconstitutional and, although at least one person was sued, no one was ever convicted of violating them. Negro realtors, like John M. Royall, ridiculed the proposal for a voluntary line of segregation as an agreement to "capitalize on prejudice." He said: "The colored people are in Harlem to stay . . . they are coming each year by the thousands." In spite of the many protests of Harlemites, St. James Church was permitted to move into the area and was even granted a large loan to build a new church. In 1913 the Lafayette Theatre was sold to promoters who realized that it was foolish to run a segregated theatre in "what is destined to become a colored neighborhood." The new owners opened their doors to Negroes ("our doors are open to all"), and even contributed regularly to Negro charities. The large basement of the building in which the theatre was housed, Lafayette Hall, was later leased as a temporary armory to Harlem's Negro National Guard unit. In 1919, the entire building, including the theatre, was sold to a group of Negro businessmen. In the twenties, the Lafayette was noted for its fine troupe of Negro actors.

The basic cause for the collapse of all organized

efforts to exclude the Negro from Harlem was the inability of any group to gain total and unified support of all white property owners in the neighborhood—and without such support it was impossible to organize a successful neighborhood-wide anti-Negro movement. Landlords forming associations by blocks had a difficult enough time trying to keep people on individual streets united. Nor was it possible—and this is the major point—to create a well-organized, well-financed movement of Negro restriction (one plan called for the contribution of one-half of one per cent of the assessed valuation of all property to a community fund) in the disrupted and emotional atmosphere that prevaded Harlem in the first two decades of the twentieth century. The very setting in which whites were confronted with Negro neighbors for the first time led to less than level-headed reasoning.

The first impulse of many whites was to sell out at whatever price their property would bring and move elsewhere. Realtors called this "panic selling" and, in spite of efforts to prevent it, it went on. Between 1907 and 1914 two-thirds of the houses in or near the Negro section were sold—practically all at substantial losses to the original owners. Since the already weak real estate market was flooded with property in a short time, and only a relatively few Negroes were wealthy enough to buy ("there was no market for real estate among the newcomers"), prices continued to depreciate rapidly: "realty values have tumbled by leaps and bounds." In the 1870's and 1880's fortunes were made from soaring Harlem land prices; by 1917 white realtors tried to encourage interest in the neighborhood by advertising how cheap property had become: "Changes in the character of Harlem population," wrote a member of the white Harlem Board of Commerce, have led to "remarkable bargains, both for rental and purchase. . . . Such properties in good condition can now be purchased at less than the assessed value of the land alone." The minority of Harlem landlords who tried to adhere to their original restrictive covenants suffered serious economic consequences. Many were unable to find white people willing to rent their apartments. To encourage white tenants already in them to remain, some were forced to reduce rents drastically: "The introduction of Negro tenants . . . has caused . . . many white tenants to move and [has] required a substantial reduction of rents to those who remained," complained a group of Harlem landlords in 1907. Those who had mortgage payments to meet were threatened with foreclosure by banks and other lending institutions, and many found it "impossible . . . to hold out." The opponents of Negro settlement were faced with the dilemma of maintaining a "White Only" policy and probably losing everything, or renting to Negroes (at higher prices) and surviving. Most chose what seemed to them the lesser of two evils and published or posted such revealing notices as this one which appeared in 1916:

We have endeavored for some time to avoid turning over this house to colored tenants, but as a result of . . . rapid changes in conditions . . . this issue has been forced upon us.

The creation of Negro Harlem was only one example of the general development of large, segregated Negro communities in many American cities in the years preceding and following the First World War. That Harlem became the specific center of Negro population was the result of circumstance; that some section of the city was destined to become a Negro neighborhood was the inevitable consequence of the migration of southern Negroes to New York City. Harlem was New York's equivalent of the Negro ghettos of the nation. "Niggertowns," "Buzzard's Alleys," "Nigger Rows," "Black Bottoms," "Smoketowns," "Bronzevilles," and "Chinch-Rows," had emerged elsewhere by 1913. "There is growing up in the cities of America a distinct Negro world,"

18
HARLEM U.S.A.

wrote Urban League director George Edmund Haynes
in that year. These were neighborhoods "isolated from
many of the impulses of the common life and little
understood by the white world. . . ."

Of all the Negro ghettos, however, Harlem was unique.
Its name was a symbol of elegance and distinction,
not derogation; its streets and avenues were broad,
well-paved, clean and tree-lined, not narrow and dirty;
its homes were spacious, replete with the best of modern
facilities, "finished in high-style." Harlem was not a
slum, but an ideal place in which to live. For the first
time in the history of New York City, Negroes were
able to live in decent homes in a respectable neighborhood ("the best houses that they have ever had to live
in"): "It is no longer necessary for our people to live
in small, dingy, stuffy tenements," editorialized a Negro
newspaper in 1906. Harlem was "a community in which
Negroes as a whole are . . . better housed than in any
other part of the country," concluded an Urban League
report in 1914. "Those of the race who desire to live
in grand style, with elevator, telephone and hall boy
service, can now realize their cherished ambition."

Practically every major Negro institution moved out
of its downtown quarters and came to Harlem by 1920:
churches, insurance companies, small businesses, real
estate firms, fraternal orders, settlement houses, social
service agencies, the YMCA and YWCA, branches of
the Urban League and NAACP. The "Fighting Fifteenth," Harlem's Negro National Guard unit, was out-
fitted in 1916. Harlem's first Negro assemblyman was
elected in 1917. Harlem Hospital hired its first Negro
nurses and a Negro doctor in 1919. P.S. 89, on Lenox
Avenue (three-quarters Negro by 1915), opened a night
school, reading rooms and a community center to keep
Negro children off the streets. P.S. 68, the former "Silk
Stocking School," became noted for its regular skir-
mishes between white and Negro pupils.

The community that had been advertised as a place

of exclusive residence in the 1890's was now claimed to be the perfect area in which to locate factories. Land was cheap, it was argued, transportation was good, and the neighborhood was full of unskilled, lower-income families willing to accept any kind of employment. The heterogeneity of Harlem's population was then seen to be one of its principal assets: "Only 17 per cent of its people are native white of native parents," concluded a survey of the Harlem Board of Commerce in 1917. "Racial colonization shows distinctly." Parades were held on local streets to stimulate public interest in Harlem's business and industrial opportunities. The merchants adjusted as best they could to new conditions while those who remembered the expectations of previous generations sadly moved away: "Harlem has been devastated as a result of the steady influx of Negroes," bemoaned an old resident in 1913. The "best of Harlem is gone," thought another in the same year, and it "will be all colored in ten years."

In 1914 Negroes lived in at least 1,100 different houses within a twenty-three block area of Harlem. The Negro population of Harlem was then conservatively estimated at just under 50,000—the entire Negro population of Manhattan in 1910 had been 60,534. By 1920 the section of Harlem bordered by 130th Street on the south, 145th Street on the north, and west of Madison and Fifth Avenues to Eighth Avenue was predominately Negro—and inhabited by some 80,000 people. As the immigrants (Italians and Jews) who lived in surrounding areas moved to better quarters in other boroughs in the 1920's, their homes were filled by Negroes. The Negro section remained and expanded as the other ethnic ghettos distintegrated. By 1930 Negro Harlem had reached its southern limit, 110th Street—the northern boundary of Central Park. Its population was then approximately 200,000. Harlem became the "largest colony of colored people, in similar limits, in the world." And so it remains to this day.

Eugene C. Holmes

⚜

THE LEGACY OF ALAIN LOCKE

THE RISE of a genuine New Negro Movement was fostered and encouraged by one person, Alain Leroy Locke,[10] who became its creative editor and its chronicler. It may be true that the term Renaissance, as Sterling Brown[11] so perceptively pointed out, is a misnomer because of the shortness of the life span of the Harlem movement. Also, much of the best writing of the decade was not always about Harlem, for most of the writers were not Harlemites. Yet Harlem was the "show window," the cashier's till, though it is no more "Negro America" than New York is America. The New Negro had temporal roots in the past and spatial roots elsewhere in America and the term has validity only when considered to be a continuing tradition.

It may be argued that the so-called Negro Renaissance held the seed of defeat for a number of reasons, among them being the general anti-intellectualism of the new Negro middle class. But, by every admission it represented a re-evaluation of the Negro's past and of the Negro himself by Negro intellectuals and artists. For the rise of the New Negro Movement coincided with an ever increasing interest in Negro life and character in the twenties. American literature was being re-evaluated and overhauled as a revolt against the genteel tradition and the acquisitive society of the last decade of the nineteenth century.

Charles Johnson[12] characterized Alain Locke as "the Dean of this group of fledgling writers of the new and lively generation of the 1920's." Johnson wrote, "A brilliant analyst trained in philosophy, and an esthete with a flair for art as well as letters, he gave encouragement and guidance to these young writers as an older practitioner too sure of his craft to be discouraged by failure of full acceptance in the publishing media of the period."[13] Johnson referred to Alain Locke as "an important maker of history" at a "dramatic period in our national history." Locke had this to say about these young writers being launched on their careers: "They sense within their group a spiritual wealth which, if they can properly expound it, will be ample for a new judgment and re-appraisal of the race." This, then, is only a part of the backdrop of what has been called the Negro Renaissance, what Charles Johnson referred to as "that sudden and altogether phenomenal outburst of emotional expression unmatched by any comparable period in American or Negro American history."

No one, not even the older Du Bois,[14] could have been better equiped to have been the architect of the New Negro Movement and maker of history. Philadelphia, Locke's birthplace, was the one city where one could speak of culture. Negro artists were encouraged and Negro literary, musical and painting groups were encouraged. Young Locke was aware of this personally and always kept these artists in mind as reminders of the awakening of Negro art in America. The literary movement had many of its origins in Philadelphia, but, because of social, economic and political reasons, it flowered in New York. For a racial dilemma in Negro art, a racial solution was necessary. This came in the mid-twenties from the inspiration of the New Negro

Movement with its crusade of folk expression in all of the arts, the drama, painting, sculpture, music and the rediscovery of the folk origins of the Negro's African heritage.

The racial dilemma was a distinct carry-over from the same dilemma encountered by the Negro writers of the late nineteenth century. In most of these writers, there was to be found the same tendentious, pedestrian and imitative style as observed in many of the painters. There was the dialect poetry of Dunbar and his later English poems in which he was the exponent of the romantic tendencies which were to be decried by the next generation of Negro poets. There were the propaganda novels of Frances Harper, Martin Delaney, Frank Webb and William Wells Brown. The novels of Charles Chestnutt[15] were outstanding for their genre, style and impact. The political essays, the pamphleteering, the autobiographical slave accounts, the polemical essays were all to be merged with and channelized into that renaissance which came to be known as the New Negro Movement.

As a burgeoning critic and student of Negro life in Philadelphia, in Boston and New York, at Howard University where he had gone to teach in 1912, Locke had been working in his way, in concert with many friends, to help lay to rest the mawkish and moribund dialect school of poetry. William Stanley Braithwaite, Locke's friend and mentor while he was at Harvard; William Monroe Trotter,[16] the editor; W. E. B. Du Bois, all helped in hastening the demise of Negro dialect poetry. Friendly critics such as Louis Untermeyer also helped by labeling the traditional dialect as "an affectation to please a white audience." And, along with James Weldon Johnson,[17] who had genuine poetic talent, this critics' coterie saw that dialect poetry had neither the wit nor the beauty of folk speech, but was only a continuation of the stock stereotypes about gentility, humility and buffoonery, and an evasion of all of the realities of Negro life.

One counteraction, however, to this dialect poetry was a conscious reverting to Romanticism and neo-Romanticism which reflected a middle-class recognition of Europeanized esthetic values. In some ways, this was a result of the rejection of the minstrel-buffoon stereotype.

In addition, as the middle-class Negro became better educated, there was an increase in his desire to share in the legacy of general culture, to participate in it, even though in a lesser fashion. As Sterling Brown put it, in too many instances "these poets were more concerned with making copies of the 'beauty' that was the stock-in-trade of a languishing tradition." These imitators were, for the most part, only too anxious to avoid any mention of a Negro tradition or to look into their own experiences as Negroes. The result, in their poetry, was escapist, without vitality or understanding.

Along with this counteraction there developed in the same period, the movement which assisted in the Negro writer's spiritual emancipation. As Locke himself wrote in his last published account (1952) of the movement: "For from 1912 on, there was brewing the movement that, in 1925, explicitly became the so-called Renaissance of the New Negro. The movement was not so much in itself a triumph of realism, although it had its share of realists, but a deliberate cessation by Negro authors of their attempts primarily to influence majority opinion. By then, Negro artists had outgrown the handicaps of allowing didactic emphasis and propagandist motives to choke their sense of artistry. Partly in disillusionment, partly in newly acquired group pride and self-respect, they turned inward to the Negro audience in frankly avowed self-expression."

Langston Hughes,[18] one of their number, thus phrased this literary declaration of independence:

We younger Negro artists who create now intend to express our individual dark-skinned selves without fear or shame. If white people are pleased, we are glad. If they are

*not, it doesn't matter. We know we are beautiful. And ugly
too. If colored are pleased, we are glad. If they are not,
their displeasure doesn't matter either. We build our tem-
ples for tomorrow, strong as we know how, and we stand
on the top of the mountain, free within ourselves.*

Once again, there was a common denominator between the advance guard elements of the majority and
the minority. The anti-slavery collaboration had forged
a moral alliance; this was an esthetic one, which spelled
out a final release from propaganda and its shackling
commitments both for Negro materials in American art
and literature and for the Negro artist and writer. And
from 1925 to the present, realism and Southern regional-
ism on the one side, and the promotion of racial self-
expression on the other, have informally but effectively
combined to form a new progressive atmosphere in
American letters.

One of the then new poets, James Weldon Johnson,
sensitive, socially aware, and a founder of the NAACP,
had a considerable influence on the younger generation
of Negro poets. His poems of race consciousness, his
fine commemorative elegy of the fiftieth anniversary of
Negro freedom, praised the Negro's contribution to
American heritage; they were more militant than anything heretofore written. After Du Bois' "Litany of
Atlanta,"[19] Johnson depicted the horrible brutalization
of lynching in his poetry, "grimly prideful and resistant
to the lynch-mad South."

Although the younger Locke had not always seen eye
to eye with the older Du Bois on every issue concerning
the Negro's struggle for artistic emancipation, he had
always admired "The Souls of Black Folk" and "Dark-
water." He had only sympathy for the "Litany" from
whose loins "sprang twin Murder and Black Hate." He
knew of Du Bois' biography of John Brown, he sym-
pathized with the Du Bois attack on the philosophy of
Booker T. Washington.[20] He supported the Niagara
movement and voiced his support for the intellectual
and literary leadership which signalled Du Bois' found-

ing of *The Crisis*, the journal of the NAACP. In the early years, Locke supplied the journal with an annual review of Negro literature, art and music. And Locke joined with those Negro intellectuals who supported Du Bois as the leader of the "talented tenth" movement and of Negro liberalism.

Under the directorship of Du Bois, *The Crisis* became the instrument which led to the vocal and verbal expression of Negro political and artistic leadership. Du Bois was one of the first American scholars to turn to the new scientific approach in the social sciences and this meant new approaches in history and sociology by way of philosophy and scientific method. All of this appealed to the philosophically trained Locke who knew of Du Bois' history, "The Suppression of African Slave Trade to America," whose technique of scientific research and its results might well be applied for the settlement of the Negro problem in America. Locke knew of Du Bois' investigations of the treatment of Negro soldiers by the American army in 1918. Locke supported Du Bois' calls for the Pan-African Congress of 1919, 1921 and 1923. And Locke withdrew from his active role in the NAACP when its Board refused to support Du Bois' Pan-Africanism. He maintained this support until Du Bois' return to Atlanta and supported the "old man's" founding and editorship in 1940 of *Phylon, The Atlanta Review of Race and Culture*. To this journal Locke contributed another annual critical review of literature by and about Negroes.

Opportunity, An American Journal of Negro Life, the organ of the National Urban League, was first edited by Charles S. Johnson. This organ was another impetus to the literary movement with the establishment in 1924 of cash prizes for original literary work. *The Crisis* prizes were established through the sponsorship of Mrs. Amy E. Spingarn and the *Opportunity* prizes through that of Caspar Holstein.[21] Additional prizes were offered later by Carl Van Vechten through *Opportunity* and by Carl Brandt through *Crisis*. Also through *The Crisis*, the

Charles W. Chestnutt Honorarium was given. These prizes were given for many years and had quite an effect upon the younger writers. The title poem to Langston Hughes' first volume won an *Opportunity* prize. "The 'New Negro' was the distillation of the ferment of the preceding decade."

The post-war decade which ushered in the Harlem Renaissance was the age of triumph for big business and the consolidation of industry and monopoly capitalism on a world wide scale. This was conducted by white capital with Negro and immigrant labor, a mass of cheap and potentially efficient labor, unlimited natural power and a use of unequaled technique, reaching all of the markets of the world and leading to the emergence of America as a force in twentieth century world imperialism.

The profits promised by the exploitation of this quasi-colonialism were endangered by labor difficulties; wholesale scabbing by Negroes threatened to flare into race war. Relations between Southern poor whites and Negroes became increasingly exacerbated. The northward emigrations to the cities depleted the rural South and made new ghettos in the North. The shadows of race riots and lynchings remained. And they seared. The Vardamans and Tillmans still ruled the Congress. The Thomas Nelson Pages and Dixons[22] were in the ascendancy in literature. There was bound to be an inevitable conflict between the new graduates of the Negro colleges and the Northerners who had supported the new schools, all of which was symbolized in the struggle and conflicts between Booker T. Washington and Dr. W. E. B. Du Bois. The organization of the Rockefeller-supported General Education Board and the Rosenwald Foundation launched the new racial educational philosophy of the South. By the second decade, a legal caste system based on race and color had been openly grafted onto the democratic conscience of the United States. And the representatives of the New

Negro Movement allied themselves to a man with Du Bois, Locke, Charles Johnson and James Weldon Johnson.

Locke had the auspicious fortune to begin his educational experience at Howard University, where, as an instructor in education and philosophy, he came into contact with many scholars who welcomed the Harvard-, Oxford-, Berlin-trained youth of twenty-five. Meeting and working with Ernest E. Just, the English teacher turned zoologist, was an event, and the two became inseparable friends until Just's untimely death in 1941. The young Locke was accepted and acclaimed by the first Negro to teach sociology, the former classicist and mathematician, Kelly Miller. There were many others such as his classmate, Montgomery Gregory, with whom he organized the Howard Players. Together, these Negro scholars organized into a group known as the Sanhedrin under the joint leadership of Locke and Miller. Locke organized the first literary movement at Howard and remained the faculty advisor of the university literary journal, the *Stylus*, from its beginning until its demise. He helped in the organization of the art gallery and the music department, for he saw that general and cultural education was a desideratum for Negro students. His own educational philosophy predisposed him to manifest the broad approach and an interdisciplinary point of veiw. In so doing, he devoted much of his own teaching to the new science of anthropology, social conflict and social theory. He wrote "Race and Culture Conflict" in 1916.

No one could have been better equipped for the leadership and sponsorship of the New Negro Movement than Locke, who described himself "more of a philosophical midwife to a generation of younger Negro poets, writers and artists than a professional philosopher." For years he had been encouraging artists and musicians to study the African sources at first hand. He was an avid collector of Africana. He wrote expertly about the lost ancestral arts of Africa and traced the influence of African art on European artists in the early twentieth century. He knew a great deal about African influences in Haiti and other Caribbean islands, and he consistently pointed out African influences on the Negro American, both before and after the abolition of slavery.

Alain Locke did not make many original researches into American Negro history or into the golden lore of African history, but he grew in stature as he learned more and more of this history. It taught him that the Negro scholar's ability to withstand the infirmities of the American scene is a dialectic phase of the democratic process. And this dialectic must necessarily aid in bringing into fruition the dream of a community of Negro scholars. This was his sensitivity about American history and it led him to an identity with the great leader, the self-taught Frederick Douglass,[23] about whom he wrote a biography. Locke was deeply appreciative of Du Bois' scientific approach to history and Carter G. Woodson's[24] pioneer scientific work in the history of slavery and the Negro past. His contributions to the New Negro Movement always turned out to be re-evaluations of Negro history as it affected the Negro writer, the Negro scholar, and the lives of all sensitively aware Negroes.

As an author, Locke knew that the story of the Negro writer had to be told, because of the social history involved. He understood that the position of the Negro in American culture had come to mean a great deal more than merely the artistic activity of the Negro minority. It came to mean for him a pointing toward a goal of a "natively characteristic national literature as being one of the crucial issues of cultural democracy." And this had to be evaluated against the slavery and anti-slavery background from which this literature emerged.

The harsh effects of slavery had to be viewed as contributing to the recognition of the Negro's role as partici-

pant and contributor to American culture. "Just as
slavery may now (1952) in perspective be viewed as
having first threatened our democratic institutions and
then forced them to more consistent maturity, the
artistic and cultural impact of the Negro must be
credited with producing unforseen constructive pressures and generating unexpected creative ferment in the
literary and artistic culture of America. In cutting the
Negro loose from his ancestral culture, slavery set up
a unique and unprecedented situation between the
Anglo-Saxon majority and the Negro minority group.
The peculiar conditions of American slavery so scram-
bled Africans from the diverse regions and culture of
our entire continent that with the original background
culture, tribal to begin with, neither a minority language
nor an ancestral tradition remains. The American Negro
was left no alternative but to share the language and
tradition of the majority culture."[25]

The Negro had never set up separate cultural values,
even though he had been forced on many occasions to
take on defensive attitudes of racialism, "an enforced,
protective, counter-attitude, stemming the worst of pro-
scription and discrimination." Locke believed that, despite historical interludes, the Negro's values, ideals and
objectives, have always been integrally and unreservedly
American. He wrote, "The crucial factors in group relationships are social attitudes and literature-recording;
and reflecting these in preference, even in social fact,
becomes the most revealing medium."[26]

Locke wrote more than a dozen books and articles
on Negro art, music and literature, tracing these developments from 1760 up to 1920. He began with the
first Negro poets, essayists and novelists, showing that
the earliest indictments of slavery from the articulate
free Negro displayed signs of a strong race consciousness. He showed that if slavery had molded the emotional and folk life of the Negro, that also it was the

anti-slavery movement which developed the intellect of the Negro and pushed him forward to articulate, disciplined expression. The edifice of chattel slavery was shaken to its foundation by the combined efforts of the literary and oratorical efforts of Negro leaders and self-taught fugitive slaves. The emergence of the "slave narrative" supplied the incandescent spark, to be added to the abolitionist tinder.

In making America aware of the Negro artist and his work, an important part was played by the *Harlem Number* (1925) of the *Survey Graphic* which was edited by Locke. This issue of the *Survey* contained a hundred pages. There were twenty contributors, fifteen Negro and five white, and twelve belonged to the Harlem group. Among the articles were, "Enter the New Negro," "The Making of Harlem," "Black Workers and the City," "Jazz at Home," "Negro Art and America," "The Negro Digs Up His Past," "The Rhythm of Harlem," and many others pertaining to Harlem. This issue of the *Survey* had the largest circulation of any in its history. Several editions had to be run off before the demand was satisfied. In "Black Manhattan" (1930), James Weldon Johnson wrote, "It was a revelation to New York and the country. Later the symposium, somewhat enlarged, was brought out as a book, entitled 'The New Negro,' under the editorship of Alain Locke. It remains one of the most important books on the Negro ever published."

The movement, for a while, *did* thrive in Harlem. Then the "influence of Locke's essays and of the movement in general, spread outward over the country, touching writers in Missouri, Mississippi, in Boston, Philadelphia and Nashville and Chicago."27

Unknowingly, there was being cultivated a middle-class nationalism within the protective folds of the capitalist ethos. The majority did not rebel, but rather hearkened to the voice of bourgeois authority. American capitalism had prospered in the redivision of the profits and spoils of the war. Many of the New Negroes were unwilling victims of an inverted racialistic nationalism, looking upon themselves as having arrived, and priding themselves that they could sing, paint and write as well as their white-skinned patrons.

But, the movement was true "renaissance" in another sense—the antiquity which Negroes wanted to revive from a "lost" African past. However they might share in the leavings of their new found prosperity, if they were to rediscover their racial souls, they had to go back, at least mentally, to the African past. There were the successes and the failures of Du Bois' leadership in the 1921, 1923 and 1925 Pan-African Congresses. The efforts of Locke to instill in the younger poets, artists and musicians, some sense of this African heritage bore fruit in the work of Toomer, Cullen, McKay[28] and Hughes.

The most developed poet and literary figure of the New Negro Movement, Langston Hughes, wrote on all manner of subjects and always movingly of Africa. In 1926, in "Weary Blues," Hughes displayed his artistry of particular power and beauty pursuing his own course more than any other of the New Negroes. Hughes' antecedents were bound up in a family tradition where the struggle for freedom was always a strong memory and inspiration. A grandfather died fighting beside John Brown. An uncle was a Reconstruction Congressman and the first Dean of the Howard Law School. Even Hughes' blues, melodious and rhythmic are full of African feeling as in "Homesick Blues:"

> De railroad bridge's
> A sad song in de air
> Every time de trains pass
> I wants to go somewhere.

The black world of America and Africa came to have a new meaningful nationalistic pride for so many of

these poets. It was not always very deep or couched in
any scientific anthropological understanding, but no
matter, there was precious little understanding at the
time for anyone. What mattered was that this flowering
was a true renaissance of feeling, a prideful evocation
of the dark image of Africa, germinated from a fructi-
fied seedbed but one which took on a new form and
content.

The Harlem Renaissance, substantively, transformed
the Negro as subject and as artist from the old stereotype into the New Negro, militant, no longer obsequious,
more of a paragon because he had shown that he was
nearly on equal terms with his white counterpart. He
won coveted prizes, fellowships, he was being published
and he won his spurs the hard way in creative writing.
These artists were not organized but theirs was a strong
spirit of cohesion, a bond of group consciousness, toward some goal of achievement which would make the
Negro artist proud of his work. It was a self-confidence
which grew and proliferated into an outburst of emotional expression, never matched by any comparable
period in American history. The new generation of
writers began to carve out a niche in the hitherto im-
permeable walls of American literary culture. Hence the
self-confidence, the self-assurance and the pride of
craftsmanship.

The New Poetry Movement embraced every facet of
Negro experience from lyricism, African heritage, social
protest, folk song and blues, Negro heroes and episodes,
lynchings, race riots, treatment of the Negro masses (frequently of the folk, less often of the workers), and
franker and deeper self-revelation, social injustice and
intolerance. Claude McKay's famous "If We Must Die"
became the touchstone for the dynamics of the social
forces and conflicts of the twenties. His was an answer
to the growing crescendo of race riots and lynchings
which characterized the times. Toomer's eloquent out-
cries in "Cane" were race conscious and challenging.

In Cullen's "Shroud of Color," his sense of race is one
of loyalty, pride and group consciousness, "almost the
tone of a chosen people."

Lord, I would live persuaded by mine own
I cannot play the recreant to these:
My spirit has come home, that sailed the doubtful seas.

Hughes' "Brass Spittoons" tells of the distasteful
tasks of menial labor:

Hey, Boy!
A bright bowl of brass is beautiful to the Lord
Bright polished brass like the cymbals
Of King David's dancers
Like the wine cups of Solomon.

These poets, in their different ways, were all in-
fluential in the twenties and thirties, influencing an entire generation of younger poets. Cullen and Toomer in
New York and all over America, Hughes in New York
and all over the world, McKay in New York and the
socialist world, Sterling Brown at Howard and all over
the South, all expressing ideas that were representative
of the New Negro Movement. In "Strong Men," Brown
pens:

They dragged you from your homeland,
They chained you in coffles
They broke you in like oxen
They scourged you
They branded you
    You sang:
        Keep a-inchin' along
        Lak a po' inch worm . . .
    You sang:
        Walk togedder, chillen,
        Dontcha get weary
    The strong men keep a comin' on
    The strong men get stronger.

After Frederick Douglass' fictionalized "Madison Washington" and the short stories of William Wells Brown and Chestnutt, the Negro as short story writer could only emerge from a vacuum even though the short story as literary genre had taken creditable form in America. Negro writers were unable to gain any entree into the magazines. Charles Chestnutt's experiences in 1887 with the *Atlantic Monthly* when the editors did not wish to publicize his racial identity was an infamous blot on American literature. Chestnutt's story "The Goophered Grapevine" was accepted by Walter Hines Page, and later Page accepted "The Wife of His Youth" and belatedly admitted that the author was a Negro, claiming to the editor of the magazine *Critic* that he did not want to do damage to the author's reputation. Dunbar's stories were popular because of the plantation tradition of his dialect style, and they did not offend.

In the late twenties, Langston Hughes faced the problem when *Esquire* published "A Good Job Gone." Hughes wrote about this in *Fighting Words:*[29]

Here are our problems: In the first place, Negro books are considered by editors and publishers as exotic. Negro material is placed, like Chinese material or Bali material, into a certain classification. Magazine editors will tell you, "We can use but so many Negro stories a year." (That "so many" meaning very few.) Publishers will say, "We already have one Negro novel on our list this fall."
When we cease to be exotic, we do not sell well.

These have been the circumscriptions placed on the Negro short story writer on all sides in the publishing world.

When the Negro writer was published in *The Crisis* or in *Opportunity*,[30] the pay was paltry and the stories were predictable. They were concerned with lynchings, race riots, race praise or passing. Many new writers of the Movement wrote well constructed stories which won *The*

Crisis and *Opportunity* prizes.[31] Eric Walrond's "Tropic Death," Langston Hughes' "Ways of White Folks" came close to penetrating into the innermost workings of Negro life which were overlooked by the racial idealists who wrote cloyingly of the new Negro middle-class escapists.

Perhaps the novel as an art form was grist to the mill of the Negro writer at any time or place, whenever he began to write about his own experiences or those of others.[32]

The New Negro Movement produced the first really competent novelists.[33] The forefield of this New Negro literature was an artistic awakening. Publishers may have had only one Negro on their lists, but as the late E. Franklin Frazier[34] pointed out, the audience was not Negro, but white. These writers were very important in the development of the Negro novelist as a craftsman. With these new writers there was great fire and enthusiasm, a creative dynamism of self-conscious racialistic expression which at the time was a healthy manifestation of the problems which beset the Negro people. Thurman, in "Infants of the Spring," satirized the exaggerations and Bohemian aspects of the movement. Fisher, a physician, the first Negro to write a detective story and a writer of social comedy, in "Walls of Jericho," wrote of Harlem jive, a socially intelligent satire of the foibles of the new Negro middle class.

The Negro had come to stay as a novelist and the novelists of the New Negro Movement prepared the way for all of those who were to come later. The genius of Richard Wright[35] burgeoned out of the thirties. Many, like Ralph Ellison, relied heavily on the New Negro novelists' experiences. The writers of the Federal Writers Project of the thirties looked back only a decade to their New Negro precursors. As Sterling Brown wrote in his essay, "The New Negro in Literature (1925–1955)",[36] "Negro authors of the thirties, like their compatriots, faced reality more squarely. For the older light-hearted-

36   HARLEM U.S.A.

ness, they substituted sober self-searching; for the bravado of false Africanism and Bohemianism, they substituted attempts to understand Negro life in its workaday aspects in the here and now. . . . Alert to the changing times, a few critics—Alain Locke among them—charted new directions."

In nineteen thirty James Weldon Johnson in "Black Manhattan" wrote: "Harlem is still in the process of making. It is still new and mixed; so mixed that one may get many different views—which is all right so long as one view is not taken to be the whole picture. This many-sided aspect, however, makes it one of the most interesting communities in America. But Harlem is more than a community, it is a large-scale laboratory experiment in the race problem and from it a good many facts have been found."

And Alain Locke, more prophetic and Cassandra-like than he could have ever known, in the last article written before his death said, "It is to this mirror that I turn for the salient changes of majority attitudes toward the Negro, and equally important, for a view of the Negro's changed attitude toward himself. For the Negro seems at last on the verge of proper cultural recognition and a fraternal acceptance as a welcome participant and collaborator in the American arts. Should this become the realized goal, the history of the Negro's strange and tortuous career in American literature may become also the story of America's hard-won but easily endured attainment of cultural democracy."

Richard B. Moore

AFRICA-CONSCIOUS HARLEM

CONSCIOUSNESS OF AFRICA, if not coeval, certainly existed very early in the development of the Afro-American community in Harlem. This consciousness grew almost as rapidly as the community itself expanded. From the few occupants of two houses on 134th Street west of Fifth Avenue in 1900, this unique community had grown by 1920 into a city within the City of New York. Embracing many thousands, this Harlem enclave then reached from 127th Street on the south of 145th Street on the north and from Fifth to Eighth Avenues. Now some 300,000 people of African descent reach down below 110th Street and up into the Washington Heights area, spread almost from the East to the Hudson rivers.

Harlem's main thoroughfare in 1920 was 135th Street between Lenox and Seventh Avenues, with an almost solid block of houses and stores on its north side owned by St. Philip's Protestant Episcopal Church. In one of these stores, number 135 to be exact, sharing space with the weekly *New York News*, George Young conducted the first Afro-American book shop in Harlem. A pullman porter who had made good use of his travels through the country to assemble a fine collection of Africana and Afro-Americana, Young also endeavored to supply such literature to his people.

In Young's Book Exchange, known then as *The Mecca of Literature Pertaining to Colored People*, there was to be seen what would seem to many, even today, an astonishing array of material treating of Africa and her dispersed descendants. In this small establishment during 1921, a visitor would have seen several copies of the compact book by Dr. W. E. B. Du Bois, which bore the all too current title "The Negro," though this was chiefly devoted to Africa. Alongside would be seen "From Superman to Man" by J. A. Rogers, which exposed racism and pointed to the ancient history and culture of the African peoples.

On the shelves at Young's there reposed histories written by Afro-Americans and African authors. Numerous books by European and Euro-American authors included important references to Africans by Abolitionists. Revealing volumes expressed the consciousness of Africa and marshalled evidence of early African culture and its significant contribution to Europe and the world in crushing refutation of the racist theories of inequality.

Further indication of this consciousness of African provenance and common heritage were the writings by scholars native to the Caribbean area.

That this consciousness of Africa was active and widespread was perhaps significantly shown in the reprinting and distribution by George Young in 1920 of "The Aims and Methods of a Liberal Education for Africans," the Inaugural Address delivered by Edward Wilmot Blyden, LL.D., President of Liberia College, January 5, 1881. Nor was this interest in Africa a new thing. For despite ruthless repression under the chattel slave system, the transplanted Africans could never be reduced to total cultural blankness.[37]

Consciousness of their ancestral homeland has thus been historically evident from the first arrivals when some of these Africans, brought as slaves into the Americas, killed themselves believing that they would thereby return to Africa. Awareness of their heritage of culture and dignity continued during the colonial period and the early days of this republic.

At that time, the name *African* was preferred and used instead of the slave-masters' degrading epithet "Negro." Witness thus The Free African Society, founded in Philadelphia in 1817 by Richard Allen and Absalom Jones. This was the forerunner of the African Protestant Episcopal Church of St. Thomas and also of the African Methodist Episcopal Church. Note also the African Lodge of Prince Hall Masons in Boston; the African Mehodist Episcopal Zion Church, African Society for Mutual Aid, African Grove Playhouse in New York; and many so named throughout the country.

As early as 1788 an organized body of Afro-Americans in Newport, R. I., which included Paul Cuffee who was soon to make history in this respect, wrote to the Free African Society of Philadelphia proposing a plan for emigration to Africa. In 1811 Paul Cuffee sailed in his own ship to Sierra Leone to investigate the feasibility of founding a settlement there. In 1815 at his own expense, amounting to some $4,000, Captain Paul Cuffee, consummating twenty years of thought and effort, sailed forth again to Sierra Leone, this time commanding the good ship *Traveler* with 38 Afro-American emigrants aboard, which included several whom he had boldly rescued from slavery along the Atlantic seaboard.

Paul Cuffee's achievement gave impetus to the founding of the American Colonization Society in 1817. But this body was dominated by slaveholders with the object of getting rid of free Afro-Americans whose very presence and example encouraged the slaves to seek freedom. Hence the American Colonization Society was powerfully opposed by free-spirited Afro-Americans and their Abolitionist allies.

Nevertheless, several Afro-American leaders took advantage of the operation of the American Colonization Society to foster self-government in Africa through the founding of Liberia. By 1848 the population of Liberia included some 3,000 persons of African descent who had emigrated from the United States of America and the Caribbean.

The distinguished Afro-American scholar, Rev. Alexander Crummell, after graduating from Cambridge University in 1853, spent twenty years teaching and laboring in Africa. Commissioned in 1858 by a convention of Afro-Americans held in Chatham, Canada, West, Martin R. Delaney led an expedition into what is now Nigeria and in 1861 published his "Official Report of the Niger Valley Exploring Party." This mission had even signed a treaty with African rulers at Abeokuta which authorized a projected settlement, but this project lapsed after the outbreak of the Civil War in the U.S.A. The other commissioner of this expedition, Professor Robert Campbell, published his report in "A Pilgrimage to My Motherland. "

After the Civil War and Reconstruction, interest was revived in African settlement as a great exodus began from the South, due to the wholesale massacre of some 40,000 Afro-Americans by such terrorist organizations as the Ku Klux Klan. This reign of terror reached monstrous proportions after the withdrawal of federal troops from the South. A new movement for migration to Africa was fostered jointly by Afro-American Baptists and Methodists. Organizations were established in several states, notably the Liberian Exodus and Joint Stock Company in North Carolina and the Freedmen's Emigration Aid Society in South Carolina. This last acquired the ship *Azor* for $7,000, and this ship actually carried 274 emigrants to Africa on one of its trips, despite the efforts of prejudiced European-Americans to impose outrageous costs and to hinder its operation. The *Azor* was soon stolen and sold in Liverpool; the attempts to recover it failed when the U.S. Circuit Court refused even to entertain the suit brought to this end.

About 1881 a descendant of Paul Cuffee, Captain Harry Dean, sailed to Africa commanding his ship the *Pedro Gorino* with the object "to rehabilitate Africa and found an Ethiopian Empire as the world has never seen." Another expedition took 197 emigrants from Savannah, Georgia, to Liberia. "Chief Sam" of Kansas launched a movement to sail ships and build a state in Africa, but this movement failed to achieve its goals.

This tradition was known in Harlem, and interest in Africa was constantly stimulated by the generally well-informed outdoor speakers of the twenties, who lectured on African history and stressed unity with the African people.

Militant socialists steadily emphasized the liberation of the oppressed African and other colonial peoples as a vital aim of their world view. Above all Hubert H. Harrison[38] gave forth from his encyclopedic store a wealth of knowledge of African history and culture which brought this consciousness to a very great height. A vigorous press which circulated widely in Harlem also intensified this consciousness of Africa.

Vibrant echoes too had reached Harlem of the Pan-African Conference, organized in London during 1900 by Henry Sylvester-Wiliams, a barrister-at-law born in Trinidad of African ancestry. This Conference elected as general chairman Bishop Alexander Walters of the African Methodist Episcopal Zion Church, and W. E. B. Du Bois as chairman of the Committee on Address to the World. Stimulating news had come of the Second Pan-African Conference organized by Dr. Du Bois and held in Paris early in 1919, following the significant though unsuccessful attempts made independently by William Monroe Trotter and Dr. Du Bois to present the case of the oppressed peoples of African descent before the Versailles Peace Conference in 1918. Several distinguished visitors to Harlem contributed greatly to this ever growing consciousness of Africa, among them F. E. M. Hercules, a native of Trinidad and founder of an organization seeking to unify all the descendants of Africa everywhere. Dr. J. Edmeston Barnes, born in Barbados, came directly from London with a similar program calling also for the rejection of the disrespectful and denigrating name "Negro," which he condemned as "a bastard political colloquialism." Likewise, Albert Thorne of Barbados and Guiana projected the ideas of his African Colonial Enterprise, which was designed to embrace all peoples of African origin.

Harlem had thus become considerably Africa conscious, and this consciousness was soon to build the movement which was carried to great heights of mass emotion, widespread projection, and stupendous endeavor by the skillful propagandist and promoter, Marcus Garvey. When Garvey arrived from Jamaica in 1916, Harlem was emerging as the vanguard and focal point, "the cultural capital" of ten million Afro-Americans and to some extent also of other peoples of African origin in the Western Hemisphere. The demand for labor, due to the First World War, rapidly augmented the growth of Harlem, as thousands poured in from the South, the Caribbean, and Central America.

Harlem then seethed with a great ferment, bitterly resenting oppression and discrimination, particularly the treatment meted out to its crack Fifteenth Regiment. Harlem reacted vigorously also against the brutal lynchings then growing throughout the country, and especially against the frightful wholesale massacre in East St. Louis in July 1917. Some 10,000 of Harlem's citizens marched down Fifth Avenue carrying placards in the Silent Protest Parade led by the National Association for the Advancement of Colored People. The hanging of thirteen Afro-American soldiers following the Houston affair, when they had retaliated against wanton attack by prejudiced Southerners, stirred mounting anger, frustration, and despair.

Marcus Garvey saw the opportunity to harness this upsurge against oppression and to direct the existing consciousness of Africa into a specific organized movement under his leadership. Realizing the deep-seated if unconscious desire of the disinherited people of African origin for equal or similar status to that of others in every phase of human thought and endeavor, Garvey projected various means and enterprises which appealed to and afforded expression of this basic human desire.

After a poor initial meeting at St. Mark's Hall and some outdoor attempts, Marcus Garvey secured his first favorable public response when introduced by Hubert H. Harrison at a huge meeting held at the Bethel AME[39] Church. Following several abortive attempts, Garvey finally launched the reorganized New York Division of the Universal Negro Improvement Association and African Communities League. With the publication of the *Negro World* in January 1918, carrying sections in French and Spanish as well as in English, the movement spread through the United States and abroad.

The founder of the *Negro World* was astute enough to secure the editorial services of Professor William H. Ferris, graduate of Yale University and well versed in African lore, Hubert H. Harrison, and of such skillful writers as W. A. Domingo, Eric Walrond, and Hudson C. Pryce. Duse Mohamed, the Sudanese Egyptian nationalist who had formerly employed Garvey in London, and from whom Garvey derived the slogan "Africa for the Africans," also worked for a time on the *Negro World*.

The convention held in August 1920 in Liberty Hall,

Boston, the dramatic, colorful, and impressive parade, costumes, and pageantry, and the mammoth meeting at Madison Square Garden, established the Garvey movement as a powerful international force. Stirring hymns with African themes, especially the UNIA[40] anthem composed by Rabbi Arnold J. Ford of Barbados, were rendered by choral groups and massed bands. Thousands joined the UNIA, the African Legion, the Black Cross Nurses, and later the African Orthodox Church. Enthusiastic supporters poured their savings into the enterprise started by Garvey, the restaurant, hotel, grocery, millinery, tailoring and dressmaking establishments, publishing concern, and finally the Black Star Line and the Negro Factories Corporation.[41]

It is difficult and still perhaps somewhat hazardous to attempt an objective estimate of the Garvey movement, yet this is necessary if we are to learn from its lessons and apply them wisely in our present endeavors. To this writer it appears that the founder and leader of the UNIA demonstrated two powerful drives which were basically opposed to each other. One was clearly the progressive tendency which projected "the redemption of Africa" and the "Declaration of Rights of the Negro People of the World." The other was obviously reactionary in its Nepoleonic urge for personal power and empire, with the inevitable accompaniment of racial exclusiveness and hostility. This latter tendency was evident when Garvey declared, on taking the title of Provisional President of Africa in 1920, "The signal honor of being Provisional President of Africa is mine. . . . It is like asking Napoleon to take the world."

Unfortunately, Marcus Garvey veered toward the more extreme forms of empire building, unlimited individual control, and unrestrained racism. At length these destructive forces were allowed to overshadow and outweigh the constructive, pristine ideas of African nationalism, liberation, and independence. Stridently advocating "racial purity," Garvey came at length to

agree openly with the worst enemies of the Afro-
American people—the white supremacist leaders of the
Anglo-Saxon clubs and even of the murderous Ku Klux
Klan—in declaring America to be "a white man's
country."

Besides, the constant attacks which Marcus Garvey
made upon people of both African and European ancestry, whom he derisively called "the hybrids of the
Negro race," did not conduce to the unifying of all
people of African descent, who, regardless of varying
shades of color and other physical characteristics, were
compelled to suffer similar oppressions whether as
colonial subjects or as oppressed minority groups. Likewise, Garvey's condemnation of the principal leaders
and organizations, which were striving for human rights
and equal citizenship status for the Afro-American
minority group in this country, was bound to arouse
opposition and internal strife.

Finally, the open condemnation of Liberian officials
by Marcus Garvey, his severe reprisals against several
of his chief associates, his poor choice of certain officers,
and the inept conduct of the business enterprises which
he controlled, left the movement wide open to the
disastrous blows of those who began to fear its growing
power. Following his conviction and imprisonment on
February 8, 1925, upon a charge of using the mails to
defraud in connection with the sale of Black Star Line
stock, the Garvey movement split into wrangling factions, and despite efforts to revive it, only a few splinter
groups remained. Nevertheless, the Garvey movement
did heighten and spread the consciousness of African
origin and identity among the various peoples of African
descent on a wider scale than ever before. This was its
definite and positive contribution.

Developing almost parallel with the Garvey movement
was what has come to be known as the Harlem Literary
Renaissance.

This was no Minerva sprung full-fledged from the

head of Jove, for while its immediate inspiration lay in the surrounding social conditions, its roots, too, went back through earlier Afro-American writers to the bards of ancient Africa. Alain Locke observed two constructive channels: "One is the advance guard of the African peoples in their contact with twentieth century civilization; the other, the sense of a vision of rehabilitating the race in world esteem. . . ."

How these Harlem avant-garde writers felt, expressed, and stimulated consciousness of Africa may be observed in a few typical outpourings. In the sonnet "Africa" published in "Harlem Shadows," the Caribbean born poet, Claude McKay, extolled:

The sun sought thy dim bed and brought forth light,
The sciences were sucklings at thy breast;
When all the world was young in pregnant night
Thy slaves toiled at thy monumental best.
Thou ancient treasure-land, thou modern prize,
New peoples marvel at thy pyramids!

The rather pessimistic note on which this sonnet ended still persisted in "Outcast" when McKay lamented the ancestral motherland in a mood of wistful nostalgia:

For the dim regions whence my fathers came
My spirit, bondaged by the body, longs;
Words felt, but never heard, my lips would frame;
Thy soul would sing forgotten jungle songs.

In "Enslaved" the poet broods over his people:

For weary centuries despised, oppressed,
Enslaved and lynched, denied a human place
In the great life line of the Christian West;
And in the Black Land disinherited,
Robbed in the ancient country of its birth; . . .

At length this searing consciousness gave rise to that famous cry of passionate revolt in "If We Must Die":

What though before us lies the open grave?
Like men we'll face the murderous, cowardly pack,
Pressed to the wall, dying, but fighting back!

And in "Exhortation: Summer, 1919" Claude McKay turns toward the future confidently with this clarion call:

From the deep primeval forests where the crouching leopard's lurking,
Lift your heavy-lidded eyes, Ethiopia! awake!
For the big earth groans in travail for the strong, new world in making—
O my brothers, dreaming for long centuries,
Wake from sleeping; to the East turn, turn your eyes!

Similarly, in "The Negro Speaks of Rivers" in his first published volume "The Weary Blues," Langston Hughes sang profoundly:

I've known rivers
I've known rivers ancient as the world and older than the flow of human blood in human veins.
My soul has grown deep like the rivers.
I bathed in the Euphrates when dawns were young.
I built my hut near the Congo and it lulled me to sleep.
I looked upon the Nile and raised pyramids above it. . . .

Langston Hughes further expressed his retrospective identification with Africa:

We should have a land of trees
Bowed down with chattering parrots
Brilliant as the day,
And not this land where birds are gray.

Again, in the poem "Georgia Dusk" included in "Cane," Jean Toomer, while etching the toilers in southern canefield and saw mill, recalls the ancestors from the long-past life of dignity and freedom in Africa:

Meanwhile, the men, with vestiges of pomp,
Race memories of king and caravan,

High priests, and ostrich and a ju-ju man,
Go singing through the footpaths of the swamp.

Countee Cullen mused long and lyrically in the poem
"Heritage" which is outstanding in the book "Color":

What is Africa to me:
Copper sun or scarlet sea,
Jungle star or jungle track,
Strong bronzed men, or regal black
Women from whose loins I sprang
When the birds of Eden sang?
One three centuries removed
From the scenes his fathers loved,
Spicy grove, cinnamon tree,
What is Africa to me?

Plaintively pondering his "high-priced conversion" to
Christianity and humility, the poet needs must transmute
this experience in terms consonant with his deeper ancestral self:

Lord, I fashion dark gods, too,
Daring even to give You
Dark despairing features where,
Crowned with dark rebellious hair,
Patience wavers just so much as
Mortal grief compels, while touches
Quick and hot, of anger, rise
To smitten cheek and weary eyes.
Lord forgive me if my need
Sometimes shapes a human creed.

The sense of dignity and power derived from Africa
led this poet to an anguished effort to restrain with
reason from a premature revolt against intolerable oppression:

All day long and all night through,
One thing only must I do:
Quench my pride and cool my blood,
Lest I perish in the flood,

Lest a hidden ember set
Timber that I thought was wet
Burning like the dryest flax,
Melting like the merest wax,
Lest the grave restore its dead.
Not yet has my heart or head
In the least way realized
They and I are civilized.

Following the failure of the Garvey movement, consciousness of Africa was bolstered in Harlem by the campaign of the American Negro Labor Congress for the liberation of the colonial peoples of Africa and Asia. Representing this body, this writer went as a delegate to the Congress Against Imperialism held in Brussels in 1927. As the forerunner of the Asian-African Conference held at Bandung in April 1955, the Brussels Congress was recalled and noted by President Sukarno of Indonesia in his opening address, "At that Conference many distinguished delegates who are present here today met each other and found new strength in their fight for independence."

The Commission on the African Peoples of the World elected at the Brussels Congress Against Imperialism included the brilliant Senegalese leaders Lamine Senghor, who died shortly afterward in a French jail, and Garan Kouyatte, who was shot by the Nazis during their occupation of Paris in 1940. Other outstanding members of this Commission were Mr. Makonnen of Ethiopia, J. T. Gumede, vice president of the African National Congress of South African, and J. A. La Guma, secretary of the South African Non-European Trade Union Federation. The writer served as secretary of the Commission.

The resolution prepared by the Commission and adopted by the Brussels Congress Against Imperialism, called for the complete liberation of the African peoples, the restoration of their lands, and several other measures including the establishment of a University at Addis

Ababa for the training of candidates for leadership in
the trade union, cultural, and liberation movements of
the oppressed African peoples.

A new wave of consciousness spread through Harlem
as people reacted to Mussolini's fascist, military aggres-
sion against Ethiopia in October 1935. Organizations
were set up to mobilize support; the executive director
of the International Council of Friends of Ethiopia, Dr.
Willis N. Huggins, was commissioned to deliver an appeal on behalf of Ethiopia to the League of Nations in
Geneva, Switzerland. Arden Bryan, president of the
Nationalist Negro Movement, sent petitions to the
League and protests to the British Foreign Office and
the U. S. State Department against their failure to aid
Ethiopia. These appeals, had they been listened to, could
have helped to prevent both the establishment of concentration camps and the Second World War.

When invading Italian airplanes monstrously rained
down deadly yperite gas on the Ethiopian people,
huge protest meetings were organized by the people of
Harlem. The Ethiopian Pacific Movement, from a gigantic rally at Rockland Palace,[42] forwarded protests and
also sent telegrams to Asian, African, Australian, Central and South American nations, appealing for action
in defense of Ethiopia. Several organizations joined in
the United Aid to Ethiopia.

A delegation composed of the organization's officers
was sent to the First Congress of the International Peace
Campaign meeting in Brussels, early in September 1936,
with instructions to try to influence the Congress to take
action in support of Ethiopia. The delegation inter-
viewed Emperor Haile Selassie in London and requested
him to send a representative to cooperate in the work
here. Dr. Malaku E. Bayen, cousin and personal physician to the Emperor, was appointed and was greeted
with acclaim at a great meeting at Rockland Palace.
Meanwhile funds were raised in Harlem and medical
supplies sent through the Medical Aid to Ethiopia.

The Ethiopian World Federation, then organized in Harlem, spread through the country, the Caribbean, and elsewhere. *The Voice of Ethiopia* published news from the Ethiopian front and further stimulated the campaign of resistance. Haile Selassie's memorable and immortal speech to the League of Nations in Geneva was printed and distributed in pamphlet form. Men and women of Harlem tried to join the Ethiopian Army but were prevented from doing this by the State Department, which refused to issue them passports. Nevertheless, the Afro-American aviator, Colonel John C. Robinson, known as the "Brown Condor," got to Ethiopia and executed many heroic missions. *The Pittsburgh Courier* sent J. A. Rogers as a war correspondent. Since that time, Mr. Rogers has written a number of the best and most authentic books on Africa, its history and its culture.

After the Italian invaders were driven out of Ethiopia in 1941, this intense fraternal consciousness in Harlem subsided into a residual sense of unity with all African peoples. When the Suez Canal was invaded in October 1956 by Britain and France, and massacre and destruction threatened the people of Port Said, Suez, Alexandria and Cairo, Harlem demonstrated its solidarity with President Nasser and the people of Egypt. Harlem rejoiced when the note sent by Premier Khrushchev of the Soviet Union, demanding that withdrawal of the invading forces begin within twenty-four hours, led to the timely evacuation of these aggressors.

Consciousness of Africa mounted again as more and more African nations regained their independence. The inhuman atrocities of the French colonialists against the Algerian people aroused widespread sympathy and fraternal support among the people of Harlem. Active consciousness reached its zenith when the Congo was betrayed and dismembered and its dedicated leaders, especially Prime Minister Patrice Lumumba, were foully and brutally done to death. Harlem boiled with fierce resentment against the failure of the United Nations to support the government of the Congo Republic and to prevent the murder of its Prime Minister and other officials.

This fierce indignation among the people of Harlem gave rise to the outburst in the visitors' gallery of the United Nations on February 15, 1961. Reactionary forces loudly denounced this protest upsurge, and pseudo-liberals presumed to lecture and to condemn the protesting Afro-American people while excusing the Belgian and other colonialist seceders and murderers.

Harlem remains today conscious of its African heritage and basic kinship. This consciousness is by no means limited to the various groups which call themselves "nationalists," and who are quite vocal but who actually contribute little or no substantial, direct support to the African liberation movements. Yet such effective support is vitally needed at this very moment in the present critical and decisive struggle now being waged for the liberation of the peoples of Central and South Africa.

The limits of this survey preclude more detail here. It should be stated, however, that these Harlem "nationalist" groups are as yet unable to unite among themselves, due largely, it appears, to self-centered power drives and competition for leadership. The tendency persists among them, unfortunately, to oppose other organizations which have the largest following of the Afro-American people and to condemn these leaders caustically and constantly. Obviously, this hinders rather than helps to achieve the *united action* needed to support the African liberation movements and to further the struggle for civil liberties and human rights here in the U.S.A.

Returning to the main currents of Harlem life, it is fitting to recognize the chief intellectual forces which have heightened consciousness of Africa since the 1930's. Outstanding is the Schomburg Collection of literature on Africa and people of African descent, established as a special reference library by the New York Public Library. The development of this institution has been carried forward by Mrs. Catherine Latimer and Mrs. Jean Blackwell Hutson.[43] The Countee Cullen Branch displays and features books on Africa for general circulation. Stimulating study classes were led by Dr. Willis N. Huggins, and of special note were the several profound and scholarly lecture series given by Prof. William Leo Hansberry. Significant also has been the activity of the Association for the Study of Negro Life and History, founded by Dr. Carter G. Woodson.

Today, in the main stream of life and thought in Harlem, interest as well as identification with Africa grows apace. In homes, more books on African life and development are seen and read. This concurs with the increasing sale of African literature in Harlem bookshops; the trend in the Frederick Douglass Book Center has been markedly away from general fiction and toward the history and culture of peoples of African origin. Among fraternal societies and clubs, in church and school, library and lecture hall, more programs than ever before are being presented on various aspects of African life and liberation.

Along with its work to emphasize the names *African* and *Afro-American* as fitting and honorable designations, the Committee To Present The Truth About The Name "Negro" has conducted and plans more lecture series on the history and culture of African peoples.

A new approach to history buttresses the Afro-American's pride in his heritage. Today, the arrogant assumption that the black man should be grateful for the crumbs of civilization and culture which have fallen to him from the white man's table is being blown away by the hurricane of change. It is a change which is writing a new page in history as it sweeps over Africa, as it brings millions of Afro-Americans into a determined stand to make the Civil Rights Bill work.

The pioneer historian, Dr. Carter G. Woodson, in-

itiated and popularized the practice of celebrating the
second week in February as a seven-day commemora-
tion of the role of our people in America and in the
world, and as an occasion for the Afro-American to
deepen his knowledge of his own rich and prideful
history.[44]

Significant was the American Negro Leadership Conference held November 1962 at Arden House in Harri-
man, New York. For this involved the principal Afro-
American organizations active or represented in Harlem
and the country—the NAACP, CORE, the Brotherhood
of Sleeping Car Porters, National Council of Negro
Women, National Urban League, the Southern Christian
Leadership Conference, and the American Society For
African Culture.
    Utterly reprehensible is the disruptive campaign
being waged by newspaper columnist George S. Schuyler
and his accomplices in mind-twisting which has rendered
aid and comfort to the Belgian and other neo-colonialist
oppressors in the Congo Republic and to the Portu-
guese imperialist butchers of the peoples of Angola and
Mozambique.
    Completely disproving the false and venomous general
accusations made by George S. Schuyler et al. in the
N.Y. Courier of the African statesmen's indifference
and hostility to Afro-American people was the reported
reaction of African Foreign Ministers at the Conference
of African States held in the Addis Ababa, Ethiopia.
The New York Times of May, 1963 published their
special correspondent's report that the Foreign Minister
of Nigeria rose "to denounce racial discrimination in
South Africa and the United States." This report also
states, "American observers have been dismayed to hear
Alabama linked with South Africa in attacks on
apartheid inside and outside the conference hall," and
further that "American correspondents approaching
members of delegations frequently hear the question,
'What's the latest news from Birmingham?'"

The Ethiopian *Herald*, which is the official publication of the Ministry of Information, is quoted as having commented:

What happened in Birmingham last week shows the United States in its true light. To be black is still a crime . . . The colored American must fight hard for freedom rather than waste time and much needed energy belly-aching about Communism. The United States version of "civilized apartheid" must be fought.

Acting on behalf of the thirty African nations assembled in this Conference at Addis Ababa, Prime Minister Milton Obote of Uganda sent a letter to the late President Kennedy which condemned the "most inhuman treatment" perpetrated upon Afro-Americans at Birmingham, Alabama, and which further stated:

Nothing is more paradoxical than that these events should take place in the United States at a time when that country is anxious to project its image before the world as the archetype of democracy and champion of freedom.

At a news conference held on May 23rd, 1963, as reported in *The New York Times*, Prime Minister Obote recognized that those "who had been doused with blasts of water from fire hoses in Birmingham were 'our kith and kin,'" and declared further that, the eyes of the world were "concentrated on events in Alabama and it is the duty of the free world, and more so of countries that hold themselves up as leaders of the free world, to see that all their citizens, regardless of color, are free."

It may be predicted confidently, despite the malicious efforts of a few venal slanderers, that consciousness of Africa will continue to grow in Harlem and among Afro-Americans generally. An even more vigorous and healthy development of this consciousness will come when it is more fully realized that rationally no conflict really or properly exists between vital interest in our

African heritage and the liberation of the African peoples, and deep and active devotion to the cause of human rights and equal citizenship status in the U.S.A. For the social forces which spawned colonialist subjugation in Africa and other areas are the identical forces responsible for brutal enslavement and racist oppression in the Americas and elsewhere.

Freedom and the full development of the human personality, therefore, require independence for the African peoples as well as full citizenship rights with equal status and opportunity for the minority people of African descent wherever they now exist. The same inherent self-respect and will to be free, which led Paul Cuffee to wage a successful struggle for the vote and equal citizenship rights in Massachusetts immediately after the American Revolution of 1776, also led this great pioneer leader to promote self-determination through migration and the development of Sierra Leone in Africa. An enlightened awareness of African lore and liberty is, and will continue to be, the inevitable expression of the indomitable will to self-knowledge, self-determination, self-realization, and self-development on parity with all mankind.

Langston Hughes

MY EARLY DAYS IN HARLEM

On a BRIGHT September morning in 1921, I came up out of the subway at 135th and Lenox into the beginnings of the Negro Renaissance. I headed for the Harlem YMCA down the block, where so many new, young, dark, male arrivals in Harlem have spent early days. The next place I headed to that afternoon was the Harlem Branch Library just up the street. There, a warm and wonderful librarian, Miss Ernestine Rose, white, made newcomers feel welcome, as did her assistant in charge of the Schomburg Collection, Catherine Latimer, a luscious café au lait. That night I went to the Lincoln Theatre across Lenox Avenue where maybe one of the Smiths—Bessie, Clara, Trixie, or Mamie—was singing the blues. And as soon as I could, I made a beeline for Shuffle Along, the all-colored hit musical playing on 63rd Street in which Florence Mills[45] came to fame.

I had come to New York to enter Columbia College as a freshman, but *really* why I had come to New York was to see Harlem. I found it hard a week or so later to tear myself away from Harlem when it came time to move up the hill to the dormitory at Columbia. That winter I spent as little time as possible on the campus.

Instead, I spent as much time as I could in Harlem, and this I have done ever since. I was in love with Harlem long before I got there, and I still am in love with it. Everybody seemed to make me welcome. The sheer dark size of Harlem intrigued me. The fact that at that time poets and writers like James Weldon Johnson and Jessie Fauset lived there, and Bert Williams, Duke Ellington, Ethel Waters, and Walter White,[46] too, fascinated me. Had I been a rich young man, I would have bought a house in Harlem and built musical steps up to the front door, and installed chimes that at the press of a button played Ellington tunes.

After a winter at Columbia, I moved back down to Harlem. Everywhere I roomed, I had the good fortune to have lovely landladies. If I did not like a landlady's looks, I would not move in with her, maybe that is why. But at finding work in New York, my fortune was less than good. Finally, I went to sea—Africa, Europe— then a year in Paris working in a night club where the band was from Harlem. I was a dishwasher, later bus boy, listening every night to the music of Harlem transplanted to Montmartre. And I was on hand to welcome Bricktop[47] when she came to sing for the first time in Europe, bringing with her news of Harlem.

When I came back to New York in 1925 the Negro Renaissance was in full swing. Countee Cullen was publishing his early poems, Aaron Douglas was painting, Zora Neale Hurston, Rudolph Fisher, Jean Toomer and Wallace Thurman were writing, Louis Armstrong was playing, Cora La Redd was dancing, and the Savoy Ballroom was open with a specially built floor that rocked as the dancers swayed. Alain Locke was putting together "The New Negro." Art took heart from Harlem creativity. Jazz filled the night air—but not everywhere —and people came from all around after dark to look upon our city within a city, Black Harlem. Had I not had to earn a living, I might have thought it even more wonderful than it was. But I could not eat the poems I

wrote. Unlike the whites who came to spend their money
in Harlem, only a few Harlemites seemed to live in even
a modest degree of luxury. Most rode the subway downtown every morning to work or to look for work.

Downtown! I soon learned that it was seemingly impossible for black Harlem to live without white downtown. My youthful illusion that Harlem was a world
unto itself did not last very long. It was not even an
area that ran itself. The famous night clubs were owned
by whites, as were the theatres. Almost all the stores
were owned by whites, and many at that time did not
even (in the very middle of Harlem) employ Negro
clerks. The books of Harlem writers all had to be published downtown, if they were to be published at all.
Downtown: *white*. Uptown: *black*. White downtown
pulling all the strings in Harlem. Moe Gale, Lew Leslie,
Harper's, Knopf, *The Survey Graphic*, the Harmon
Foundation,[48] the racketeers who kidnapped Caspar
Holstein and began to take over the numbers for whites.
Negroes could not even play their own numbers with
their *own* people. And almost all the policemen in Harlem were white. Negroes couldn't even get graft from
themselves for themselves by themselves. Black Har-
lem really was in white face, economically speaking. So
I wrote this poem:

> Because my mouth
> Is wide with laughter,
> And my throat
> Is deep with song,
> You do not think
> I suffer after
> I have held my pain
> So long?
>
> Because my mouth
> Is wide with laughter,
> You do not hear
> My inner cry?

Because my feet
Are gay with dancing,
You do not know
I die?

Harlem, like a Picasso painting in his cubistic period.
Harlem—Southern Harlem—the Carolinas, Georgia,
Florida—looking for the Promised Land—dressed in
rhythmic words, painted in bright pictures, dancing to
jazz—and ending up in the subway at morning rush
time—*headed downtown*. West Indian Harlem—warm
rambunctious sassy remembering Marcus Garvey.
Haitian Harlem, Cuban Harlem, little pockets of tropical
dreams in alien tongues. Magnet Harlem, pulling an
Arthur Schomburg from Puerto Rico, pulling an Arna
Bontemps all the way from California, a Nora Holt
from way out West, an E. Simms Campbell from St.
Louis, likewise a Josephine Baker, a Charles S. Johnson
from Virginia, an A. Philip Randolph from Florida, a
Roy Wilkins from Minnesota, an Alta Douglas from
Kansas.[49] Melting pot Harlem—Harlem of honey and
chocolate and caramel and rum and vinegar and lemon
and lime and gall. Dusky dream Harlem rumbling into
a nightmare tunnel where the subway from the Bronx
keeps right on downtown, where the money from the
nightclubs goes right on back downtown, where the jazz
is drained to Broadway, whence Josephine goes to Paris,
Robeson to London, Jean Toomer to a Quaker Meeting
House, Garvey to the Atlanta Federal Penitentiary, and
Wallace Thurman to his grave; but Duke Ellington to
fame and fortune, Lena Horne to Broadway, and Buck
Clayton to China.

Before it was over—our New Negro Renaissance—
poems became placards: Don't buy where you can't
work! Adam Powell with a picket sign; me, too. Buy
black! Sufi long before the Black Muslims. First to be
fired, last to be hired! The Stock Market crash. The
bank failures. Empty pockets. *God Bless The Child*

That's Got His Own. Depression. Federal Theatre in Harlem, the making of Orson Welles. WPA, CCC, the Blue Eagle, Father Divine. In the midst of the Depression I got a cable from Russia inviting me to work on a motion picture there. I went to Moscow. That was the end of the early days of Langston Hughes in Harlem.

E. U. Essien-Udom

჻

THE NATIONALIST
MOVEMENTS OF HARLEM

A COUNT OF contemporary Afro-American "nationalist" organizations in Harlem discloses more than two
dozen and a combined membership of about 5,000
—considerably smaller than the 30,000 membership
scored forty years ago by the New York City division
of the Garvey movement. They vary in size from
crackpot-type sects, with a handful of members, to
more serious, well-organized, and highly disciplined
Muhammad's Mosque No. 7, led by Minister Malcolm
X. Shabbazz, or the Yoruba Temple of "New Oyo"
(the congregation named Harlem "New Oyo" after the
historic Kingdom of Oyo, West Africa), led by the
Babalosha (chief priest), Nana Oserjeman Adefunmi.[50]
These groups reveal a wide range of organizational
patterns (most are run as petty "fiefs" of their leaders), ideologies, and objectives, though all pretend to
have the same basic objective: Afro-American liberation. At any rate, they subscribe to one or more variants
of Negro nationalism. Nearly all are woefully weak,
insignificant organizations, and apart, from the Nation
of Islam, they have been completely ineffective in
evolving a nation-wide nationalist movement in the

United States. On the whole, the leadership of these groups is inadequately educated or informed; hence, they tend to misunderstand their role in the contemporary Negro freedom movement in the United States; they are equally misunderstood by their countrymen.

If we are to comprehend the social manifestations generally called Black Nationalism among Afro-Americans in Harlem and elsewhere in the United States, if we are to appreciate its place in the Negro freedom movement, we must dispel a few prejudices which are obstacles to our understanding. First, a widespread belief that there exists in the United States a consolidated body of black nationalists, explicitly and unswervingly committed to a political program for achieving political self-determination.

The second, derived from the first belief, is what I call the "conspiracy theory" of Black Nationalism. This theory explains nationalistic tendencies among Negroes as a vast conspiracy against the government and people of the United States. Evidence of this view is to be found in statements of some legislators, in at least one official report, viz., the "Eleventh Annual Report" of the State of California's Senate Committee on Un-American Activities, in newspaper and quasi-scholarly accounts, and in "trigger happy" attitudes of some local law enforcement officers, especially toward the Muslim movement. The conspiracy theory fails to recognize Black Nationalism as a variant of Negro protest, obscures issues, and tends to divert public attention from the deplorable conditions of the masses of Negroes. Implicitly, this theory explains away the legitimate protest of the oppressed against an unjust social situation and helps to mask the absence of long-term self-help and "uplifting" programs for the social and cultural elevation of the masses of Negroes. Furthermore, the conspiracy theory serves to perpetuate the erroneous belief that the Negro will endure suffering with Job-like patience and sphinx-like silence.

A third obstacle to our understanding of Negro nationalism is widespread public ignorance of the history
of Negro protest in the United States. This is because
no serious effort has been made at any level of white-
dominated educational institutions to incorporate the
historic struggles of the Negro people in the learning
experience of generations of white Americans.[51] Had
this been done, the conspiracy theory of Black Nationalism, the hysteria generated in the press, would
have little currency. For this history would reveal,
among other things, the basic and continuing theme of
nationalism in Negro protest. It would show the fundamental weakness of Negro nationalism and its rejection
by successive generations of Negro leadership. This
point needs to be emphasized both for the "benefit of those who hate the Negro more than they love
their country," as Frederick Douglass once said, and
for apostles of a "black Zion."

The history of Negro nationalism during two "classical" periods testifies to the correctness of what may be
called the "Douglass Dictum":

It is idle—worse than idle, ever to think of our expatria-
tion, or removal . . . We are here, and here we are likely
to be. To imagine that we shall ever be eradicated is absurd
and ridiculous. We can be remodified, changed, and assimilated, but never extinguished. We repeat, therefore, that
we are here; and that this is our country; and the question
for the philosophers and statesmen of the land ought to be,
"what principles should dictate the policy of action towards
us?" We shall neither die out, nor be driven out; but shall
go with these people, either as a testimony against them,
or as evidence in their favor throughout their generations.
. . . The white man's happiness cannot be purchased by
the black man's misery. . . . It is evident that white and
black must fall or flourish together.

Douglass' dictum, published in the North Star, November 16 ,1849, under the heading, "The Destiny of
Colored Americans," served two purposes. First, it was
an expression of the overwhelming opposition of the

freed African population against various emigration
schemes sponsored by whites, and second, as a reply
to a growing sentiment for voluntary emigration represented by a faction of Afro-American intelligentsia
whose nationalistic agitation later found expression in
the Cleveland (Ohio) National Emigration Convention,
August 24–26, 1854. The period 1840–1858, may be
said to represent the first classical period of Negro
nationalism. This nationalism derived its inspiration in
part from the social unrest among freed Africans during the 1840's and 1850's and in part from the theoretical nationalistic propositions advanced by Martin
R. Delaney in his book, "The Condition, Elevation,
Emigration and Destiny of the Colored People of the
United States, Politically Considered" (1852). His
views, setting forth the advantages of emigration to
Central and South America and the West Indies, were
adopted by the 1854 Convention as a "Report on the
Political Destiny of the Colored Race on the American
Continent." The movement failed for several reasons—
principally because nationalism or emigration was a
peripheral objective to the overwhelming issue of the
day, emancipation of the slaves. Douglass' dictum was
unshaken during the second classical period, approximately 1915–1925, when the Garvey movement held
considerable attraction for the Negro worker. Negro
nationalism of this period derived significantly from the
social unrest which accompanied intensive urbanization
of Negroes, their continued subordination, and in part
from Garvey's theoretical formulation of the "Negro
Problem," embodied later in the "Philosophy and Opinions of Marcus Garvey" (2 Vols. 1925). There appears
to be no evidence that the contemporary manifestation
of Negro nationalism as a political phenomenon has
better chance of success than it did during the previous
periods.

Nearly all Negro nationalist organizations incorporate
explicit or implicit political goals. At any rate, they

subscribe to one or more variants of Negro nationalism.
These manifestations may be classified according to the
degree of emphasis placed on political or other goals or
with respect to their functions and ideologies. Those
movements which have sought specifically political goals
have been few. Both the National Emigration Convention
movement during the nineteenth century and Garvey's
Back-to-Afrca movement in this century may be said to
have been largely political in objective. We should not,
however, ignore the cultural and economic emphasis
in the ideology of the Garvey movement. Neither succeeded. At best, both served during their respective
periods as "gadfly" in the Negro protest, first against
the ruling whites, then against the conservative wing of
Negro leadership. Garvey, moreover, is generally credited with instilling pride and morale in the urban Negro
proletariat.

Contemporary nationalist organizations in Harlem
which advocate specific political goals are few and insignificant. Among these are splinter groups of the
Garvey movement, e.g. African Nationalist Pioneer
Movement or the recently founded African Nationalist
(Alajo) Independence-Partition Party of North America.
Some secular political goals are implied by the Nation
of Islam, but its ideology is too ambiguous and confused, its leadership too uncommitted to a political
program to warrant inclusion among movements with
explicit political goals. It belongs, in part, to the religiously-oriented variant of nationalism discussed later.
It incorporates, however, economic and cultural nationalism.

Political goals advocated by Harlem nationalists vary
with organizations and with time. The most persistent
of these goals has been emigration from the United
States; in the nineteenth century the region of emigration preferred was Central and South America and the
West Indies. During the twenties, Africa south of the

Sahara was advocated; the Muslims appear to prefer an area in the Nile valley. However, a new variation on the theme of emigration has been added by the Muslim movement and the Alajo Party: the partition of the United States between blacks and whites. The Muslims have suggested that they would be satisfied with five or seven states, although they have not specified which of the states they would prefer. The "Provisional Government of the African-American Captive Nation" arm of the Alajo Party is more specific. In its "Declaration of Self-Determination of the African-American Captive Nation," issued January, 1963, the Provisional Government states:

> Therefore, be it resolved, that this powerful nation (The United States of America), that was built with the unrequited slave labor of our African ancestors, be as magnanimous as it is great, and relieve our oppression with restitution;
> Be it further resolved that all land south of the Mason Dixon line where our people constitute the majority, be partitioned to establish a territory for Self-Government for the African Nation in the United States; and
> Be it further resolved that the United States Government take full responsibility for training our people for self-government in all its ramifications, and
> Be it finally resolved that the Provisional Government of the African-American Captive Nation be recognized by the Government of the United States as of now.

Critics of these proposals argue that the partition goal is impracticable. Furthermore, they point out that the example of American tutelage over the Republic of Liberia for more than a century should discourage any idea of a black republic adjacent to the United States. In fact, it is argued that the overwhelming obstacles created by neo-colonialism and neo-imperialism for African states thousands of miles away ought to dampen the enthusiasm of the partitionists.

Closely related to emigration or partition themes has

been the nationalists' demand that the United States should pay reparations to Afro-Americans as restitution for the free labor of their ancestors during slavery. The sums demanded vary from $5,000 per Negro to a bulk sum of five billion for the entire Negro population in the United States. Some argue that the Negro question can properly be viewed as one of "under-development" just as much as those of countries in Africa, Asia, South and Central America. They claim that the purpose of American foreign aid, quite apart from making friends, is aimed at helping these countries and their peoples develop rapidly. Hence, they insist (and I believe with justification) that part of American foreign aid grants or peace corps arrangements could be utilized more profitably to attack the economic and cultural basis of inequality of the Negro people. They do not, however, consider restitution in cash or in kind to be full restitution—although it would be a step in the right direction. Others have demanded that the United States government should settle her "historic wrong" against Africa by payment of five hundred billion to all Independent African States. These, I believe, exhaust concrete political demands made by contemporary Harlem nationalists—one group has recently drawn up a petition which is intended to be submitted to the United Nations Refugee Committee ("as soon as we can find a sponsor among the U.N. delegations"), requesting that the Committee take up the "Negro question" as an international problem of refugees.

A variant of Negro nationalism manifested itself earliest in religious terms. While this religiously-oriented nationalism has, in effect, tended to dissipate the emergence of secular political nationalism, it is significant that the organization of the Negro church as well as early African societies during the eighteenth and nineteenth centuries provided a viable framework for Negro self-assertion. It is my contention that a study of early

literature of Negro religious bodies would reveal a high
poltical and nationalistic content. Hence, the frequent
appeal by many Negro Christians and nationalists to the
Biblical statement, "Ethiopia shall stretch forth her
hands . . ." interpreted by them as a promise of their
liberation and emancipation. This religious nationalism
is most central in the teachings of Mr. Elijah Muhammad,[52] spiritual leader of the Nation of Islam. Religiously-oriented nationalism is, perhaps, the most
widespread form of Negro nationalism. In practical
terms, however, the separate Negro Church, like the
Muslim movement, in the formative years provided a
framework for self-assertion by the Negro people. The
following passage from Benjamin T. Tanner's "An
Apology for African Methodism" (1867) highlights an
expression of the Negro's need for self-assertion as a
group:

> The *giant crime committed by the Founders of the Afri-
> can Methodist Episcopal Church against the prejudiced white
> American and the timid black*—the crime which seems
> unpardonable—was that they dared to organize a Church
> of men, men to think for themselves, men to talk for them-
> selves, men to act for themselves. A Church of men who
> support from their own substance, however scanty, the
> ministration of the Word which they receive; men who
> spurn having their churches built for them and their pastors
> supported from the coffers of some charitable organization;
> men who prefer to live by the sweat of their own brow
> and be free. *Not that the members of this communion are
> filled with evil pride, for they exhibit a spirit no more
> haughty nor overbearing than Paul, who never neglected
> to remind the world that he was a man, and a Roman
> citizen.*

The position of the AME Church then, like that of
contemporary Muslims, was constantly branded by opponents as "ignorant, fanatical, and proscriptive." The
AME Church was even attacked by better-placed
Negroes as "ignorant and degrading."

To this accusation, Tanner replied:

Methodism—the organization that builds more churches, supports more preachers and missionaries, gives more money to the poor, and has done more to prove the absolute ability of black men to do everything which [white] men do than all the colored organizations in the United States —that is the organization which in the eyes of Rev. Mr. (Charles H.) Thompson demoralizes the Negro. And he a Presbyterian! Who built the Church which the Reverend gentleman now ministers? The white Brethren. Who built four-fifths of all the colored Presbytherian Churches and one-half of the other fifth? The white Brethren. Who is it that assists in the support of four-fifths, if not every individual one, of the colored Presbyterian pastors? The white Brethren. Who is it that makes their books, good or bad? The white Brethren. Who edits their papers, ably or only with mediocrity? The ever present, ever generous white Brethren.

And yet the religious organization that does all this, inter se, degrades itself by so doing, in the eyes of our wise Bro. Thompson. Surely from his standpoint, independency and suppliancy, freedom and bondage, have become inverted terms.

The sentiments expressed by Tanner, I believe, have been the most important theme of Negro nationalism. To this religio-nationalism, which stresses not only worship but also self-assertion and self-help of the Negro people, should be added variants expressed in economic and cultural terms. However, all represent positive and constructive contributions to the Negro freedom movement.

The nationalists constitute that wing of Negro protest which is most insistent on self-assertion and self-help by the Negro people as a group—though they tend to undermine important contributions of Negro effort, energy, resources, and talent to this three-century-old struggle.

A variant of this theme of self-sufficiency stresses the economic position of Negroes in the United States. This we call "economic nationalism." It is advocated by nearly all Harlem nationalists and stridently voiced by the Muslims. The weaknesses of Negro economic nationalism have often been stressed. It is said that a separate Negro economy in the United States is a myth: that whatever capital exists within the Negro community is insignificant in the total economy of the United States. In any case, it is said that Negroes lack both capital and experience for effective participation with the giant corporations of America in large scale industrial and financial undertakings. There is no doubt that the improbability of the emergence of an economically significant Negro capitalist class far outweighs its probability.

I am convinced the liberation of the Afro-American in Harlem and elsewhere in America ultimately lies in an understanding, appreciation, and assertion of his Afro-American and African cultural heritage. It is the exploitation and assertion of cultural and spiritual heritage that will help to usher him into freedomland during the second century of emancipation. In this, he will be engaging in tasks comparable to those of his African brother. Herein lies the foundation of our freedom and liberation; and such is the meaning of the "voices from within the veil" represented, though inadequately, by the nationalist movements of Harlem.

Ollie Harrington

❦

HOW BOOTSIE WAS BORN

As I REMEMBER it the year was 1936, a bad year in most everybody's book. Ellis the cabdriver used to say that even the grays[53] downtown were having it rough but I don't know about that because I lived in Harlem and stayed in Harlem like most members. Anyway, there were a terrible lot of us brethren squeezed in between Central Park, which was as far south as most of us were willing to let our thoughts dwell, and the 155th Street bridge across the Harlem River to the north. To the west it was St. Nicholas Avenue and Park Avenue to the east. That was Harlem and that was where Brother Bootsie was born.

I remember that it was 1936 because it was the year of the Berlin Olympics and Obie McCollum, the chief editor of the *New York Amsterdam News*, had one of his rare bad days and sent his star, all-round newshawk to cover the event. Since one of the duties of the Berlin-bound member had been providing the "Dam" News with cartoons, his departure left a hole in the staff which I was supposed to plug up temporarily. Luckily, not much imagination was needed for the job. I simply recorded the almost unbelievable but hilarious chaos

around me and came up with a character. It seems that
one of the local numbers runners dug my cartoon, and,
as you probably know, nobody covers as much Harlem
territory as the numbers man. And so the cartoon's
popularity grew by word of *his* mouth . . . which was
very big. About the same time an enterprising root man
got into the act.

Now as any P.S. 139 schoolboy could have told you,
the root man's job isn't nearly finished when he sells
you a bag of old stones and some High John the Con-
queror to provide you with staying power. After all,
what good is technology in the boudoir without money
in your pockets? So the root man[54] also sold you a dream
book and several possible hits. Advertising this fantastic
offer he began pasting copies of my humble cartoon in
his little shop window with the previous day's number
written across the top. Well, between the numbers cat,
the root man and the rising circulation, I was a made
man. McCollum jumped my salary from seven dollars
a week to ten, and I was able to resign from Father
Divine's famous eatery in 135th Street where you could
knock yourself out for two bits and a fervent avowal
of "Wonderful Peace." I immediately transferred my
chowing activities to Rosalie's, a basement hash joint
next door to the newspaper which boasted a more
socially select herd of feeding members. The rarefied
social atmosphere of this eatery was due to a combination of circumstances . . . part pigs' tails and collard
greens, part hot rolls and deep dish peach cobbler and
that part of the clientele which sneaked down off Sugar
Hill to partake of these gastronomic delights, lured no
doubt by Rosalie's congenital inability to say "no" to
any proposition. Incidentally, the cat who was sent to
cover the Olympics in Berlin never made it. A post-
mortem on the case revealed that he'd gotten hung up
in a Paris juice joint. But our man was cool. He sent
back about twenty postcard-sized photos showing a
bird's eye view of the stadium and all 100,000 specta-

tors. On the back of each photo, which reeked of Guerlain's Parfum, he had written captions with what appeared to be a Max Factor eyebrow pencil. The captions read: "Jesse Owens[55] winning the 100 meters". . . "The great finish of the 200 meter sprints with U.S. Jesse Owens in first place!"

Now I ask you, how could a cartoonist miss? There I was right in the middle of all of this action. I didn't have to think up gags. All I had to do was walk across to The Big Apple, or Smalls, latch on to a shorty[56] and watch. The cartoons drew themselves. After a while a jolly, rather well fed but soulful character emerged and crept into each drawing. Ted Poston, the world's loudest and fastest-talking journalist, who was city editor on the *Amsterdam,* named the character Bootsie and Bootsie it has been ever since. And I was more surprised than anyone when Brother Bootsie became a Harlem household celebrity, not only among the colored proletariat but among the literati as well. It could be dangerous though. Like what happened one Saturday morning.

Some unschooled, contemporary cats may believe that the center of the universe during the "hungry thirties" was the Savoy Ballroom but nothing could be farther from the truth. The real center was the Elite Barber Shop, old man Garrison's wire clipping emporium on Seventh Avenue just a few doors above 135th Street. Although by modern standards it would go down as a small joint (there were only five chairs and two raised shoeshine stands) every known Home of the period was shorn or fried regularly on these premises. Each Saturday morning some of America's top second class citizens filled the Elite air with spirited public debate on such varied subjects as women, horses, politics, show business, surgery (both amateur and professional) and on what the s.o.b.'s were doing to keep the colored man down. The famous heads which demanded the tonsorial attentions of Pop Garrison and Co. included such notables as Bojangles, Joe Louis, The Black Eagle, Judge

Hubert Delaney, Dr. Louis Wright, the Mills Brothers, Walter White, Lester Granger, "Pig Meat" Markham, and Broadway Rose.[57] When Joe Louis was in the chair, traffic was tied up on both sides of Seventh Avenue and to get into the Elite that day you had to have a B.A., a B.S. (which didn't always mean Bachelor of Science), an M.D., Ph.D., or D.T.'s. But let me tell you about *that* Saturday morning.

I had just liquidated a real crazy *Poisson neunière à la reine* . . . or, fried fish and rice (Rosalie had visited France once) at Rosalie's counter and I felt like digging some way-out tales and light signifying, and so, when I left the eatery I headed for the Elite. Just as I reached the entrance there was a flash and a whoosh . . . man, just like the launching pad at Cape Canaveral! A cat shot out of the door, face covered with lather and new fried hair flying in the breeze. Behind him, waving a razor with an air of dedicated concentration, sprinted Brother Walker, one of the venerable barbers. Alas, the track was too fast and Brother Walker lost his quarry around about 138th Street when his poor old barber's feet cut out on him. But the fleet-footed client had to take his head elsewhere for future conking[58] and general beautifying. Dismukes, my barber, explained that it was all about a tactless remark the missing member had made to the effect that Brother Walker reminded him of the cartoon character, Mister Bootsie . . . and didn't he pose for the cartoonist? The joint was in a merry uproar for hours after and each new batch of clients got a complete rundown on the action from Mister Chappie, the shoeshine "boy." Brother Walker maintained a dignified but hurt silence while I tried to play it cool although I was newly awakened to the dangers of having created a popular Harlem cartoon. But Brother Bootsie thrived on it!

To really dig Brother Bootsie, his trials and tribulations, you'd have to see Harlem from the sidewalk. Everyone in Harlem had trials and tribulations because

everyone in Harlem was colored. Or almost everyone . . .
John Hammond, Archer Winston and the Baron Timmie
Rosencranz[59] were not colored and yet they were de-
voted Harlemites.

But being colored—even in an enlightened northern
burg like New York—could be a drag. Well, of course,
there were a few restaurants downtown where the grays
wouldn't panic if a member appeared and ordered a
meal. But it would take a strong constitution to pass off
the ground glass and other delicate spices they were apt
to drop into that particular serving. And so most members stayed and laughed and cried in Harlem. There was
some integration, however.

Practically all of the gentlemen of the police were
Paddys. Hoods[60] like Dutch Schultz, Owney Madden
and Jimmy Hines came to Harlem nightly . . . and departed in the morning with the loot. All on the up and
up though, because they owned practically all of the
lucrative real estate like Connie's Inn and the Cotton
Club. Thousands of other ofays came up nightly to
"study the Negro." At times these study groups became
so enthralled in their scholarly pursuits that the vice
squads had broken down the doors and pulled back the
blankets before they realized that their research was
about to be tampered with. One of the world's most
publicized aristocrats, who later became a king (though
he would have much preferred being made queen),
danced nightly in a fruity joint called Chez Clinton. A
girl child named Billie Holiday poured out her broken
heart at the Elk's Rendezvous while a young laundry
girl named Ella made new, unheard-of sound with Chic
Webb[61] at the Savoy. The Black Eagle took off on the
first nonstop flight to Africa and landed out of gas
twenty-eight miles away in the Flushing mud flats, while
there were persistent rumors that Father Divine would
step from another airplane onto a cloud to show Harlemites the true road.

Downtown, the psychoanalyst's couch joined the cast-

ing couch as style Americana, and the grays beat their
shallow breasts and sobbed, "Where, oh where, Lord, did
we goof?" It was the time of the great guilt and they
flocked to the Roxy and the Palace to watch evil
Indians sink feathered arrows into the good guys, who
kicked a couple of times and then split the scene. The
sobs and groans of the audiences were heard deep
underground where the "A" Train sped home to Harlem. And the same flicker would hit the Alhambra and
the Regent[62] a couple of months later but here, when
the long-suffering pioneers collected red arrows and
bullets in their pale frames, the colored folks rolled in
the aisles, laughin' and laughin'. And Brother Bootsie
was right in there laughin' and gigglin', too . . . but he
could never figure out why. And one night in the Harlem
Moon, over a few gins with gingerales, Langston Hughes
told Bootsie it was very simple. He was just laughin' to
keep from cryin'. And out front at the bar, Yar-
borough, the Bishop's chauffeur, yelled, "Bartender.
Give the professor another shorty of gin there."

A little scoople-headed runt walked along 117th Street
munching on a bag of day-old buns. As I passed him he
stopped working his jaws and said, "Hey Mithter, you
know one thing? White folks shore is dumb. Why?
Well, I'll tell ya why. Now take this Mithter Kelley . . .
he's my white teacher over at the school. And I'm settin'
there in my seat in the las' row, an' he says, 'Leroy'. . .
tha's me. 'Leroy is you asleep?' Man, I didn't say
nothin'. I jest set there lookin' at him. So he says, 'Leroy,
is you asleep?' An' I kept settin' there lookin' at him. An'
then I says . . . 'yeah! yeah! yeah!' "

Another rat chewed up another colored infant over in
one of the Fifth Avenue slums and a downtown tabloid
editoralized that perhaps something ought to be done because so many rats were eating up so many Harlem
babies, and the rats might become so well fed and bad
enough to move downtown and start chewing on the
grays! But alack and alas . . . real estate operators in

other parts of the city couldn't be expected to go along
with letting the coloreds break out of Harlem into their
nice real estate because the "values would drop." So New
York's mayor started reading the comics over the radio
every Sunday morning!

Ras Something-or-other put on a turban and a black
uniform and, perched up on a ladder in 125th Street in
front of Herbert's Diamonds, hipped the crowd on the
virtues of the color black. *Buy black, act black, be black.*
As a matter of fact, screamed the good Ras, all the great
cats in history were black, from Caesar to Beethoven,
President Harding, Mickey Mouse and even Santa Claus.
His listeners filled the streets and for the first time
Harlem saw Paddy cops tip-toeing.

The Snakeman, who naturally enough was called
Snakes, roamed Harlem teasing giggling women and
children with his wooden snakes and alligators and occasionally selling one. And all the time he was laughin'
and laughin'. Every member loved old Snakes and every
schoolchild knew that he'd once been caught in a Texas
mob which was joyously barbecuing another Negro.
And when old Snakes began laughing the pecks[63] stared
in amazement and let him walk right through. He never
stopped walking until he reached the Big Apple . . . and
he ain't stopped laughing yet.

The Black Eagle sent a telegram to Hermann Goering, Hitler's Luftwaffe marshal. It was a challenge to an
air duel at 40,000 feet above the English Channel.
Brother Bootsie happens to know that it was all done
with the aid of a bottle of Haig and Haig. That irrepressible rascal, Ted Poston, then with the *Pittsburgh
Courier,* just happened to need a story that night, just
happened to have the pinch-bottle, and just happened to
run into the Eagle. A little light signifying and Goering
was a challenged cat. It could have been a coincidence,
but Poston beat the metropolitan dailies with his story
and the record will show that the *Courier* paid for the
Haig and Haig and the telegram. But Max Schmeling

punched the Brown Bomber into blissful slumber and all of the pimps had to sell their golf clubs and move down off the Hill. Ellis, the taxi driver, was overheard to say that this was going to be a night for the three efs, which I gathered meant Fightin', Love-makin' and Footracin'.

But Harlem was flexing her muscles and had eyes for Washington Heights.[64] Ben Davis[65] was elected to the New York City Council and Paul Robeson sang to an election rally in front of the Theresa Hotel.[66] The grays downtown were in a state of panic. When the mounted cops moved in to break up a torchlight parade outside the Theresa Hotel the stuff hit the fan. The tactic used by these Cossacks was usually successful since it involved backing their horses' behinds into colored faces and hollering "back up." But since this was a torchlight parade, well, the brothers were quite naturally carrying magnesium torches held straight out in front of them like Little David's sword. And so, glossy horse behinds backed right into magnesium torches and Harlem was suddenly witnessing its own Kentucky Derby. Many of the blue uniformed jockeys were left at the post, but the hustlers were placing bets on a fast field heading for the Central Park lake. Brother Bootsie shook his head and chuckled . . . or maybe it was me who shook his head and chuckled. Anyway, by that time I didn't know who was Bootsie and who was me!

Kenneth B. Clark

HARYOU-ACT IN HARLEM—THE DREAM THAT WENT ASTRAY

AT THE same time the President's Committee on Juvenile Delinquency provided funds for the operation of the Mobilization for Youth Program,[67] it granted funds to Harlem Youth Opportunities Unlimited (HARYOU) to conduct a study and to plan a program for the control of delinquency in the Central Harlem area. The HARYOU approach was similar to that of Mobilization. It recognized that an indispensable stage of the program would have to be diagnosis and treatment of pervasive conditions in the community which stunted and dehumanized Harlem's youth.

The HARYOU document "Youth in the Ghetto" analyzed the community, its strengths and its weaknesses, its power and its stagnation, its momentum and its inertia and put forward a program for increasing the personal and social effectiveness of that community's youth. The HARYOU document went beyond concern with the immediate community and sought to understand the problems of the community and its youth in terms of the nationwide intensification of the civil rights struggle and fundamental questions of social and political power and justice. Probably the document's most significant contribution was that it built into the core of its recommendations the insistence that community action was the indispensable factor in obtaining social change. Just as the Mobilization Program expanded the view of juvenile delinquency to include the framework of the community, the HARYOU program added the idea of social action and social change as fundamental requisites for dealing with the problems of disadvantaged youth. This emphasis on social action and social change precipitated a dilemma: the anti-poverty program demanded the mobilization of a depressed community to achieve social action and social change on its own, and at the same time, it sought to finance such programs through federal and local government funds. The following remarks on the nature, organization, operation and effectiveness of the community action components of the anti-poverty program deal with this fundamental problem.

In New York City, the MFY (Mobilization For Youth) and HARYOU (Harlem Youth Unlimited) programs both gave promise of serving as models of an effective, new community-action approach to the problems of the poor. Each was precise in its definition of the nature and goals of social action. In the case of MFY, proposals were implemented by programs. After three years of planning, organizational tooling-up and program pretesting, MFY had nearly two years of administering community-action programs financed by the President's Committee on Juvenile Delinquency. The MFY staff was in fact urging the people of the Lower East Side of New York to come forward with their problems in such areas as housing, jobs, welfare and education and was teaching them how to petition the appropriate governmental agencies for redress.

Prior to the publication of the HARYOU document "Youth in the Ghetto," in which the political implications of the community-action approach to the problems of the poor were more explicitly spelled out, the community-action activities of MFY did not result in raging controversy and conflict with the press and city officials. It is significant that the serious attacks on MFY, its philosophy, its methods and its top staff came after the Harlem riots of June, 1964. Though MFY operated on the Lower East Side, MFY was charged by some members of the press with instigating the Harlem riot and publishing inflammatory material concerning a policeman who had killed a Negro youth. MFY was also charged with harboring leftists and subversives on its staff and with poor administration. The local superintendent of schools and the police department were naturally irritated and disturbed that the MFY staff was organizing the people in their community for direct confrontation and action.

The newspaper attacks on MFY, by no means unanimous,[68] were not countered by any meaningful support on the part of local officials. Paul Screvane, then president of the City Council, conducted an "investigation" and released a report which not only failed to clarify the facts but contributed to the distortions of the attacking press. The board of directors of MFY at times seemed sure and firm but at crucial times vacillated in backing its top staff. The result of the MFY controversy was that two of its three top staff members resigned. The agency was reorganized under the direction of a distinguished social service administrator; during the first year of his tenure it tended to play down its more abrasive or disruptive community-action programs.

MFY still works with groups of poor and provides some of them with legal aid and representation in seeking redress from the Department of Welfare and the New York City Housing Authority, but its programs are now more service- than action-oriented. The results of the conflict add up to victory for the anti-community-action forces—or at best to a temporary defeat and regrouping of the poor in preparation for a more sophisticated and hopefully more effective future struggle. As in the Syracuse CATC conflict, the momentum of serious, controversial community-action programs undertaken in the past may eventually generate more significant activity on the part of the poor and their allies.

The HARYOU controversy is not to be understood in the same terms as the MFY conflict. In the case of MFY the conflict arose out of the program's direct work with the poor, the threat to the power order inherent in its organization, and its confrontation with governmental agencies over the poor's grievances. HARYOU's controversy arose out of a struggle for control over the program prior to any actual work with the poor of Harlem. Adam Clayton Powell was the first major political figure to recognize the political implications in the community-action components of the HARYOU planning document. He insisted that if HARYOU were going to operate in his district, it would have to be under his control. It is quite probable that the publicity surrounding Powell's intervention alerted other officials in New York and other cities to the built-in threat in community-action programs and set the stage for controversies over MFY, CATC in Syracuse and programs elsewhere.

The fact is that HARYOU's difficulties preceded any direct or serious attempt to organize the poor of Harlem for community action. The Powell forces were victorious in the initial stage of controversy; the program was damaged and its momentum stopped before any overt encounter with the government and institutions of the city could take place. Previously independent HARYOU and the Powell-sponsored Associated Community Teams (ACT) now merged into HARYOU-ACT. A former assistant to Powell was designated as executive director, and Powell supporters dominated the board of directors of the new organization. Powell's victory was made possible by the failure of the HARYOU board of directors to understand and resist the power and persuasiveness of the Powell forces; by failure of the federal government, the President's Commission and the newly emerging OEO, to defy the then-powerful chairman of the House Education and Labor Committee, through which all anti-poverty legislation and appropriations must initially pass; and by the refusal of political officials in City Hall to face a fight with Adam Powell before a crucial mayoral election.

Aside from the administrative and fiscal difficulties of HARYOU-ACT, reflecting the inexperience, if not incompetence, of its administrators and the general muddle and inefficiency of its staff, it remains a fact that HARYOU-ACT postponed implementing the core of its community-action programs for no less than eighteen months. Even at present, the community-action program—organization of neighborhood councils and groups—is among the least effective of HARYOU-ACT programs, less effective even than the present MFY community-action programs. The controversy over control of the HARYOU program and the ensuing victory of the Powell forces effectively blocked any systematic, serious work with the poor in Harlem. The poor were fought *about* but not for, another instance of their pathetic condition. The poor were hostages, instruments to the forging of other peoples' profit and power. The Harlem poor did not have even the dubious emotional satisfaction obtained in certain other programs from conflict with governmental agencies. They did not even have the chance to be defeated in action as MFY did. HARYOU-ACT's programs during the first two years seemed confined to social services of maximum public-relations value and to programs aimed at curbing the disruptive potential of the ghetto's restless and frustrated elements. Indeed, the leaders of HARYOU-ACT based their claims of program effectiveness on the fact that there was no riot in Harlem during the summer of 1965!

The Bedford-Stuyvesant and anti-poverty programs

among the Puerto Ricans in New York City encountered similar difficulties in organization and in struggle for control. These programs have also failed to involve the poor in any direct-action confrontation and conflict-producing activity, and have spent their available energy in intramural power struggles. Here, too, the needs of the poor were ignored while the struggle for control of them raged and waned.

The controversies which plague anti-poverty programs in New York City suggest the possibility that the effectiveness of these programs is limited by problems peculiar to New York City. Not the least of these is the sheer size of the city and its agencies. Then, too, New York City probably has a larger number of poor people in a given municipal unit than any other American city. The problems of New York's poor are complicated by population density, ethnic diversity among the poor, and the fact that the poor are distributed in large pockets throughout the five boroughs, rather than concentrated in a single manageable location. Given these and related factors, it is impossible to predict with any degree of confidence whether community-action components of current anti-poverty programs can effectively address the problems of the poor in New York City.

Claude Brown

◈

GROWTH AND SURVIVAL
IN HARLEM

Most of the cats my age, sixteen, seventeen, eighteen, were just coming out of the house. They were just
being cut loose from their parents. The first thing they
usually did was run out and start using drugs to be
hip, to be accepted into the street life, to be down.
I didn't have to do that, because I had come up in
the street life. I knew all the old hustlers, the hustlers
who had become successful now, the hustlers who used
to be fences, used to be whores, the hustlers I used
to sell stolen goods to when I was just ten, eleven,
twelve. I knew these people from way back, and
now they had big Cadillacs, they had restaurants. Some
of them had little nightclubs, after-hour places. I'd see
these people on the street, and we'd stop and talk.
All the young cats my age envied me and looked upon
me as an older cat. Most people thought I was older.
They had put out the story at one time that I was a
young-looking midget, a cat who was really twenty-
one or twenty-two. It was the only way some of the
cats my age could explain my being so far ahead of
them in street life.

Mama used to get down on me about hanging out
with Reno. She'd say that she knew he'd be going to

jail one day soon and that I'd be going with him. At the same time, she was always getting down on me about bringing certain chicks to the house. She used to say I always brought nasty girls to the house. It became a real hassle.

Dad knew I was doing something, but he didn't know exactly what. They didn't know I was dealing pot, because I didn't have people coming to the house. He'd say, "Yeah, you gon be up there in jail where all them other bad boys is you used to hang around with." He was always riding me.

I got tired of it after a while. I got tired of them telling me who to hang out with and who to associate with. I felt that this shit was childish, and since I was out working, I didn't have to take it.

I got fed up one day and moved out. I told Mama I'd found a place up on Hamilton Terrace and was moving. Mama didn't believe me until I started packing my stuff. Dad didn't say anything; he started mumbling to himself. Mama started crying and said I shouldn't be leaving, I didn't have anybody outside. She said a boy of sixteen should still be living with his family.

I didn't feel that way about it. I told them that I was tired of living with them, that I just couldn't take that sort of thing any more. They were kind of old-fashioned and countryfied. The way I saw it, they couldn't understand anything. I just packed up one night and pulled out. I left Dad squawking and Mama crying and moved up on Hamilton Terrace to a nice little room. This was where all the young hustlers lived.

The only other fellow I knew in Harlem who used to sell a lot of nice pot was Tommy Holloway, and he lived on Hamilton Terrace too. He was the one who got me my room up there. Tommy dressed real nice. He showed me a lot of stuff. He showed me what fences to buy clothes from if I wanted to get the best. He even cut me into the dry-goods thieves so that I would never get burned by fences.

This was where I felt I was supposed to be; it

was where all the slick people were living. This was the set I wanted to be in.

It hurt Mama. Dad didn't care. He thought I was going to end up in jail anyway. Behind this, I could associate with anybody I wanted to. Mama kept telling me, "You can come home," every time I came around. I told her that I had my own home now and that I wasn't going to come back there any more. She said, "Come by and get a good meal." I'd stop by and give them money. After a while, they stopped asking me where I'd gotten it.

After I'd moved, Reno got busted, and he was in the Tombs. I didn't swing with anybody for a while. There was Tony Albee, who was about a year older than me, but he was just coming out. He'd been a nice boy, and he had just come up from the South in 1950. He had never gone through all the stuff that I had gone through. He hadn't been through the gang-fighting stage. He'd never smoked pot until I gave him a reefer one night. The cat was at a party, and I gave him a joint. He said he liked it, and started trying to get tight with me, but the cat was a farmer. I didn't let him get but so tight. I used to let him run errands for me. He used to do what I told him to. If I went someplace and told him to wait, he'd wait. After a while, I started liking the guy.

He started hanging around. He said he wanted to start dealing pot. I said okay, and I gave him a couple of ounces and told him, "You can give me fifty dollars when you sell the stuff." I had to show him how to roll pot. He was a real country boy all the way.

People started saying that he was my partner. He turned out to be a real nice guy, so I didn't mind. He stayed close to me and used to try to dress the way I did. He'd buy clothes from the same people I got mine from. He'd never worn anything but cheap Charlie's shoes before, but now he started wearing custom-made. I guess he wanted to start acting just like me, and he had to start someplace. If he wanted to get into the street life, he had to start swinging with somebody who was already into it. I was into it kind of good, so I was a good person for him to start with.

When Reno came back on the street scene, he found out that Tony and I were tight. He said he didn't like him and that I shouldn't be hanging out with a farmer. I told him that the cat was all right with me and that I was going to swing with him for a while. Reno started staying away from me, and he started telling other cats that I was swinging with a lame, an old farmer. He was putting me down. I thought, Fuck it, I don't need him. But I still liked the cat and still admired him. I'd see him, and if he needed anything, I'd whip some money on him. Or we'd get high together.

Sometimes Tony would come around and try to talk with him. Tony might say, "Hi, Reno," but Reno would ignore him and then walk.

I guess it was something that Tony deserved, in a way, because he had been a nice boy for so long. Reno and Danny and Butch the Kid and I were with the dirty side. We were always the ones that people said would probably be in jail or dead before we were twenty-one. I think a lot of those "good boy" cats believed their parents when they were telling that kind of stuff. Guys like Reno had to get their revenge on those cats, I guess, and now the "bad boys'" day had come. We were the elite in the neighborhood. We were the people who were into all the happenings, and these cats were trying to get in.

I guess we all kind of had it in for the righteous-doing folks in the neighborhood because they had messed with all of us when we were just kids coming up. They were always squealing on us and stuff like that. But I don't think anybody had as much reason to get back at them as Reno and his family. Most of them were pretty nice. Bucky was a nice guy. Mac was kind of lame and didn't have a lot of heart, but he

was damn nice. He was a natural athlete. He was tall
and lanky; he could play a whole lot of basketball,
and he could run real fast. He had everything needed
to become a good athlete, everything but confidence.
Maybe if Miss Jamie had just shown him a little bit
that she cared and tried to give him a little bit of
self-respect, he would have made out all right. But
she didn't do that, so the cat just never had any heart.

I guess it was harder on the girls than it was on
anybody. Dixie started tricking when she was thirteen.
She was big for her age, and "nice" ladies used to
point at her and say, "Oh, ain't that a shame." But
it wasn't. The shame of it was that she had to do it
or starve. When she got hip and went out there on the
street and started turning tricks, she started eating and
she stopped starving. And I thought, Shit, it ain't no
shame to stop starvin'. Hell, no.

Babe, Dixie's younger sister, was kind of ugly. She
tried tricking, but she was just too ugly to make any
money. Babe and Dixie were both sent to Hudson State
Training School for Girls. When Dixie came out, she
moved from Miss Jamie's and got a nice little place
downtown. She made it on her own. Babe was too
young to make it, so she just kept going back to Hudson.
She said she liked it there. It was the first place she'd
been where people didn't make her feel she was out
of place.

When Dixie got to be thirteen, there was nobody to
tell her not to trick. She figured that since her mother
was laying so many cats, why shouldn't she be tricking,
especially if it was going to mean money and food.
She used to feed the whole family sometimes, and that
was a damn job, but the people in the neighborhood
just kept looking down on her. They used to say that
they didn't want their daughters hanging out with Dixie.
But some of their daughters were giving away more
cunt than Dixie was selling.

Reno was always in the Tombs for jostling. The
Tombs used to be his winter home. He said he didn't

mind being down there in the wintertime, but he liked to be out on the streets in the fresh air and living and partying in the summertime, when so much was happening out on the streets. I guess to most people, it would have seemed like a hard life to be spending all your winters down in the Tombs, but it wasn't so bad. Life out on the street for some people was harder. It was much harder to be out there working every day than to be in the Tombs. Jail wasn't hard for anybody who knew how to live down there and get by.

A few weeks after I moved to Hamilton Terrace, a panic was on. You couldn't get any pot. Cocaine was pretty nice, but nobody used cocaine much but the hustlers, and it wasn't an all-night thing with them. You could sell a hundred dollars' worth of cocaine if you made all the bars up to 148th Street. You could sell it to the pimps, the whores, all the hustlers out there at night. But there weren't many customers for cocaine on the street, not like pot. Cats who were working would hardly come up and give you five dollars for a tiny cap of cocaine or ten or twenty dollars for a little tin of cocaine. It was too expensive for the average person, and you couldn't be selling it to the hustlers every night, because they couldn't afford to be blowing all their money on cocaine.

I had a little money in the bank, but I was scared that wasn't going to last too long. So I got a job working at a joint called Hamburger Heaven. This was a real drag. It was something terrible. It was on Madison Avenue, and you had to be a real Tom. Most of the cats there were from the South and weren't too hip. They hadn't been in New York long, and they didn't know anything. Most of them were really dumb—farmers.

I stayed with that for a while. The thing that bothered me most—I didn't know it would, because I'd never thought about it before—was that only white people came in there. I started off as a busboy. Later I became a waiter—white coat, black tie, and black pants. You had to smile at the white folks, hoping they'd throw a big tip on you. You had to watch what you said, and you had to watch the way you acted, because they had an old, dumbhead waiter who was a real Tom. If you said anything to one of the customers and didn't put a "sir" on it, he'd tun up there and say, "Boy, what's wrong with you?" and all this kind of simple shit. It was pretty hard to take, but I needed a job.

I stayed on for about a year. Behind the panic coming on, I couldn't get any pot, so I wasn't dealing anything then. I still had my contacts, and as soon as the stuff came in again, I would go back into business.

The first time I heard the expression "baby" used by one cat to address another was up at Warwick in 1951. Gus Jackson used it. The term had a hop ring to it, a real colored ring. The first time I heard it, I knew right away I had to start using it. It was like saying, "Man, look at me. I've got masculinity to spare." It was saying at the same time to the world, "I'm one of the hippest cats, one of the most uninhibited cats on the scene. I can say 'baby' to another cat, and he can say 'baby' to me, and we can say it with strength in our voices." If you could say it, this meant that you really had to be sure of yourself, sure of your masculinity.

It seemed that everybody in my age group was saying it. The next thing I knew, older guys were saying it. Then just about everybody in Harlem was saying it, even the cats who weren't so hip. It became just one of those things.

The real hip thing about the "baby" term was that it was something that only colored cats could say the way it was supposed to be said. I'd heard gray boys trying it, but they couldn't really do it. Only colored cats could give it the meaning that we all knew it had without ever mentioning it—the meaning of black masculinity.

Before the Muslims, before I'd heard about the

Coptic or anything like that, I remember getting high
on the corner with a bunch of guys and watching
the chicks go by, fine little girls, and saying, "Man,
colored people must be somethin' else!"

Somebody'd say, "Yeah. How about that? All those
years, man, we was down on the plantation in those
shacks, eating just potatoes and fatback and chitterlin's
and greens, and look at what happened. We had Joe
Louises and Jack Johnsons and Sugar Ray Robinsons
and Henry Armstrongs, all that sort of thing."

Somebody'd say, "Yeah, man. Niggers must be some
real strong people who just can't be kept down. When
you think about it, that's really something great. Fatback, chitterlin's, greens and Joe Louis. Negroes are
some beautiful people. Uh-huh. Fatback, chitterlin's,
greens, and Joe Lous . . . and beautiful black bitches."

Cats would come along with this "baby" thing. It
was something that went over strong in the fifties with
the jazz musicians and the hip set, the boxers, the
dancers, the comedians, just about every set in Harlem.
I think everybody said it real loud because they liked
the way it sounded. It was always, "Hey, baby. How
you doin', baby?" in every phase of the Negro hip
life. As a matter of fact, I went to a Negro lawyer's
office once, and he said, "Hey, baby. How you doin',
baby?" I really felt at ease, really felt that we had
something in common. I imagine there were many
people in Harlem who didn't feel they had too much
in common with the Negro professionals, the doctors
and lawyers and dentists and ministers. I know I didn't.
But to hear one of these people greet you with the
street thing, the "Hey, baby"—and he knew how to
say it—you felt as though you had something strong
in common.

I suppose it's the same thing that almost all Negroes
have in common, the fatback, chitterlings, and greens
background. I suppose that regardless of what any
Negro in America might do or how high he might rise

in social status, he still has something in common with
every other Negro. I doubt that there are many, if
any, gray people who could ever say "baby" to a
Negro and make him feel that "me and this cat have
got something going, something strong going."

In the fifties, when "baby" came around, it seemed
to be the prelude to a whole new era in Harlem. It
was the introduction to the era of black reflection. A
fever started spreading. Perhaps the strong rising of
the Muslim movement is something that helped to
sustain or even usher in this era.

I remember that in the early fifties, cats would stand
on the corner and talk, just shooting the stuff, all
the street-corner philosophers. Sometimes, it was a
common topic—cats talking about gray chicks—and
somebody might say something like, "Man, what can
anybody see in a gray chick, when colored chicks are
so fine; they got so much soul." This was the coming
of the "soul" thing too.

"Soul" had started coming out of the churches and
the nightclubs into the streets. Everybody started talking
about "soul" as though it were something that they
could see on people or a distinct characteristic of
colored folks.

Cats would say things like, "Man, gray chicks seem
so stiff." Many of them would say they couldn't talk
to them or would wonder how a cat who was used to
being so for real with a chick could see anything in a
gray girl. It seemed as though the mood of the day was
turning toward the color thing.

Everybody was really digging themselves and thinking
and saying in their behavior, in every action, "Wow!
Man, it's a beautiful thing to be colored." Everybody
was saying, "Oh, the beauty of me! Look at me. I'm
colored. And look at us. Aren't we beautiful?"

HARLEM AND THE ARTS, SCIENCES, AND PROFESSIONS

Elton C. Fax

❧

FOUR REBELS IN ART

I F YOU ARE looking for an appraisal of artists and their
art all done up in fancy esoteric jargon you will not find
it in the paragraphs written here. This is a statement
about four distinguished Americans whose works speak
to the world in forceful reproach at what they see and
feel as gross injustice. They are Negroes—three men
and a woman. Their mood is rebellious. Because they
are true artists they speak in voices strong, articulate,
and shattering to the national conscience: voices pro-
claiming that the mantle of dignity and greatness fits
our nation badly because Uncle Sam has become grossly
overweight from excess fear, bigotry, and hatred.

To understand the rebellion in these artists one has to
look long and honestly at the times and places that bred
them, and to remember that there are many Negroes
who do not meet adversity with a smile and negative
placidity. Thus, viewed in the order of their arrival on
the scene, the quartet is led by Elizabeth Catlett.

Elizabeth Catlett is a sculptor, painter, and print
maker. She is tall, strong, handsome, and not given to
easy smiling, small talk, or idle chatter. For the last
decade she has lived in Mexico. There, amid the shades
of Hidalgo, Morelos, Obregón, and other great Mexican

freedom fighters, Elizabeth Catlett draws and carves, rears her family, and lives among Mexicans in the manner of Mexicans. In return she finds an acceptance she never found in Washington, D. C. where she was born, or in Iowa, Louisiana, Texas, Virginia, and New York where she pursued the study and practice of her craft. Her compassion for oppressed human beings is deep and eternal; her portrayal of them glows with a warmth that is as real as it is unsentimental.

The year was 1915. Eighty Negroes and thirteen white men were lynched by U.S. mobs. The nation's colleges awarded bachelors' degrees to two hundred eighty-one Negroes.

A daughter, Alice Elizabeth, was born to the Catletts. Before she was five, Elizabeth had come to know the small child's terror of mob violence. She also learned that her people did not hesitate to strike back in defense of their lives and property.

A group of white soldiers, sailors, and marines on leave in Washington launched an unprovoked attack upon Negro citizens of the city's southwest section. The attackers, infuriated over the social acceptance overseas of Negro servicemen by Europeans, had taken this means of "putting the Negroes in their place." That was on Saturday, July 19, 1919. The next day the assailants, reinforced by white civilians, raided street cars and other vehicles, dragging out Negroes and beating them into unconsciousness. One Negro was beaten in front of the White House. Three hundred others were wounded by gunfire and assorted weapons.

Another siege, planned for the next day, found Washington's Negroes "ready"; the raid on a large Negro section resulted in the death of four whites and two Negroes, the wounding of scores of whites, *and the end of the Washington riot!*

Six years later a Ku Klux Klan parade, two hours long, marched down Washington's Pennsylvania Avenue. The klansmen were in full regalia and their demonstration had the permission of the U.S. Government.

Elizabeth Catlett was eleven, old enough to understand —and to remember. Today she remembers Negroes less "privileged" than she was: work-worn men and women of the slums and the rural cabins. And she remembers their children with whom she went to school, with whom she played and fought and contemplated the wonders and evils of segregated life.

When Elizabeth Catlett depicts humble working people and their children, Mexican or American Negro, they spring alive under her skillful hand. When she does them in sculpture she is superb. Her figures of Negro mothers are strong and, like her terse conversation, bereft of non-essentials. Their heads tilt upward at defiant angles, their feet are planted squarely. And why not? Elizabeth Catlett learned early that to survive as an individual she must lift her head and plant her feet firmly in the good earth.

Following the outbreak of the First World War Negroes migrated from the South to northern cities in two massive waves: the first between 1916 and 1919, the second between 1921 and 1923. They streamed into New York, Chicago, Philadelphia, Pittsburgh, Cleveland, Detroit, and St. Louis, looking for work and for better treatment from white folks than they had been getting in Dixie. Jacob Lawrence's family came with that first migration. They tried Atlantic City where Jake was born. Later they moved to Philadelphia; by the time Jake was twelve his folks had arrived in Harlem.

The Harlem of 1927 was indeed the legendary Harlem of the roaring twenties—the Negro capital of jazz, of sultry night spots owned by white mobsters, of policy kings, bootleggers, assorted hustlers, and fabulous stage personalities. It was the Harlem of writers, painters, hardworking domestics and day laborers, of Bojangles, The Barefoot Prophet,[69] Kid Chocolate,[70] and Ethel Waters. And it was also the Harlem of A'Leilia Walker, whose mother, a one-time laundress, made a fortune ironing the "naps" out of Negro hair.

In 1929, the Depression hit Harlem like a thunder-bolt. By 1933, half of its congested population depended upon unemployment relief. Its infamous "Lung Block" housed more than 4,000 Negroes whose death rate from pulmonary turberculosis doubled that of all white Manhattan. Rats and roaches swarmed through its fetid tenements. Rags and old newspapers were stuffed into broken windows to keep out the winter blasts, and Negroes paid from forty to fifty per cent of their slim incomes to live in such hovels. The Harlem of the gay and reckless twenties was no more. "Depression Harlem" was the Harlem Jake Lawrence lived in and came to know so dreadfully well. It was the Harlem of his early paintings.

A blind man is led along a squalid street. A child pauses hungrily before a dingy shop window where hang a few scrawny chickens. Children play in the concrete forest dense with refuse and filth. The colors are flat and sombre, with contrasting areas of black and white balanced within the composition. Figures, buildings, pavements, and sky bite into the consciousness of the viewer. This is HARLEM, man! It is the dozens of Harlems all across America seen through the sensitive eye and mind of an aroused inhabitant. In those early days the career of Toussaint L'Ouverture fascinated Jack Lawrence and he made a series of forty-one paintings of the great Haitian general. Later he painted commentaries on John Brown and the struggles of the American revolutionists; he also painted the powerful group he called "The Migration."

As he continues to paint, Lawrence's technical advancement becomes increasingly evident. Even more striking is his constant awareness of the changing scene. The current demonstrations of Negro youth against white tyranny and the cruel ineptness of that tyranny in meeting youth's challenge are themes Lawrence handles with strikingly personal symbolism. To those who know him closely, Jake Lawrence matures in a way that is beautiful to see. The fire of his outrage burns bright, and deep inside the flames he forges the tools of retaliation. When he replies, orally or in paint, he does so with deadly clarity. Jake Lawrence shakes you up. His experiences and his power to transmit them give him the right to do so.

Like Jacob Lawrence, Charles White was born in poverty during the first wave of the Negro migration to Chicago. His mother worked in domestic service and his father was a steel worker who later entered the U.S. postal service.

Violence stalked the surroundings into which Charles White was born and in which he spent his childhood. The year before his birth, a gruesome massacre took place in the southwestern Illinois city of East St. Louis. Between one and two hundred Negroes were shot, burned, and hanged to death by white mobs of men, women, and children. Six thousand Negroes were driven from their homes. Negro laborers, newly arrived from the South, had been used as strikebreakers at three major meat packing houses. Fear, suspicion, and hatred spread throughout the white community and mobs quickly formed to drive all Negroes from the city. They nearly succeeded.

Anti-Negro feeling in Chicago was on the upsurge. Between 1910 and 1920 the city's Negro population had tripled. One fourth of the laborers in the Armour stockyards were Negroes. The specter of a migration to Chicago of even more employable Negroes panicked the white worker. Having been led to believe that Negroes were too shiftless to be serious labor competition, they demanded a subservience of Negroes in employment opportunities. The latter, many of them battle-conditioned veterans of the First World War, were having no part of it. In the three day riot that ensued thirteen Negroes and eleven whites were reported killed.

Charles White had scarcely reached his third birthday before twenty-five bombs had been thrown at the homes of Chicago's Negroes who could afford to buy homes. Eight bombings occurred on the residences of whites who had dared to sell to Negroes; but nobody bothered to waste bombs on the houses occupied by Charley's family and the other Negroes on that street.

Chicago, 1925: Boom! Another hate bomb smashed the north side of the newly acquired Negro Bethesda Baptist Church. No one was injured. Damage estimated at $50,000. Charley White was seven years old. When he tells us that he began to draw at the age of seven we conclude that then and there he somehow sensed *why* he had to draw and *what* he had to draw about. He speaks about rebelling against formal schooling. Yet he made it through high school with honors! With professional study at Chicago's Art Institute, The Art Students League of New York, and the Taller de la Gráfica in Mexico, White was on his way to a powerful mode of self-expression and communication.

Charley White paints murals and makes lithographs and woodcuts. What he no longer remembers about the science and art of draughtsmanship would do a lesser professional a lot of good. His theme: the struggle of the American Negro for the dignity of full manhood. In murals and prints he reflects a serious study of the Mexican masters. The Orozco influence is particularly strong in White's panel installed at Hampton Institute. Titled "The Contribution of the Negro to American Democracy," it depicts Negro abolitionists, educators, soldiers, and working people welded in a strikingly rhythmic and solid design. This is Charley White's answer to those who would deny the Negro's strength. He gives us a portrait of a people who have withstood lynching and privation, who have come through the great Depression of the thirties, and who have given America its current young Negro leadership. This panel embodies the forces that organized the sit-ins, kneel-ins, wade-ins, and the March on Washington. And there are also those who, tomorrow, will free the nation from her own bondage.

HARLEM: HER ARTISTS AND SCULPTORS

The art of Charles White

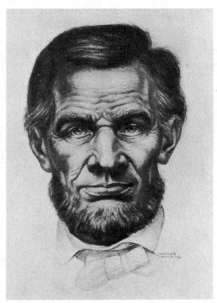

The art of John Biggers

The art of Elizabeth Catlett

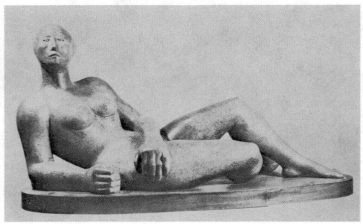

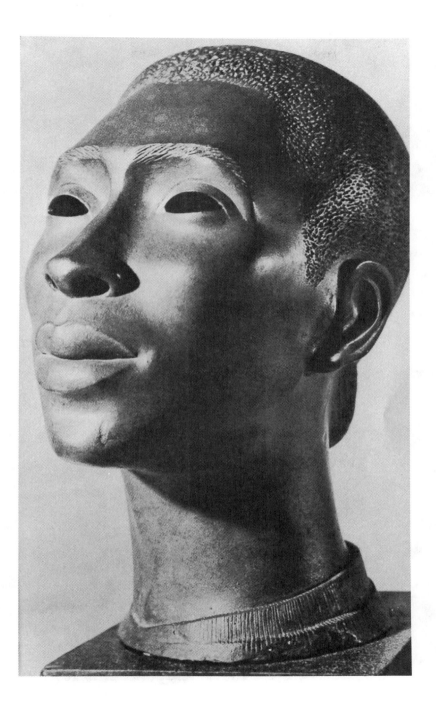

The art of Jacob Lawrence

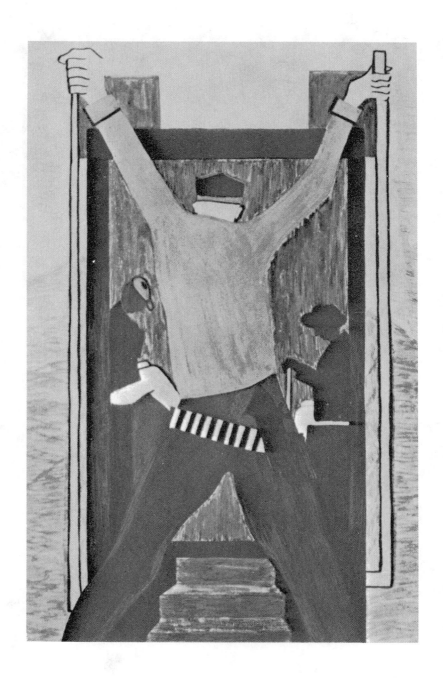

The art of Richmond Barthé

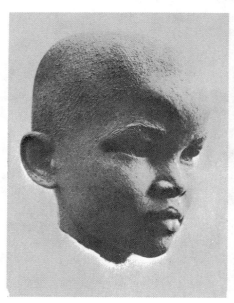

BOOTSIE CARTOONS

by Ollie Harrington

"Doctor Jenkins, before you read us your paper on
inter-stellar gravitational tensions in thermo-nuclear
propulsion, would you sing us a spiritual?"

"Oooh look, Sis, a robin red breast, and it must be spring. Do you reckon Uncle Bootsie was lying when he said spring comes three weeks earlier over 'cross town where the white folks live?"

"I think I messed up in the civics class and ain't gonna git promoted this term. The teacher, Miss McCharles, been saying we be spreading freedom all over the world. Then I opens my big fat mouth and asked when it would git to Georgia and Florida . . . and Harlem!"

"General Blotchit, you take your tanks and feint at Lynchville; General Pannick, you move into the county seat. And then in the confusion, my infantry will try to take little Luther to school!"

A BRUMSIC BRANDON, JR.
CARTOON

All of this is said and implied in one painting because of what Charley White has been forced to feel and see from childhood.

Today his statements of conviction roll across our land like sustained thunder. Only a man fully and proudly aware of what he is and what he will yet be can speak in tones so commanding. Charley White is that kind of man.

The drawings, paintings, and sculptures of John T. Biggers that brought him initial acclaim speak for the anonymous Negroes of the rural South. His are the interpretations of the hopes and aims of those who, spurning migration, remain behind to carry on the freedom fight on the hottest lines of battle. The Negroes whom Biggers draws are the rustics whose manners and customs are ridiculed and rejected by many whites and middle-class Negroes. More recently John Biggers has been to Ghana and to Nigeria. Out of that experience he has given us a magnificent book, "Ananse, The Web of Life in Africa"; and in typical Biggers fashion he has reported mainly on the common folk of the towns and villages he visited in those two West African countries.

The youngest of these four artists, John Biggers is a native of Gastonia, North Carolina. While his home state is not considered one of the "hard core" areas of segregation neither can it be considered a Southern oasis of pro-Negro attitudes. In the thirty-five years preceding Biggers' birth (1924) North Carolina had lynched over forty Negroes. It had lynched seven more before young Biggers had reached his eighteenth birthday. In 1930, when President Hoover nominated John T. Parker, a North Carolina circuit court judge, to the U.S. Supreme Court, the NAACP waged a fierce and successful struggle to block Judge Parker's appointment—the judge had previously declared political activity of Negroes "a source of evil and danger to both races." As recently as 1951 the nation was aghast at the conviction and sentencing to prison of Mack Ingram, a Negro farmer of Caswell County, North Carolina, for the crime of "looking at a white woman." Understandably, Ingram became known to readers of the Negro press as "Evil-Eye Ingram" and "What-A-Man Ingram."

Gastonia is a thriving mill town whose 1955 population was 23,000. Negroes in surrounding rural communities work the land yielding cotton for the mills. They are the people from whom John Biggers draws inspiration for his murals and prints.

After his schooling in North Carolina, Biggers attended Hampton Institute in Virginia. There he met Victor Lowenfeld, who later headed the Department of Art Education at Pennsylvania State University.

"It was Victor Lowenfeld who helped me firm up my convictions of who I really was," Biggers says. John Biggers is a man of academic and aesthetic achievement who knows that it is not his doctorate which makes him an important artist.

As a muralist he looks for inspiration to Orozco and Charles White. "The Contribution of American Negro Women to American Life and Education" is the subject of the Biggers mural panel for the Negro YWCA of Houston, Texas. This panel is an expertly organized interpretation of the matriarchy embodied in the subject. The artist is no less skillful when handling smaller works. His drawings and lithographic prints have a grandeur that lend a dignity to the simple people represented in them. John Biggers occupies a place of distinction with Elizabeth Catlett, Jacob Lawrence, and Charles White.

Collectively these four artists voice in clear, resolute, and eloquent terms, their dissatisfaction with their country's reneging on its own declared principles.

Just think of it! We are the only people on earth who could produce this particular quartet of artists, together with Odetta, Miles Davis, Sidney Poitier, Mahalia Jackson, and Ray Charles.

Loften Mitchell

༺❀༻

THE NEGRO THEATRE AND
THE HARLEM COMMUNITY

A SCENE in the play "Star of the Morning" describes the disbanding of the Williams and Walker
Company[71] in 1909.

Bert Williams asks Jesse Shipp, the company director: "Jesse, where'll you go?"

Jesse answers: "Uptown. A hundred thousand
Negroes in New York now. Lots of them moving to
Harlem. I'll go there. Maybe they'll be needing a the-
atre."

Fifty-three years after Jesse Shipp's statement, Ed
Cambridge, the director of "Star of the Morning," read
these lines at an audition. The shoulders of a number of
theatre people sagged as the lines left Cambridge's lips.
A sharp pain stabbed me. I wished the lines had not
been written.

Later that night Gertrude Jeanette, Esther Rolle,
Lynn Hamilton, Louis Gossett, Rick Ferrell and Irving
Burgie[72] sat in the home of Michael Allen, rector of
St. Marks in the Bowery, discussing the fact that there
was a theatre in Harlem when there were only a hundred thousand Negroes in the city, and not one now
when the population approximated one and a half mil-

lion black people. Our trembling fingers spilled coffee into overflowing saucers and onto Priscilla Allen's tablecloth.

Ed Cambridge shuddered, banged his cup into the saucer, and growled: "It's a good thing Jesse Shipp didn't go up there this year looking to work in theatre. He'd have been hungry as hell!"

The Harlem to which Jesse Shipp went—like the Harlem of today—was peculiarly a part of the society created by an impoverished, decaying Europe which reached out, searched for a new route to India and found instead a new El Dorado in the west. The European underprivileged raced to these shores, staked claims, then warred with the red man and with rival European groups. Other Europeans found the rich African continent, enslaved its people, then attempted to justify these atrocities. "The image of Africa," says John Henrik Clarke in his essay "Reclaiming the Lost African Heritage," "was deliberately distorted by Europeans who needed a moral justification for the rape, pillage and destruction of African cultural patterns and ways of life."

The image of the African was also distorted in America, where a ruling aristocracy sought to break its ties to the old world. Grandiloquent phrases declared equality of all—with the exception of those who were black or those who were white and owned no property. Patrick Henry demanded liberty or death, but he ignored the twenty-three slaves in his possession.

America was, for the African, a strange, hostile land. Everywhere people spoke of freedom, yet he was not free. Everywhere he heard others speak of their glorious ancestry, yet he was told his Africa was a huge jungle, inhabited by cannibals. Sometimes the Negro believed these distortions and saw himself as others saw him—as something sub-human, deserving a cruel fate. Yet, somehow he dared to dream that someday he would be free.

His dreams were not idle ones. He fought the nation's wars. His hands built the economy. His cultural gifts were either stolen or ignored by white historians who interpreted the nation's history in biased terms. In his essay "Negritude and Its Relevance to the American Negro Writer," Samuel Allen[73] describes the Negro's subjection to the cultural imprint of a powerful, dominant majority in an unfriendly land. Mr. Allen tells us that the American Negro group became—if not the only—one of the few black minorities in world history. Despite colonialism, those in Africa had the sheer weight of numbers for allies, plus the realization that the land was rightfully theirs. The West Indian Negro also had the advantage of numerical strength, plus an infrequency of contact with the ruling group.

The American Negro, however, underwent a physical and spiritual alienation without parallel in modern history. He was overwhelmed militarily and economically, transplanted from his native soil, then subjected not only to a dominant elite, but to what the poet Claude McKay called a cultural hell—a hell created by a powerful, materialistic, brutal frontier society that was uncertain of its own identity, yet seeking to assure itself of status by denying status to its victims.

The slave system crumbled. The Reconstruction Era followed, but this was sabotaged by those who sold the Negro back to his former owners. Jim crow legislation further oppressed him. The Southern slaveholding oligarchy remained unchallenged and now, more than one hundred years later, as the Negro struggles to complete the first American Revolution, it seems remarkable indeed that he ever owned a house, let alone a theatre.

Despite hostility, the Negro was part of the drama long before the United States became a nation. John Leacock's "The Fall of British Tyranny" (1776) described recalcitrant slaves who promised to kill their masters upon attaining freedom. "Yorker's Stratagem" (1795) dealt with a New Yorker's marriage to a West

Indian mulatto. Murdock's[74] "The Triumph of Love" (1795) featured the cackling, comic servant, despite the fact that black Crispus Attucks was not comic when in the American Revolution and black Phoebe Fraunces[75] did not cackle when she saved the life of George Washington.

In the early part of the nineteenth century a group of free New York Negroes, spearheaded by James Hewlett,[76] organized the African Company at Bleecker and Grove Streets. In 1821 this group performed Shakespearean plays before mixed audiences. Disorderly whites forced the management to segregate them and also to lament that whites did not know how to behave at entertainment designed for ladies and gentlemen of color. This theatre, eventually destroyed by white hoodlums, is reported to have influenced the great Ira Alridge[77] who went abroad where he was acclaimed by European royalty.

In the middle of the nineteenth century a number of plays attempted to deal with the Negro as subject matter. The nineteenth century was, however, chiefly the era of the minstrel tradition—*the tradition originally created by slaves to satirize their masters*. White performers copied this pattern, popularized it, and spread the concept of the shuffling, chicken-stealing Negro to a society willing to embrace any representation of the Negro that denied his humanity. Following the Civil War, Negroes themselves joined the minstrel tradition, blackened their faces and imitated whites imitating them.

The wave of minstrelsy overflowed into the latter part of the nineteenth century. A group of showmen[78] objected to this and saw to it that the break with minstrelsy was complete. They produced a series of musicals with plot, characterization, and meaning.

But Thomas Dixon's "The Clansman," later filmed as "The Birth of a Nation," echoed existing attitudes towards the Negro. Race riots flared. The robber barons built their empires and the Theatrical Trust Syndicate brought the big business concept to the American theatre. This Syndicate controlled the theatre, and, because Mrs. Fiske and Sarah Bernhardt[79] incurred its disfavor, the former was compelled to play in second rate theatres and the latter in a tent. The Negro artist found himself unable to get inside the Broadway theatre as performer or patron. Only Bert Williams worked on the Broadway stage.

In 1910 the Negro performer had to go to Harlem. Some Negro actors welcomed the exile to Harlem. There they could perform roles previously denied them. They could play love scenes—something that was "taboo" while performing before whites. There, too, they could escape the raging hostility rampant in downtown areas. Many remembered too well the 1900 race riot when the mob yelled: "Get Williams and Walker!" Many knew, too, that comedian Ernest Hogan had to lock himself in a theatre overnight to escape from a lynch mob.

Harlem, therefore, offered the new Negro resident a haven from an unfriendly world despite the fact that he often had to fight neighboring whites in hand to hand battles. Many classes of Negroes poured into Harlem. Although a large number came from the South, this group had either heard about the theatre or seen Negro touring companies. In America at the turn of the century there existed approximately five thousand theatres as well as tent shows and civic auditoriums. To these came the Williams and Walker Company, Black Patti's Troubadours, and others. The movie industry had not yet challenged the economics of theatre. Despite the rise of the Syndicate, theatre was then a primary form of entertainment. It had not yet become a totally middle-class luxury.

The Negro who moved to Harlem, therefore, was receptive to the theatre movement that grew around him. For one thing, he could not go into any other theatre. Had he been able to go, he would have witnessed vapid Cinderella stories unrelated to his daily life. Therefore, he flocked readily to the Harlem theatres, the Crescent, the Lafayette, the Lincoln and Alhambra, which presented Negro versions of Broadway plays, originals, dance-dramas, classics, and musicals. Florenz Ziegfeld bought the finale of "Darktown Follies" for his own production. Another show, Darkydom," saw many of its sketches sold to Broadway producers.

On April 5, 1917 the Negro drama again moved towards downtown circles. Ridgely Torrence's "Three Plays for a Negro Theatre," directed by Robert Edmond Jones, opened at the Old Garden Theatre. Charles Gilpin[80] appeared in John Drinkwater's "Abraham Lincoln" and in Eugene O'Neill's "The Emperor Jones" (1920) at the Provincetown Theatre. Later, O'Neill's "All God's Chillun Got Wings" fanned flaming headlines because the play dealt with miscegenation. The Negro theatre artist had returned to the downtown area, doing what he felt whites would pay to see, or performing plays that reflected a white point of view.

The Negro Renaissance flowered and various types of productions[81] became major downtown offerings during the 1920's.

Theatrical activity continued in Harlem. Night clubs flourished. This was the period when the Negro was in vogue. Commercialism flooded the community. Stage presentations gave way to vaudeville sketches as the commercial-minded sought to sell to whites what they wanted to see and hear about Negroes. And then the movie industry reared its head. Where there had been approximately five thousand American theatres in 1900, the arrival of talking pictures reduced this amount drastically. By 1940 there were only two hundred in the nation. The moving picture replaced the stage, and in addition to the novel form, the prices were considerably cheaper. And many Negroes frankly sought this type of entertainment because at least it was honest. It did not attempt to represent them in any light.

One of the ventures that suffered as the movies rose to power was the Theatrical Owners and Bookers Association. This group, known as "Toby," was organized, owned, and managed by Negroes, who controlled a nationwide circuit. It assured Negro performers of continued work. The Depression, the movies, and the extended influences of white managers destroyed Toby. Theatre veterans have declared that Negro actors did not know unemployment until Toby went out of business.

The Depression temporarily halted the Harlem theatre movement. Still, Negroes appeared in a number of professional shows.[82] Besides the lighter themes, there were such serious plays as Hall Johnson's "Run Little Children," Langston Hughes' "Mulatto," John Wexley's "They Shall Not Die," Paul Peters' and George Sklar's "Stevedore." "Four Saints in Three Acts," "Mamba's Daughters," "Roll Sweet Chariot," "Porgy and Bess," "The Swing Mikado," and "The Hot Mikado" were other successes of the era.

Rose McClendon and Dick Campbell[83] organized the Negro People's Theatre in the 1930's.

The Harlem Players, a stock company, presented Negro versions of "Sailor, Beware" and "The Front Page" at the Lafayette Theatre. This group tried to speak to a community that concerned itself with eating regularly, with being dispossessed, and with relatives being lynched in the Southland. The troubles of a sailor and the problems of a newspaperman hardly interested Harlem. The Harlem Players soon went out of business. Another group, the Harlem Experimental Players, produced Regina Andrews' plays, directed by Harold Jackman.[84] The Harlem Suitcase Theatre presented Langston Hughes' "Don't You Want To Be Free?" and Dick Campbell and Muriel Rahn organized the Rose McClendon Players, who performed at the 124th Street Library Auditorium.

Best known of the uptown groups, however, was the Negro Unit of the Federal Theatre.[85] At the Lafayette, it presented numerous fine plays by famous dramatists. Its most highly acclaimed production was the Orson Welles-John Houseman[86] offering, "Macbeth," on April 14, 1936. Canada Lee[87] was a member of the cast. This Federal Unit was a solvent, skillful group that attracted theatre-goers of all incomes. When an Act of Congress ended the Works Progress Administration, it left Harlem without a low-priced professional theatre.

The Negro Playwrights Company, organized towards the end of the 1930's, attempted to supply the community with professional theatre. Theodore Ward's "Big White Fog," directed by Powell Lindsay, opened at the Lincoln Theatre and introduced Frank Silvera to New York audiences.[88] Financial difficulties brought this organization to an untimely end.

During the 1940's the Negro was involved on Broadway as well as in Harlem. The Richard Wright-Paul Green play, "Native Son," starring Canada Lee, and Paul Robeson's "Othello" were significant achievements. "Cabin in the Sky" enjoyed a successful run. In Harlem, Abram Hill, Frederick O'Neill, Austin Briggs-Hall, and a number of talented theatre people formed the American Negro Theatre and housed it in the auditorium of the 135th Street Library.[89] It was the Abram Hill-Harry Wagstaff Gribble adaptation of "Anna Lucasta" that created a sensation and later moved to Broadway. That sensation also brought the American Negro Theatre into commercial focus—a move not welcomed by the group's founders. Despite its continued efforts to build a community theatre, the group discovered that, because of its success with "Anna Lucasta," it was judged in terms of Broadway fare.

With the end of the Second World War a number of dramatists turned to the post-war adjustment of the Negro. All of their plays[90] involved Negro artists.

American attitudes towards the Negro underwent a

change in the post-war world, a change reflected in
many avenues of the nation's life. Nationalism roared
from colonial lands. American Negroes echoed this
roar. Some whites found it easier to accept this roar
as the voice of the "New Negro." To some extent this
concept alleviated numerous guilt complexes and permitted the ruling group to believe it had only subju-
gated the "old, non-protesting Negro." What was not
faced was the truth that Negroes had been protesting,
agitating, and fighting for human rights since 1619.
But now, after the Second World War, sharper lines of
communication brought the revolts in Asia and Africa
into the lives of Americans. The revolt of suppressed
peoples became a reality that had to be met.

A number of barriers relaxed. Negroes now found
they could purchase seats to Broadway houses—seats
that were not on the aisle. Prior to 1945 only three
Broadway houses sold seats to Negroes that were not
on the aisle. This practice was based on the belief that
whites did not want Negroes climbing over them. The
Playwrights Company's declaration of principles in
1945 had much to do with this shift in policy. In addition, the company also declared its members would deal
specifically with Negroes in dramatic terms. Interesting
examples of the integration of the Negro in white
shows followed. "Detective Story" (1948) and "The
Shrike" (1951–52) featured Negro actors in roles that
were not specifically Negroid. Actors Equity Association launched repeated drives, urging the continuation
of this pattern. The Greenwich Mews Theatre, a professional Off-Broadway company, followed this pattern.
Broadway, however, continued to use the Negro actor
in specified roles, and in roles the Negro himself did not
always find to his liking.

In November, 1950 a group of Negro playwrights
met in Harlem with representatives of four community
theatre groups: the Harlem Showcase, the Committee for the Negro in the Arts, Ed Cambridge[91] and the

"Y" drama group, and the Elks Community Theatre. The American Negro Theatre had disbanded and many of its charter members wandered into the aforementioned groups. At the meeting a Council on the Harlem Theatre was formed. A resolution noted that the use of Negro actors in non-Negro roles offered limited employment to a large group of actors. However, it neither encouraged nor assisted in disseminating the cultural values of the Negro people.

The Council noted, too, that the commercial failure of Theodore Ward's "Our Lan' " (1947)—after its initial Off-Broadway success—suggested that the commercial theatre wanted to tolerate the Negro, but it did not want to deal with him in strong, truthful, dramatic terms. The Council members declared that serious plays about Negro life met commercial failure because they were often written from a white point of view. Generally, plays involving Negroes had a "good" white character helping the black people out of trouble. The obvious implication, the Council noted, was that white theatre-goers faced psychological barriers and could not identify with central, sympathetic Negro characters.

The Council urged the representative groups to produce plays by Negro writers and to assist one another in casting, producing, and promoting. The target was the Off-Broadway area. A number of Negro-written plays appeared in library basements, in community auditoriums and lodge halls, financed quite often because the group collected money from its members and launched a production. The plays shown were written and directed and produced by Negroes; they appeared primarily during the 1950–51 period.[92]

In the midst of what Harlemites considered a new Renaissance, the Apollo Theatre sponsored two shabby productions of white plays with Negro actors: "Detective Story" and "Rain." Both productions were artistically and commercially unsuccessful. The Apollo's management stated publicly that Harlemites did not care for serious drama. The Council on the Harlem Theatre issued a statement declaring: "The owner of the Apollo has insulted the Negro people by bringing to this community two inferior pieces with little meaning to our lives. Ridiculous prices were charged, and when we exercised the buyer's right (of withholding patronage) we were accused of lacking taste."

The Apollo management's charge, however, served as a catalytic agent for productions by Negro authors. On October 15, 1951 William Branch's "A Medal for Willie" was presented by the Committee for the Negro in the Arts at the Club Baron on Lenox Avenue. The critics hailed the play, which posed in strong dramatic terms the question: should the Negro soldier fight and die abroad or should he take arms against the prejudiced Southland. In September, 1952 Ossie Davis' "Alice in Wonder" opened at the Elks Community Theatre and it, too, roared the truth about the Negro's plight in America.

The early 1950's witnessed another significant event. Large numbers of Negroes moved from Harlem to Long Island, Brooklyn, the Bronx, and Westchester. Many theatre workers and play-goers moved, too. Apartment houses in Harlem became rooming houses, occupied by those who fled the South in terror. There was a shift, too, in methods of producing plays. Community theatres all over the city broke down. The Yiddish Theatre saw an era approaching when it would no longer profit on Second Avenue. Producers were no longer anxious to own theatres, but rather to rent them, produce a play there, and let someone else worry about maintaining the property. Those Negroes who had sought so valiantly to build a theatre in the Harlem area now turned towards Broadway and Greenwich Village.

Most of the professional theatre work since that time has been performed in those areas. On September 24, 1953 Louis Peterson's "Take A Giant Step" opened on

Broadway. The Charles Sebree—Greer Johnston play, "Mrs. Patterson," also appeared on Broadway. On October 24, 1954 William Branch's "In Splendid Error" excited audiences at the Greenwich Mews Theatre. In 1955 Alice Childress' satire, "Trouble in Mind," delighted audiences at the same theatre. Luther James produced an all-Negro version of "Of Mice and Men" in the Greenwich Village area, and on March 29, 1956 Earl Hyman appeared as "Mr. Johnson" on Broadway. Despite Mr. Hyman's remarkable performance, the play failed.

The 1956–57 season brought three Negro-written plays to Off-Broadway stages: Louis Peterson's "Take A Giant Step," revived at the Jan Hus House, this writer's "A Land Beyond the River" at the Greenwich Mews, and the Langston Hughes–David Martin folk musical "Simply Heavenly" at the 84th Street Theatre. These plays should have ended the bromide that Negro audiences do not support theatre. Negro theatre-goers were directly responsible for the financial success of these plays.

On March 11, 1959 Lorraine Hansberry's "A Raisin in the Sun" opened on Broadway to acclaim and later won the Critics Circle Award. It enjoyed a long and successful run, then later toured. During the 1961–62 season Errol John's "The Moon on a Rainbow Shawl" was shown on the Lower East Side and in May, 1961 Jean Genêt's "The Blacks" settled down at the St. Mark's Playhouse for a long run. "Fly Blackbirds," a revue, won critical acclaim Off-Broadway while the Ossie Davis satire "Purlie Victorious" was hailed by Broadway theatre-goers during the 1961–62 season.

In reviewing this brief—and, of necessity, superficial—survey,[93] it seems amazing that Negro theatre workers have managed such a considerable output. It should be remembered that many of the ventures discussed here were written, directed, and produced under harrowing circumstances. The artists generally worked full time at other jobs. They had no well-to-do relatives who could maintain them. They performed at night while working or struggling during the day to pay their rents. And, too, these plays were supported by people whose incomes were, at most, uncertain.

Whether it is possible to build a Harlem community theatre in an era when community theatres are almost nonexistent remains a tantalizing question. However, people like Maxwell Glanville, Jay Brooks,[94] and other tireless workers continue their efforts in Harlem. They fight eternally rising costs, the omnipotence of Broadway, cheap movie and television fare, and a changing community.

For the theatre worker outside Harlem, we can only foresee an occasional successful production. One cannot resist noting, however, that the produced plays will be written by whites dealing with the strings attached to an interracial love affair or some other area of Negro life receptive to white audiences. We may even have the Birmingham story brought to the stage, but it will probably be written by a white author who will deal with the problem of a "good" white caught in the throes of an uprising. Theatre in America remains a middle-class luxury wherein the playwright speaks, cajoles, seduces, and lies to an expense-account audience. Until it becomes once again an art form willing to attract all people, we see no change in the type of play being produced.

Yet, a courageous producer has before him a rich opportunity. Negro playwrights are numerous and they wait eagerly for a producer who has not been "brainwashed." One of the most needed theatre workers at present is the Negro producer. He could utilize the rich dramatic history of these times, the wonderful artists, and the splendid audiences that can be attracted if the theatre speaks to them in terms of the truth of their daily lives.

Carlton Moss

⚜

THE NEGRO IN AMERICAN FILMS*

E VERY WEEK five and a half million colored Americans go to the movies. Their total admissions are a
small dent in the gross "take" from one hundred million weekly movie-goers. But not so small that the motion picture industry is indifferent to it. In a way it
can be said this concern for the "colored market" is
due to the struggle going on between rival movie companies for the largest possible market.

But, equally important in these days of struggle for
liberation by the colored peoples of the world, the movie makers look toward the colored audience with an
eye set on winning it in a struggle to maintain the status-quo. This status-quo has given the men who own the
motion picture industry—or American Investment as
it is popularly called—a substantial profit since the inception of the business.

No one will challenge the fact that American movies
have been and are one of the most powerful media of
social expression the world has ever known. There is
no part of the globe that has not been influenced by

---

* The figures quoted in this article were accurate at the time of
its writing, 1963.

the ideas, standards of taste, and information disseminated in American motion pictures.

What better time than now for the molders of public opinion in the United States to show the world that colored Americans are judges, school teachers, brave soldiers, songwriters, home owners, and that they are integrated into prosperous American life like any other person who lives on these shores.

But to what extent are Negro Americans integrated into the motion picture industry itself? To begin with it might be helpful to glance at the history of colored people in American movies.

Significantly, Negroes appeared in the first creative films ever made. In the very first film to exploit the medium as an art the plot concerned a situation in which a group of colored characters was the center of interest. The film, made in France in 1902, told this tale:

An omnibus drawn by an extraordinary mechanical horse is driven by four Negroes. The horse kicks and upsets the Negroes, who, falling, are changed into white clowns. They begin slapping each other's faces and by the blows become black again. Kicking each other, they become white once more. Suddenly they are all merged into one gigantic Negro, and when he refuses to pay his carfare, the conductor sets fire to the omnibus, and the Negro bursts into a thousand pieces.

But it was the American motion picture that set the pattern for the handling of Negroes on the screen. The presence of colored people in American life, their second class status, often defined by local law, national customs, and community mores, was a source of comedy for the early American motion picture producers. However, Negroes themselves did not appear on the screen in actuality. The characters supposedly portraying colored people were played by white actors who smeared their faces with black grease paint.

In 1905, just one year before W. E. B. Du Bois called

the founding conference of the Niagara Movement (fore-runner of the National Association for the Advancement of Colored People), the movie makers released a film which set the precedent for the treatment of colored people in films. That was to stand for more than fifty years. A short film, "The Wooing and Wedding of a Coon," showed a colored man and his bride as stupid and immoral. The producers described it as a "genuine Ethiopian comedy."

In 1907, one year after the founding of the Niagara Movement, the movie producers gave America its second film on the "place of colored people" in white America. It was as if the film were made to answer Dr. Du Bois' Niagara proclamation that Negro Americans would not accept less than their full manhood rights— for the film dealt with social relations between colored and white people. Released under the title "The Masher" it told this story:

A would-be lady-killer is unsuccessful with every woman he tries to woo. Finally, a lady wearing a veil, responds to his flirtation. However, when the lady-killer makes further advances and lifts the lady's veil, he discovers to his consternation that the lady of his choice is colored. Horrified, the lady-killer runs away as fast as his legs can carry him.

Once the industry was established, the pattern for the handling of Negroes settled into two categories— films in which colored people were the butt-end of crude and insulting jokes, and films in which colored people were portrayed as devoted slaves who "knew their place."

In 1914, Bert Williams tried to break the boycott against employing colored artists by producing his own films. The attempt met with disastrous results. His first film was badly received by white audiences and even resulted in a "race" riot in Brooklyn, New York. Elsewhere it met an undercover boycott.

Shortly after the unsuccessful attempt by Bert Williams to give Negro people a voice in the film industry, another gifted artist, D. W. Griffith, used his unusual motion picture craftsmanship to state the case of American racists. Based on a novel called "The Clansman," which depicted the Ku Klux Klan of the 1870's as a band of knights. Griffith's film told a sentimental story advocating segregation of the races—with whites as rulers.

Immediately after its release, the film was re-titled "The Birth of a Nation." Significantly, Woodrow Wilson, the President of the United States, welcomed the Griffith movie to the White House. This was the first film ever to be so honored. The President, who had consistently turned a deaf ear to the pleas of colored Americans for federal protection against the wave of lynching then sweeping the country, is said to have remarked after seeing "The Birth of a Nation"—"It is like writing history with lightning."

But despite White House acceptance of "The Birth of a Nation," the film aroused a storm of protest throughout the northern states. Colored and white people united in attacking the picture because of its extreme bias and many historical inaccuracies. Race riots broke out in Boston and other "abolitionist" cities.

Several states refused to issue a license for the exhibition of "The Birth of a Nation." Many prominent people spoke bitterly, and often, against the showing of the film. Oswald Garrison Villard, grandson of William Lloyd Garrison, the famed anti-slavery crusader, condemned it as "a deliberate attempt to humiliate ten million American citizens." New York City's distinguished Rabbi Stephen Wise declared it was "an intolerable insult to the Negro people," and Charles E. Eliot, president of Harvard University, charged the movie "with a tendency to perversion of white ideals."

Unquestionably, "The Birth of a Nation" proved the power of the screen to mold and shape opinion. Can it

be challenged that the film's justification of the Ku Klux
Klan was at least one factor which enabled the Klan
to enter upon its period of greatest expansion—reaching a total membership of more than five million by
1924? Nevertheless, Griffith and the film industry were
not completely insensitive to the protest against the
film. In an obvious attempt to atone for the harm he
had done to the colored people, he included a scene in
a subsequent picture which showed a white soldier kiss-
ing his wounded colored comrade.

Simultaneously, the industry, called upon to use the
power of its medium to rally the total population around
the slogan "Make the World Safe for Democracy," relaxed its policy toward Negroes. The most significant
change in the period following the First World War was
the introduction of colored actors to play the roles
that hitherto had been played by white men and women
using black make-up. The concept of the characters
didn't change, but their importance to the story did.
Heretofore, colored characters had played major roles
in the short film stories. Now that films were greater in
length, colored characters were relegated to incidental
roles.

Again it remained for D. W. Griffith to set the tone
for the handling of Negro actors in motion pictures.
Once more he seemed bent on avenging the defeat of
his rebel father's army[95]—for again he demonstrated
how a director steeped in anti-Negro prejudice can influence his audience.

Here for the first time film-goers were given the
cowardly black man whose hair turns white when he
meets danger in any form. He is afraid of the dark, of
thunderstorms, of firearms, of animals, of police, and
above all—of white folks. This contemptible comic relief character "stole" the show in Griffith's "One Exciting Night," released in 1922. Although the character
was played by a white man with black grease paint on
his face, every colored actor who applied for work following the release of this film was expected to imitate

the frightened, weak-kneed, stupid creature created by D. W. Griffith.

During this period, Negroes again tried to produce their own films. This second attempt found an audience in theatres catering exclusively to Negro patronage— theatres which had opened since Bert William's earlier experiment.

But it was too late in the history of the motion picture industry for anyone to make films for so limited a market. At best, there were some four hundred to five hundred colored theatres of a total of more than fifteen thousand motion picture houses throughout the United States. Basic economics intervened. The colored producer, making films for the handful of colored theatres, had to make them on a very limited budget. Further, he had to compete with the white producers— because not enough colored films were made to keep the colored houses open every week in the year.

Even more important was the handicap of experience and technique. From the very inception of motion pictures no colored man or woman was hired to work in any of the technical departments of the industry.

The Negro producer, operating with extremely limited funds and the barest necessities of equipment, found that all the facilities for making and processing films were in the hands of the white producers. With no experienced colored technicians available, he had to hire such white personnel as were available to him— the most inefficient, inexperienced, and least skilled, in the industry, whom he could only equip with the cheapest and most inadequate production facilities. As though these handicaps were not sufficient, the colored producer found himself opposing what his very own organizations were fighting for: namely, an end to jim crow. For the white theatres would not buy his product, and his films were, of necessity, limited only to jim crow houses. To add insult to injury, the content of his films had to conform to what the status-quo approved, for any film which portrayed Negro Americans in any context of militancy would have been challenged by the police and other arms of government.

The status of colored Americans during the years in which the motion picture industry was being organized made it impossible for them to control the real estate and laboratories which are the very basis of the business. True, there were a few Negro Americans who might have had the money to open a nickelodeon, but the hurdles in their path were insurmountable. Further, the kind of social and business contact which would have brought Negro aspirants into the laboratories and equipment manufacturing services was completely closed to all but whites. The only phase of the industry which was open to colored people was that of the performing artist—and even here, as we have shown, he had to stand aside and let white people "imitate" him for the first thirty years. When he finally achieved the role, he was expected to insult himself and his own people.

Today, the motion picture business represents a capital investment of $2,966,000,000. In 1962 its approximate world-wide gross income was $3,000,000,000. The investment in theatres is $2,700,000,000. It employs 25,400 production workers, a personnel of 10,-000 for distribution, and a staff of 150,000 for exhibition. Its total yearly payroll is $580,000,000. And to this day, the participation of colored Americans is basically still that of the paying audience.

Despite the advances in the trade union movement, in Fair Employment Practices, and the general awakening in the United States to the treatment of colored people, only a handful of Negro Americans can earn a living in the industry—and they are employed only in front of the cameras. All of the business and technical opportunities of the industry are to this day barred to Negroes. True, the industry has shifted its method of production and slashed the number of its personnel. Nevertheless, it hires new writers, directors, composers, and set designers constantly. Occasionally, a Negro writer is employed to work on the script for a "colored picture." Even then the Negro writer is teamed with a white writer, which is not necessarily objectionable. However, once the "colored picture" is completed the Negro writer is never heard from again.[96] The Negro public relations man gets the same treatment. He, too, is occasionally hired to work on a film that the producer believes should be of interest to colored theatre-goers.

Employment opportunities for Negroes are just as limited in the non-theatrical motion picture industry. In 1962, this branch of film-making spent in excess of $389,000,000 on sales, educational, industrial, religious, military, and institutional films. Negro participation in these films amounted to a half-dozen acting roles in a limited number of race-relation films produced by makers of religious motion pictures.

But the future of the Negro in films is not as bleak as these facts suggest. For there are other facts which, if grappled with, can lead to a new day for the Negro people in American films.

First, the myth that "white audiences are not interested in seeing Negroes on the screen" has long since been exploded. The box office returns as listed in the film magazine *Box Office Barometer* clearly show that films featuring Negro actors and actresses *do* make money. The *Box Office Annual* for 1961 credits "A Raisin in the Sun" with a rating of 144, which is 44 points above the hundred points used by *Box Office Magazine* to indicate that a motion picture is making money. "Paris Blues," starring Paul Newman, Sidney Poitier, Diahann Carroll, and Joanne Woodward, is also listed among the 1961 money-makers. It had a rating of 163.

Granted, films featuring Negro artists have not yet made millions in profits, as the producers would have the public believe a "colored interest" film must make if the industry is to continue making them. In proportion to what it actually costs to make the specific

film they don't lose money. Unless, of course, the film
is wrapped in bandannas. Further, investigation shows
that none of the "colored interest" films plays all the
theatres available to the producer. Many exhibitors
refuse to play "colored films" on the grounds that they
would attract too many colored people to the theatre.

Another film that shows the potential of motion pictures featuring Negro talent is the Brazilian-made
movie "Black Orpheus." This film succeeded on its own.
It did not have the advantage of a guaranteed release
or the budget for a high-powered advertising campaign.
Nevertheless, it found theatres and has been attracting
audiences since its release in the United States more
than three years ago. The success of "Black Orpheus"
shows that it is possible to find an audience for films
featuring Negro artists without going through the giant
motion picture distributing companies. Heretofore, as
we have shown, the Negro producer was faced with
the problem of a very limited number of small theatres
in which he could show his production. The experience
of "Black Orpheus" certainly indicates there is a profitable market in the United States for an imaginatively
made independent film.

In addition to this market a new foreign outlet is
opening up. This market has already captured the attention of the giants of American movies. Under the guidance of Eric Johnston, then president of the Motion
Picture Producers Association, a group called American Motion Picture Export Company was organized.
According to their press release, "The purpose of the
new company is to open up distribution of American
films on a sound basis in the new nations of Africa and
to bring the best American products to wide audiences
in Africa. It will create the basis for the construction
of modern theatres. I am convinced that by bringing
up-to-date film distribution to Africa the Africans,
themselves, will be given opportunities to participate
in new businesses thus stimulated." This organization

has already taken steps to open offices in Lagos, Nigeria; and Accra, Ghana.

Irrespective of what Mr. Eric Johnston and company think they are going to do in Africa, it is apparent that the new nations of Africa have no intention of giving up control of their resources. Neither is it probable that they would refuse to book a film because they would be afraid it would attract too many "colored people."

The second point of interest is the availability of skilled film craftsmen. Mainly through University Cinema Schools a number of Negroes have had the opportunity to learn how to make motion pictures. A few of these have found freelance work which has given them the opportunity to gain film-making experience. In addition, unity between Negro and white has now developed to the point that some of the most skilled and experienced craftsmen in the industry are available to colored producers, enabling them to make films of quality and content. Incidentally, the making of such films in this context would provide an opportunity for the training and developing of real skills among colored aspirants. The combination of a potential market and the availability of production talent paves the way for a new day in film making.

But the making of such a film calls for a pioneer. A pioneer in the tradition of the Negro men and women who founded our press and historical publications. There is no place for such a producer in Hollywood. The very nature of Hollywood production methods makes it impossible for a Negro producer to make an independent film. Hollywood films, in the main, are financed by banks, the same banks that provide funds for the real estate interests, southern farming and industry, northern and western ghettos, and all other facets of American investment that thrive on jim crow and gradualism. If the Negro producer is to make an independent film he must turn his back on Hollywood and draw on the experience of the film makers who have defied the industry and made successful motion pictures. An example of a successful film made outside of the industry is the recent production "David and Lisa." The producers (an inspired husband and wife) solicited investments of fifty to a hundred dollars until they had a total budget of $200,000. On this "shoestring" they produced a film devoid of the glamorous trappings and waste of Hollywood, yet sensitive in its story, and imaginative in its execution. So effective was "David and Lisa" that it won film prizes and was generally considered one of the finest films produced in 1962. With such attention it could hardly fail to make money for its investors and appeal to an extremely wide audience.

In 1964, another "shoestring" production, "One Potato, Two Potato," was highly praised by judges and reviewers at the Cannes Film Festival, although it was not an official entry. Directed by Larry Peerce, son of the opera star Jan Peerce, it was produced by Sam Weston of television and shot in Ohio. Its story does not linger on the fringe of life as the Negro-American knows it but deals with one of his problems in depth. The film's further outstanding success at a second film festival—this time in Karlovy Vary where, again, it was not an official entry—made its showing at a Broadway theatre a profitable undertaking. Here, again, it repeated its success with public and critics alike.

"David and Lisa" and "One Potato, Two Potato," do not show a trend, for they stand alone among the hundreds of motion pictures produced every year.

But there is no reason why a Negro producer cannot emulate these outstanding achievements. Certainly enough material of a tremendously inspirational nature exists within the heart of the Negro community.

Lorraine Hansberry

☙

A CHALLENGE TO ARTISTS[97]

I AM AFRAID that I haven't made a speech for a very long time and there is a significance in that fact which is part of what I should like to talk about this evening.

A week or so ago I was at my typewriter working on a scene in a play of mine in which one character, a German novelist, is trying to explain to another character, an American intellectual, something about what led the greater portion of the German intelligentsia to acquiesce to Nazism. He says this, "They (the Nazis) permitted us to feel, in return for our silence, that we were non-participants; merely irrelevant if inwardly agonized observers who had nothing whatsoever to do with that which was being committed in our names."

Just as I put the period after that sentence, my own telephone rang and I was confronted with the voice of Dr. Otto Nathan[98] asking this particular American writer if she would be of this decade and this nation and appear at this rally this evening and join a very necessary denunciation of a lingering *American* kind of travesty.

It is the sort of moment of truth that dramatists dearly love to put on the stage but find as uncomfortable as everyone else in life. To make it short, however, I am here.

I mean to say that one can become detached in this world of ours; we can get to a place where we read only the theatre or photography or music pages of our newspapers. And then we wake up one day and find that the better people of our nation are still where they were when we last noted them: in the courts defending *our* constitutional rights for us.

This makes me feel that it might be interesting to talk about where our artists are in the contemporary struggles. Some of them, of course, are being heard and felt. Some of the more serious actresses such as Shelley Winters and Julie Harris and a very thoughtful comedian such as Steve Allen have associated themselves with some aspect of the peace movement, and Sidney Poitier and Harry Belafonte have made significant contributions to the Negro struggle. But the vast majority—where are they?

Well, I am afraid that they are primarily where the ruling powers have always wished the artist to be and to stay: in their studios. They are consumed, in the main, with what they consider to be larger issues— such as "the meaning of life," etc. . . . I personally consider that part of this detachment is the direct and indirect result of many years of things like the House Committee and concurrent years of McCarthyism in all its forms. I mean to suggest that the climate of fear, which we were once told, as I was coming along, by wise men, would bear a bitter harvest in the culture of our civilization, has in fact come to pass. In the contemporary arts, the rejection of this particular world is no longer a mere grotesque threat, but a fact.

Among my contemporaries and colleagues in the arts the search for the roots of war, the exploitation of man, of poverty and of despair itself is sought in any arena other than the one which has shaped these artists. Having discovered that the world is incoherent

they have, some of them, also come to the conclusion
that it is also unreal and, in any case, beyond the corrective powers of human energy. Having determined
that life is in fact an absurdity, they have not yet decided that the task of the thoughtful is to try and help
impose purposefulness on that absurdity. They don't
yet agree, by and large, that simply being against life
as it is is not enough; that simply *not* being a "rhinoc-
eros" is not enough. That, moreover, replacing phony
utopianisms of one kind with vulgar and cheap little
philosophies of accommodation is also not enough. In
a word, they do not yet agree that it is perhaps the
task, I should think certainly the joy, of the artist to
chisel out some expression of what life can conceivably
be.

The fact is that this unwitting capitulation really does
aim to be a revolt, really does aim to indict—*something.* Really does aim to be partisan in saying no to a
world which it generally characterizes as a brothel. I
am thinking now mainly, of course, of writers of my
generation. It is they, upon whom we must depend so
heavily for the refinement and articulation of the as-
piration of men, who do not yet agree that if the world
is a brothel, then someone has built the edifice; and
that if it was the hand of man, then the hand of man
can reconstruct it. That whatever man renders, creates, imagines—he can render afresh, re-create, and
even more gloriously re-imagine. But I must repeat
that anyone who can even think so these days is looked
upon as an example of unparalleled simple-mindedness.

Why? For this is what is cogent to our meeting tonight; the writers that I am presently thinking of come
mainly from my generation. That is to say that they
come from a generation which was betrayed in the late
forties and fifties by the domination of McCarthyism.
We were ceaselessly told, after all, to be everything
which mutilates youth: to be silent, to be ignorant, to
be without unsanctioned opinions, to be compliant and,

above all else, obedient to all the ideas which are in fact the dregs of an age. We were taught that agitational activity in behalf of changing this world was nothing but an expression, among other things, of our "neurotic compulsions" about our own self-dissatisfactions because our mothers dominated our fathers or some such as that. We were told in an age of celebrated liberations from repressions that the repression of the *urge* to protest against war was surely the only *respectable* repression left in the universe.

As for those who went directly into science or industry it was all even less oblique than any of that. If you went to the wrong debates on campus, signed the wrong petitions, you simply didn't get the job you wanted and you were forewarned of this early in your college career.

And, of course, things are little different from my parents' times, I mean with regard to the candor with which young people have been made to think in terms of money. It is the only single purpose which has been put before them. That which Shakespeare offered as a curse—"Put money in thy purse"—is now a boast. What makes me think of that in connection with what we are speaking of tonight? Well, I hope that I am wise enough to determine the nature of a circle. If, after all, the ambition in life is merely to be rich, then all which might threaten that possibility is much to be avoided, is it not? This means, therefore, not incurring the disfavor of employers. It means that one will not protest war if one expects to draw one's livelihood from, say, the aircraft industry if one is an engineer. Or, in the arts, how can one write plays which have either implicit or explicit in them a quality of the detestation of commerciality if in fact one is beholden to the commerciality of the professional theatre? How can one protest the criminal persecution of political dissenters if one has already discovered at nineteen that to do so is to risk a profession? If all one's morality is wedded

to the opportunist, the expedient in life, how can one
have the deepest, most profound moral outrage about
the fact of the condition of the Negro people in the
United States? Particularly, thinking of expediency,
when one has it dinned into one's ears day after day
that the only reason that troublesome and provocative
group of people must some day be permitted to buy a
cup of coffee or rent an apartment or get a job is NOT
because of the recognition of the universal humanity of
the human race but because it happens to be extremely
expedient international politics now to *think* of grant-
ing these things!

As I stand here I know perfectly well that such institutions as the House Committee, and all the other little
committees, have dragged on their particular obscene
theatrics for all these years, not to expose "Communists" or do anything really in connection with the "security" of the United States, but merely to create an
atmosphere where, in the first place, I should be afraid
to come tonight at all and, secondly, to absolutely
guarantee that I will not say what I am going to say,
which is this:

I think that my government is wrong. I would like to
see them turn back our ships from the Caribbean. The
Cuban people, to my mind, and I speak only for myself, have chosen their destiny, and I cannot believe
that it is the place of the descendants of those who did
not ask the Monarchists of the eighteenth century for
permission to make the United States a republic, to
interfere with the twentieth-century choice of another
sovereign people.

I will go further, speaking as a Negro in America,
and impose a little of what Negroes say all the time to
each other on what I am saying to you. And that is
that it would be a great thing if they would not only
turn back the ships from the Caribbean but turn to the
affairs of our country that need righting. For one thing,
empty the legislative and judicial chambers of the vic-

tims of political persecution so we know why that lamp is burning out there in the Brooklyn waters. And, while they are at it, go on and help fulfill the American dream and empty the Southern jails of the genuine heroes, practically the last vestige of dignity that we have to boast about at this moment in our history: those students whose imprisonment for trying to insure what is already on the book is our national disgrace at this moment.

And I would go so far, perhaps with an over sense of drama, but I don't think so, to say that, maybe without waiting for another two men to die, we should send those troops to finish the Reconstruction in Alabama, Georgia, Mississippi, and every place else where the fact of our federal flag flying creates the false notion that what happened at the end of the Civil War was the defeat of the slavocracy at the political as well as the military level. And I say this not merely in behalf of the black and oppressed but (for a change, and more and more thoughtful Negroes must begin to make this point) also for the white and disinherited of the South, those poor whites who, by the millions, have been made the tragic and befuddled instruments of their own oppression at the hand of the most sinister political apparatus in our country. I think perhaps that if our government would do that it would not have to compete in any wishful way for the respect of the new black and brown nations of the world.

Finally, I think that all of us who are thinking such things, who wish to exercise these rights that we are here defending tonight, must really exercise them. Speaking to my fellow artists in particular, I think that we must paint them, sing them, write about them. All these matters which are not currently fashionable. Otherwise, I think, as I have put into the mouth of my German novelist, we are indulging in a luxurious complicity—and no other thing.

I personally agree with those who say that from here

on in, if we are to survive, we the people, still an excellent phrase, we the people of the world must oblige the heads of all governments to become responsible to us. I personally do not feel that it matters if it be the government of China presently engaging in incomprehensible and insane antics at the border of India or my president dismissing what he knows to be in the hearts of the American people and engaging in overt provocation with our sister people to the south. I think that it is imperative to say NO to all of it; no to war of any kind, anywhere. And I think, therefore, and it is my reason for being here tonight, that it is imperative to remove from the American fabric any and all such institutions or agencies as the House Committee on Un-American Activities which are designed expressly to keep us from saying—NO!

William R. Dixon

&‌⁂‌&

THE MUSIC OF HARLEM

THE MAIN DIFFICULTY one encounters when attempting to write about the music of Harlem is that unlike the other arts—the dance, theatre, literature, etc.—the music of Harlem did not necessarily concern itself only with Harlem in Manhattan but was involved with all the other Harlems that were and are abundant in America. With the possible exception of Bud Powell (piano), Sonny Rollins (tenor saxophone), Jackie McLean (alto saxophone), Bennie Harris (trumpet), and of course there are others, the musicians who made this music were not from Harlem at all, but did come there at first to live and then to explore and develop their music.

A strange paradox is that the music which did much to shape contemporary music and dance, which was largely created in Harlem, is not to be found on a large scale in Harlem today. Any student of jazz history has heard of the golden days of jazz in Harlem; the Cotton Club, Smalls, Connie's Inn, the Elk's Rendezvous, etc. The legends of the house rent parties[99] are legion where such pianists as Willie "the Lion" Smith, James P. Johnson, Willie Gant, Fats Waller, and others vied for the plaudits of the audiences.

It was at Leroy's that I first saw piano battles. Players like Willie "the Lion," James P., Fats Faller, Willie Gant. They'd last for three or four hours. One man would play two or three choruses, and the next would slide in. Jimmy was on top most of the time. Fats was the youngest, but he was coming along. They played shouts and they also played pop tunes. You got credit for how many patterns you could create within the tunes you knew, and in how many different keys you could play.[100]

And of course the old Savoy Ballroom, that home of "happy feet" which today is no more, did much to bring people from other parts of the city, country, and even the world, to hear this music and to see experts dance to it.

Much of the world's important music, music that has lasted and endured, has a great deal of the time been concerned with the dance. And if not a specific dance, something about that kind of movement. The early days of jazz were not to be an exception to that rule. In the beginning everybody danced to the rhythms of jazz. And by their dancing to it, by participating in it, created new dance steps such as the Lindy Hop, the Big Apple, the Charleston, etc.

From 1916 to 1930, James P. Johnson was the outstanding ragtime pianist and composer for piano in New York. During that time, he developed the New York style of "stride" piano from the rags of Scott Joplin and the southern Negro cotillion and set dances. . . .[101]

The first dance that I ever went to was at the Renaissance Ballroom, known affectionately as the "Rennie," located on 137 Street and Seventh Avenue. At that time I was much more knowing about the art of music through listening than I was by participating through dancing. The band was that of Jimmie Lunceford, whose music was later to become a heavy influence on the music of Stan Kenton and others. I can remember standing all night long at the bandstand, completely enthralled, listening to the music of that marvelous band. But then those bands were not dance bands in the way that a dance band is thought of today. Those bands were good jazz bands and the music they played was good music, suitable for both listening and dancing. A few weeks ago, a friend of mine played some tapes made by the Ellington band at a dance in Fargo, North Dakota, and in the light of what is played for dancing today, this was indeed a marvel. The band was simply playing Ellington's music, with such as Jimmie Blanton, Rex Stewart, and others, in the way that they play. And the people danced.

Yes, dancing is very important to people who play music with a beat. I think that people who don't dance, or who never did dance, don't really understand the beat. What they get in their minds is a mechanical thing not totally unacademic. I know musicians who don't and never did dance, and they have difficulty communicating.[102]

It has been offered as argument that the "new music" or bebop, later just plain bop, was created to discourage inferior players from participating and also to keep "outsiders" off the crowded bandstand at Minton's. But I can't fully accept this. No art is deliberately created on so small a premise. It is possible that some of the rather unusual harmonies (for the time) employed were thus devised for the purpose of making it difficult for non-"in" musicians to play or even to want to play, but the overall idea of the music, a music that was to change the direction or rather further and reinforce the direction of the older music, was much more profound in concept. And, like all art, it was simply created by doing.

There are certain advantages about the ghetto, although one may not view them in this manner if compelled against one's innate desire to live in the ghetto. Because the Negro musician was relegated to jazz and jazz only, it is easy to understand why all of the main innovators and important creators have been Negro. The Negro jazz man has never (until very recently) played anything really but jazz. And when I say jazz,

I mean that he has, for the most part only played that music which he himself created. All of his creativity, concentration, and sensitivity went into this music and this kind of playing. Unlike white musicians he could not work both in the symphonic or non-jazz world and the jazz world. And this had nothing to do with his ability or even his desires. As a result his entire concept of music, braced and supported with a background of spiritual music, work songs, field hollers, and of course, the blues, demanded heavy emotional giving and response. In jazz, unlike other forms of music, the composer, the man who wrote the music (in a literal sense), was not *that* important. All pieces of music to the jazz player simply meant that he was to extract from the music those elements he felt and responded to. In fact, in jazz the player always, if he were true to his art, played himself.

In the ghetto this kind of emotional playing flourished. And there was no time or inclination to intellectualize the music. Either it "moved" you or it didn't and if a player failed to "get to the people," he would most certainly find it difficult to work. And all jazz was not played in the clubs, at dances, or the other places commonly assumed to be *the* places where jazz was heard. Who is to say that it was not jazz that I heard as a child in those Baptist churches? It made *my* foot pat.

It is amazing to me how the full significance of the music of Parker and Gillespie has managed to escape the majority of people who lay claim to being art and music "lovers." It is a rare occasion that in one's own time one is able to witness so much innovation, transition, so much change, and so much creativity. After the initial impact of Parker and Gillespie (and of course I am not leaving out Powell, Monk, Clarke, or Lester Young) had sort of infiltrated into the non-creative areas of music (the commercial big bands and the radio and television "jingle" field, which incidentally were to reap large financial rewards for *their* "work," while Bird[103] was to die a premature death and Gillespie was unable to keep a large band together because of the financial strain) it became pretty safe to play LIKE Parker and Gillespie. (Monk's music for some reason or another never allowed that kind of "borrowing" and familiarity.) Hornmen, pianists, arrangers, composers, etc., drew excessively from not only the grammar and musical language of these men but also some of their works themselves. It reached a state, which jazz has had the fortunate pleasure to do every now and then, when the "borrowers" thought they had solved it all, when much of the music produced in and out of jazz was highly predictable. At the apogee of this period another addition and extension of this vital music appeared in the personage of the composer-saxophonist Ornette Coleman.

Ornette (like most of the revolutionaries in jazz: Parker from Kansas City; Gillespie from Cheraw, South Carolina; Monk from Rocky Mount, North Carolina; and Christian from Dallas, Texas) was not born in Harlem. He came to New York from Fort Worth, Texas, with his own ideas of what should be the ultimate in a person's application to jazz music. He indicated that the old way of playing, interpreting, and composing would no longer suffice if further creativity and extension of the music was to be desired and obtained.

With his arrival all of the old stock arguments concerning his ability to play, etc., were again heard. Every innovator has had the same experience. Ornette was both hailed and cursed. Idolized and sneered at. Understood and misunderstood. His music, however, left no one who heard it passive. And now, if being aped musically is the sign of arrival, then he most certainly has arrived. But this is in the musical sense, certainly not the financial sense. Those same musicians who at first contested even his ability to play his instrument have found it necessary to re-evaluate their own musical statements. Each day finds a new fragment of his music cropping up in someone else's music. (This writer copied part of the music for a concert recently held at Carnegie Hall and conducted by the composer-conductor Gunther Schuller of avant-garde non-jazz music, and at least one of the pieces was a composition based on the concept and approach of Ornette's playing and writing.) So it is apparent that not only has his presence been felt in the jazz world but in the non-jazz music world as well.

Had it not been for the early Cotton Club, it is quite possible that Duke Ellington might never have formulated the style of music that he did. Of course this is highly speculative because Ellington would most certainly have created some kind of important music. But Gunther Schuller, posing the question:

. . . how did Ellington develop into one of America's foremost composers?[104]

has the following highly informative answer:

It was precisely due to the fortuitous circumstance of working five years at the Cotton Club. There, by writing and experimenting with all manner of descriptive production and dance numbers, his (Ellington's) inherent talent and imagination found a fruitful outlet.[105]

That the music which virtually supports the musical theatre, theatre, television, radio, commercial jingle, and in some instances, even supplies the life blood for "serious" music, exists as a non-functional art music for so many who profess love of folk music, is for me a ridiculous situation. As Louis Armstrong has so aptly put it, "All music gotta be 'folk' music: I ain't never heard no horse sing a song." And with the emergence of spring there is hardly a Sunday that Washington Square Park in Greenwich Village doesn't play host to thousands of folk singers and folk song lovers. Of course we know that jazz, especially that of today, is no longer folk music in the sense that defines folk music, but the noted British writer-critic, Francis Newton, observing the work of Duke Ellington, has noted:

. . . . he (Ellington) solved the unbelievably difficult problem of turning a living, shifting, improvised folk music into composition without losing its spontaneity.[106]

When I was coming up, every beginning Negro band, composed of youngsters, was always formed with a dancing audience in mind. Sol Moore always had a good musical band and George Smith always played at the functions we went to as kids. Strange, as I write this I'm recalling that both of these musicians are now dead and I think we were all of the same age. . . . Of course much of the self-consciousness that is attached to much of today's playing was absent in the beginning for several reasons. In the beginning art for art's sake was not a dominant factor. Well maybe it was deep down inside, but the thing that came through was the fact that these "cats" had a story to tell; they wanted to play and they wanted more than anything to play themselves, without restrictions. And this was the most important thing.

But music was plentiful in Harlem (as it was everywhere else) in the late twenties and thirties up to the early forties. And while it was necessary to go "downtown" to make a living, the real "living" for these people was when they returned home. What was it that Bessie Smith[107] said about Saturday night? It was music, dancing, dancing and music. Not that that was all there was to life. But to face reality, who could only view the bad and sometimes terrible things and injustices twenty-four hours a day, seven days a week, three hundred and sixty-five days a year? Who could think all the time that in all those banks in New York not one black person would ask for your deposit book?

I can remember when we came from Massachusetts to Harlem in 1934. I had never seen so many people before, let alone black people. And it never really occurred to me until I went "downtown" to high school, that every person in authority that I'd seen in Harlem: the butcher, the grocer, the policeman, the man who came to read the gas meter, and even the vendor of fruit and vegetables in the block, were all white. It did seem, to a little boy, that these white people really owned everything. But that wasn't entirely true. They didn't own the music that I heard played. And although I did like Harry James (it was when I first decided I wanted to learn to play the trumpet) and the Glenn Miller band, it was Count Basie, Earl Hines, Les Hite, and Duke Ellington that I "dug," and I really didn't understand them, but I most certainly liked them.

In 1937, in three weeks, I heard a dozen big bands of quality (Duke Ellington, Jimmie Lunceford, Fletcher Henderson, Chick Webb, Earl Hines, Basie, Dorsey, Goodman, Shaw, Millinder, Willie Bryant, and Luis Russell). In 1958, in six weeks, I heard only two, both of which were assembled solely for recording purposes.[108]

At one time all of the bands (Negro and white) were large bands and it served a two-fold purpose. It enabled a musician to learn. He learned music and musicianship. He learned to play *with* other musicians. He learned to play in a section. He learned to be a "lead" man and a soloist. It was a kind of apprenticeship. Also a bandleader was able to employ more men. The average band was composed of from twelve to about seventeen men. There was more employment, and a young, inexperienced musician found work fairly easily. At the end of the Second World War, most of the large bands were unable to continue. Musical tastes had changed; the concept indicated by the younger players of what a large band should play was difficult for the older leaders to fathom. Above all the economics of the situation ruled out the large pay-rolls needed by a large band. Where formerly bands had broadcast "live" from clubs and dances, recordings began to substitute for the in-person performance. And if white bands suffered, Negro bands suffered even more. In the first place, they had always been restricted to certain areas to play. That was REAL segregation. And of course the decline in vaudeville, the doing away with the movie houses (downtown) having bands, and with the final ushering in of television, the death of the large jazz band became finalized.

But when the big band was in its heyday (in the thirties and early forties), the music that was played generally bore the stamp of one individual. The arranger. It was his job to create the style of the band. Such men as Don Redman, Fletcher Henderson, Eddie Barefield, Bud Johnson, Benny Carter, etc., were the deciding factors in how a band should play and in most instances what. It was the Henderson arrangements, played by the Henderson band almost a decade before, that enabled Benny Goodman to become "King of Swing." Sy Oliver, who had written for the Lunceford band, started to write for and shape the musical thinking in the Tommy Dorsey band. It was, in fact, really Don Redman who introduced the style of orchestration that was to become the *modus operandi* of all the jazz orchestras. Thus the large band, to some of the more creative players, served as a kind of tyrannical parent. It provided him with food and shelter (almost literally) but he was rarely to play as much individual jazz as he wanted. Because of this situation the "jam session" (also called "after-hours session") and later called simply "session" was born.

The afternoon I walked into the Rhythm Club, the corner and street were crowded with musicians with their instruments and horns. I was introduced and shook hands with a lot of fellows on the outside. Then we entered the inside which was crowded. What I saw and heard, I will never forget. A wild cutting session[109] was in progress and sitting around the piano were twenty or thirty musicians, all waiting for a signal to play choruses of Gershwin's "Liza."[110]

The after-hours session was just what its name implied. It was an occasion for musicians to gather after their regular working hours (generally after three in the morning) to play specifically for their own pleasure.

One factor in the development of many a jazz artist, a factor frequently ignored, is the now almost obsolete custom of sitting in (jamming); and the interchange of ideas between musicians in sessions has been beneficial to the development of many jazz styles.[111]

Bystanders, other than musicians who were in attendance at these sessions, were usually as creative in listening as the musicians were in playing. There were also "after-hour spots." These were places that opened after the regular places closed. Admittance to them was often viewed as a high status symbol in the days when Harlem was *THE* place to go for the people who lived "downtown," and "downtown" meant any place that was not Harlem. Monroe's Uptown House, then located on 134 Street off Seventh Avenue, was one of the more popular places and the music was generally of the kind that was not to be found in the more ordinary establishments.

With all of this background and development, however, jazz apparently to many people is not music at all. To them it is not the expression of a people, the collectivization of a group experience, coupled with a strong desire to live and enjoy living within the confines of a social system which has not completely allowed them their birthright, which has resulted in a form of musical expression indigenous only to America. For without America there could never have been jazz, such as we know it, that is, and those of us that have the good fortune to know it, love it and try to understand it.

Many great composers have, at one time or another, drawn on folk tradition for their sources of inspiration. Bela Bartok has made extensive use of this source. Vaughan Williams, Igor Stravinski, Aaron Copland are but three others who have extended some of the folk tradition by infusing it with their own personalities and experiences. But jazz, another kind of folk music, has seemingly eluded the "serious" composer. And I mean such composers as Milhaud (although his *Création du Monde* is considered to be a jazz-"influenced" piece), Stravinski (the same holds true for his *L'Histoire du Soldat*), Copland, and the Negro composer William Grant Still.

Where these men have made their mistake is in their attitude that jazz music is something a smidgin less valuable and important than other types of music. Their approach has always embodied the idea that they can be influenced by the music to write much longer "serious" pieces. As if length had anything to do with the quality of music. They almost always "love" the "quaintness" of jazz. It is always "novel" to them. It is, however, never really music to them. For some strange reason it never really lives and breathes life to them. They can never glean the hope, despair, love, hate, and all that man does and consequently is, that the music is inbued with. It is always "exotic." And there isn't a "serious" composer who isn't "fascinated" by the rhythms of jazz.

The insatiable curiosity of a gourmet anxious to try everything had brought him closer, as early as 1913, to Pierrot Lunaire, with the result that polytonality itself was for him an untried and particularly subtle form of pleasure. In fact Schoenberg interested him as much as Gershwin: for this same hunger for novelty took him also to the music hall and to jazz; he certainly reveled in American Negro music, as can be seen from the fox trots and Boston two-steps of L'Enfant et Les Sortilèges . . . and the nostalgic blues which serves as andante to the Sonata for Piano and Violin.[112]

When Igor Stravinski composed the "Ebony Concerto" for the Woody Herman band, it was because he had been so enthralled and excited about the sound of the Herman group with its exuberance and vitality. That same Herman band, however, owed much of its *raison d'être* to the writing and creativity of John Birks "Dizzy" Gillespie. The now famous unison trumpet passage in "Caldonia" was lifted directly from the work and playing of Gillespie. And I often wonder how

the work of Gillespie's own orchestra playing such
works as George Russell's "Cubano Be, Cubano Bop"
would have affected him.

I think that jazz composers and improvisers have
utilized the techniques and approaches of non-jazz
music much more definitively than has been the reverse
case. However, jazz and the jazz language have made
themselves felt, if not entirely loved and understood,
by the "serious" composer.

*. . . Even in self-consciously academic compositions we are
used to hearing quarter-tones, glissandos, Moorish wailing
on the clarinet and oboe, "dirty" tones, overblowing of
trumpets in screeching registers, and the other instrumental
effects once exclusively associated with jazz. All are now
assimilated into the common language of contemporary
music.*[113]

It is indeed a sad commentary when the people who
have created and fostered this music now feel that in
order to "better" themselves they have to deny this
music and its creators in 1963. It was painful to read
recently that William Grant Still had put down hard
the efforts of individualism in musical expression of
many of today's younger jazzmen, both instrumental
and compositional. How far from what you are can
one go? Whether he likes it or not his roots are also located in that field holler, and the blues. It was composer
George Russell who said: "Jazz is the Negro's most important gift to American culture."[114]

I find it doubly sad that the community and the people who formerly nurtured this music have for some
reason or another found it necessary to reject jazz. It
is their contribution to the arts. Jazz IS America. The
music of Duke Ellington, Miles Davis, Charlie Parker,
heard around the world, is rarely thought of as being
their music but the music of America. And all Americans should be proud. But the proudest should be the
Negro. For he has contributed when his contributions
were thoroughly undesired. He gave when both he as

the giver and what he had to give were unwanted. But
the gift was too big to lie in the shadow. It sought the
sun and the sun sought it.

There was a time around the late forties and early
fifties when sessions could be found all over Harlem.
There was a rehearsal studio at 315 Lenox Avenue,
between 125 and 126 Streets. Newby's studio was located on 116 Street. At that time Fritz Pollard had a
studio next door to the Loew's Victoria Theatre on
125 Street. And jazz could be heard at Club Harlem
(sometimes known as the Heat Wave) on 145 Street,
at Connie's on 135 Street and Seventh Avenue, Minton's on 118 Street, the Paradise on 110 Street and
Eighth Avenue, the "L" bar on 146 Street and Broadway. A private club called the Sportsmen on 145
Street and Seventh Avenue, next to the Roosevelt Theatre, had jazz on the weekend. There was also a very
colorful bar with the misleading name Lotus on Lenox
Avenue and 131 Street. Showman's on 125 Street next
to the Apollo Theatre had jazz, and the list goes on.
Of course for dancing there was the Savoy Ballroom
on 140 Street and Lenox Avenue, the "Rennie" on
Seventh Avenue at 137 Street, and the list goes on.

But what happened? What Ed Cambridge has said:

*It's a good thing Jesse Shipp didn't go up there (Harlem)
this year looking to work in theatre. He'd be hungry as
hell!!!*[115]

Yes I listen to many of the record shops on 125
Street and I don't feel elated when I hear in quantity all
of the cheap, gaudy (yes, music CAN be gaudy), sentimental hit-parade and sub-hit-parade pap and garbage
that Madison Avenue[116] has dictated should be accepted
as music. It does indeed sadden the heart to know that
if one is to hear jazz, as Thomas Wolfe[117] put it, he
"can't go home again." But then, perhaps that too is
good. Harlem, although it doesn't appear to have jazz
today, at least did, and in its way gave it to us.

Ossie Davis

~✤~

PURLIE TOLD ME!

N OTHING I HAD learned from the Baptist Bible, from Howard University, from my long association with Causes, black and white, or from my fifteen years on Broadway, prepared me in any degree for what I was to learn from Purlie Victorious,[118] as actor, as author, as Negro, and as—what I hope someday soon to be—a man!

Had not Purlie come along when he did and proceeded to shake the living daylight out of me, I would by now have had it made: I would have sidestepped completely the Negro Question (which is, to the best of my knowledge, "When the hell are we gonna be free?!"); I would have safely escaped into the Negro Middle Class, burying my head somewhere between the Cadillac and the mink; and would probably have become, by express permission and endorsement of the Great White Father, an Honorary White Man myself. But Purlie came, Purlie saw, Purlie laughed!

In pursuit of Purlie I found more than I had bargained for: the act of writing became my long moment of truth; and it took me five years to adjust my eyesight, to be able to look squarely at the world and at myself through Negro-colored glasses. And to decide on the basis of what I found: it is not enough to be only a Negro in this world . . . one must, and more important, also be a man.

For Purley Victorious is, in essence, the adventures of Negro manhood in search of itself in a world for white folks only. A world that emasculated me, as it does all Negro men, before I left my mother's breast, and which taught me gleefully to accept that emasculation as the highest honor America could bestow upon a black man. And in more ways than I thought possible, I accepted it!

Purlie, in order to get himself put down on paper at all, had to force me to examine myself; to dig deeper and deeper into my own soul, conscious and subconscious, to peel off and rip away layer after layer of sham, hypocrisy, evasion, lies; to rip up by the roots the many walls I had erected around the pretense that I was indeed a man—when I knew all along, but had never before been forced to admit even to myself, that in the context of American society today *the term Negro and the term Man must mutually exclude each other!*

Purlie showed me that, whatever I was, I was not a man . . . not yet! That I would never become a man by sacrificing everything I was, merely to become an American. That I would never ease my way into the bosom of American acceptance by pretending, like Jacob, that I was Esau; by pretending that freedom and equality could be practiced between whites and blacks purely on a personal basis; that Negroes could be integrated into American society one at a time; that the doors of opportunity would open wider and wider each day, not only for me but also for my brothers, as soon as we learned to talk middle-class talk, dress middle-class dress, behave middle-class behavior, and literally "wash ourselves whiter than snow." And above all never become too clamorously assertive of our rights as Americans lest it upset those brave and leading souls of other races who know so much better how to conduct our struggles than we do!

Purlie told me I would never find my manhood by asking the white man to define it for me. That I would never become a man until I stopped measuring my black self by white standards—standards set deeply in my own mind by a racist society which could almost define itself by its hatred and its fear of me! *And therefore felt impelled to teach me hatred and fear of myself!*

Purlie told me my *manhood* was hidden within my *Negroness*, that I could never find the one without fully and passionately embracing the other. That only by turning again homeward, whatever the cost, to my own blackness, to my own people, and to our common experience as Negroes, could I come at last to my manhood—to my *Self!*

Purlie is black laughter and like all laughter, when it is humane, is liberative. Or intends to be. Based on the simple assumption that segregation is ridiculous because it makes perfectly wonderful people, black and white, do ridiculous things, Purlie would hold all those "ridiculous things" up to universal scorn, while at the same time maintaining a loving respect for the people, white and black, caught up in this ridiculous nonsense. And when I see people, white and black, sit down side by side and laugh like hell at those ridiculous customs which still serve to keep us artifically separated, then I feel Purlie has done his job. For if men may really laugh together at something disturbing to them both it means that—for the moment—they have overleapt their separateness and are—for the moment—free to behold the universe, with sorrow or with joy—from the same point of view. Laughter, if it is wise, can lead to many things even among strangers—not the least of which is a mutual respect for people on which all other relations including the struggle for freedom in this country must ultimately depend.

In the objective sense, the public response to Purlie,

pro and con, black and white, has been no less educational. The critics, with one exception, were full of praise. (Some for the wrong reasons.) And since these gentlemen usually hold in their hands the decision whether a play will live or die, their enthusiastic reception of Purlie was, in realistic terms indeed, the kiss of life. I was disappointed that they did not comment on Purlie, good, bad, or indifferent, as *literature*; and more deeply disappointed that most of the white playwrights I had known, with two exceptions—men who were friends and mentors of mine, and whose opinions I still value highly—were silent, and still are. But it is quite possible, and I say this without rancor, that their very talents, and their concepts of what a Negro is, have left them unprepared to understand Purlie at all!

The theatre-going public, when it has taken the time to come and see, has usually been both surprised and delighted that comedy—satire in particular—could be such an effective weapon against race prejudice; that a stereotype about Negro life, which would be offensive in the hands of a white writer, might become, in the hands of a Negro writer, a totally unexpected revelation of the true substance of Negro wit and humor.

But Purlie, in spite of excellent reviews and a tremendous word-of-mouth enthusiasm generating from those who have seen it, has never been a big "hit" with the "carriage trade," the "expense-account crowd"; and though we had some early support from theatre parties, it was not enough really to see us through. As a matter of fact, had Purlie been forced to rely on the normal avenue of Broadway patronage we would long ago have sunk and disappeared from sight. But something happened with Purlie that was different. And that difference, small as it was in the beginning, steadily grew, until finally it made all the difference in the world.

Sylvestor Leaks and John H. Clarke met Purlie first hand on opening night and decided he belonged to the Negro people. That decision made the difference. They went to churches, to lodges, to social clubs, labor unions. They took Purlie directly to the Negro community, and the Negro community got the message. It was, and is, the attendance of *my own people* at the box office that made the difference: it kept Purlie alive. Did this mean that a Negro work, with Negro content, could depend on the Negro community for support, and survive? I believe it did.

Not that Purlie is a Negro play only. It is, I hope, much more than that. As Purlie himself told me: "Look at the Negro from outside and all you see is oppression. But look at the Negro from the inside and all you see is resistance to that oppression." Now oppression and resistance to oppression are universal themes. If Purlie speaks at all, he speaks to everybody—black and white: and the white audience still finds its merry way to the Longacre Theatre. But it is no longer always in the majority. Normally a black performer on Broadway will have his wages paid in white money. But for Purlie the situation is reversed. For the first time since I started working in the theatre, *my boss is the Negro People!*

And I choose to believe that this fact has implications that are revolutionary for the Negro artist, musician, performer in his struggle to express himself and survive at the same time. For if we can, in fact, create for our own people, work for our own people, belong to our own people, we will no longer be forced into artistic prostitution and self-betrayal in the mad scramble, imposed upon us far too long, to belong to some other people. We can indeed, as long as we *truly* deserve the support of our own, embrace our blackness and find the stuff of our manhood.

The Negro people, if given a chance, will cherish, defend, and protect its own: Purlie is proof of that. If we turn to them ever so little, they will turn to us in full. It is time for us, who call ourselves artists, scholars, and thinkers, to rejoin the people from whom we came. We shall then and only then be free to tell the truth about our people, and that truth shall make us free!

Only then can we begin to take a truly independent

position within the confines of American culture, a
black position. And from that position, walk, talk, think,
fight, and create like men. Respectful of all, sharing
with any, but beholden to none save our own.

*For there is hope of a tree [this is Job talking], if it be
cut down, that it will sprout again, and that the tender
branch thereof will not cease. Though the root thereof
wax old in the earth, and the stock thereof die in the ground;
yet through the scent of water it will bud, and bring forth
boughs like a plant.*

The profoundest commitment possible to a black creator in this country today—beyond all creeds, crafts,
classes, and ideologies whatsoever—is to bring before his
people the *scent* of freedom. He may rest assured his
people will do the rest.

That's what Purlie told me!

Julian Mayfield

~❦~

AND THEN CAME BALDWIN

O NE OF THE MOST interesting aspects of the phenomenon called Baldwin has been the peculiar impact he
has had on various black intellectuals. Among them
are to be found his most vociferous and unqualified
admirers and his most severe detractors. After reading
Sylvester Leaks' cleverly-titled letter, "James Baldwin
—I Know His Name" (*Freedomways*, Winter 1963),
I began to search my memory and my correspondence
files for commentary about the novelist-essayist whose
work and personality occupy so much of our thinking
nowadays.

After my perusal I am not only struck by how often
the reaction to James Baldwin has been negative but by
how much of the commentary has been couched in
extreme, almost violent, language. A couple of years
ago I talked to a very able and dedicated woman who
had spent the best years of her life promoting artistic
expression among Negro youth. Some remark of mine
provoked the angry retort from her that she was sick
and tired of hearing about Baldwin. She was convinced,
she said, that Baldwin was the most dangerous threat
to young Negro writers to appear in a generation. I

asked her to be more explicit, but she could not do so. She would only nod her head with the vigorous obdurateness that one associates with the superstitious (which she was not) and predict gloomily, "You mark my word. You will all be sorry you ever heard of that man!"

As I write now I have before me two letters from a learned college teacher who frequently reviews books. He argues that Baldwin's style and ideas have endeared him to the "arty" set, and that this writer is merely another voice which seeks to keep American literature on its knees to Gide and Proust:[119]

I liken him to a rebel cow we had . . . she had a fondness for wild onion salad. The market . . . wouldn't take her milk and the children wouldn't drink it, but she had a vast following; indeed, she was a best smeller. . . .

The two topics which are most frequently used as weapons by Baldwin's detractors are his critical and commercial success, and the theme of homosexuality which is the motif of "In Giovanni's Room," a frequent occurrence in "Another Country," and the subject of at least one essay on Gide. In sum, the argument seems to run something like this:

There must be something wrong with Baldwin because his books are on the best-seller list and his articles appear in prestige, mass-circulation magazines. Worse yet, he's always on television giving his opinion about this or that; and although I usually say "hear, hear" to his ideas, tell me – since when did Mr. Charlie White Man Boss become so interested in the opinion of any black man but an Uncle Tom? And why should Baldwin be writing about "queers" all the time when there are so many other important things to concern Negro writers.

Many militant Negro intellectuals of the Left, of nationaltist and socialist inclination, grudgingly concede that "Oh, the guy's a fine writer and he says many things that need saying," but they assert that he is deplorably ignorant of economics, history and political science and were it not for this ignorance *They*, those who control American communications media, would never have permitted him to become so prominent. By this they usually mean that Baldwin has not yet called for a socialist revolution in his essays or public appearances.

There is, I believe, some merit in this argument, but it is not so much a criticism of Baldwin as of the society in which he functions. At any rate, Baldwin is neither an historian, economist nor a political scientist, but a creative writer whose work testifies that his layman's knowledge of these fields is not as shallow as his critics suggest. His task as the creative writer is to synthesize and illuminate, in human terms, as much of the knowledge of these disciplines as is within his grasp. Would that the artist could be a scholar and vice versa, but he rarely is.

For the most part, these are superficial views of Baldwin and the society in which he functions. Neither is quite as simple as that. Baldwin, as one would expect, is a highly complex man, and the United States is of so vast and complex a weave as to defy almost any generalization. There is no board of censors which watches over the nation's television and radio networks, its magazines and newspapers, for the sole purpose of locking out the truth about racial oppression, nationalism, socialism, etc. The actual censor is the economic reality of the communications media. The people who run this country, and who also run a large part of the rest of the world, do not belong to a single club. They don't have to. They only have to have enough common sense and common self-interest not to allow socialists and spokesmen for genuine revolution to use their media. If they needed fascism to retain control, they would no doubt have it. But only fools invoke fascist methods when they can achieve the same results within the democratic structure.

To view the power elite as one giant board of directors is to credit it with a unity which does not exist.

The more enlightened among the power groups know that the nation will encounter serious difficulties unless it substantially ameliorates the condition of its twenty million black citizens. The economic benefit derived from the exploitation of Negroes in certain areas is vastly outweighed by the glittering jewel of Africa, the earth's richest continent. The world-wide publicity which attends race riots, the Ole Mississippi fiasco, the Monroe frame-up, etc.,[120] impedes the progress of these ruling groups in their campaign for the economic reconquest of Africa. To these groups a certain amount of racial integration makes common sense, and it is a small price to pay for racial harmony. Genuine capitalists possess a remarkable degree of tolerance. They may hire Roy Welenskys, Verwoerds and Eastlands,[121] but they can seldom afford to be crippled by blind racialism themselves. They will even endure the voice of the radical so long as it serves their purpose. The only thing a genuine capitalist fears, hates and will not tolerate, is a genuine socialist revolutionary.

It is in this context that we must consider Baldwin. I believe the power elite could survive a dozen Baldwins broadcasting day after day, month after month, as long he does not spell out socialist alternatives. Moreover, it redounds to the credit of present-day American society that there should be a successful and popular Negro writer who is also a radical.

Negroes have so seldom been allowed to compete in the American market place (whose dog-eat-dog values we hardly questioned until recently) that we naturally look with suspicion on a black writer who not only is allowed to enter the race, but who wins it, hands down. We do not take into account Baldwin's remarkable talent nor the charged atmosphere of racial tensions in the United States which allows that talent to flourish. Nor do we consider that not only are intelligent ruling groups aware of the rebellious mood seething in the Negro community, but nearly every American who can see and hear senses it. To take the most obvious example, the Black Muslims have about succeeded in scaring the pants off everybody. It was axiomatic that as long as Negroes remained quiescent, whites would have no need to be disturbed, but as soon as Negroes displayed any significant militancy, whites of every political complexion would want to know what was going on.

But still we may ask, "Why did the mantle of spokesman fall on a Baldwin?" A significant development of the recent period is that in the absence of a leadership group reflecting the militant readiness in the Negro community, a few intellectuals have insisted on occupying the floor, men and women who were neither leaders of national organizations, prominent athletes nor show business personalities. The description of one incident will suffice to show how displaced the "recognized" leadership was:

On May 17, 1961 a tiny group of Black Nationalists was able to prevent the Executive Secretary of the NAACP, Roy Wilkins, from speaking at a rally in Harlem, the largest community of black people in the world. In their view the moderate Mr. Wilkins was an Uncle Tom and they were prepared to do him bodily harm. Yet he was able to walk among them, unharmed and unheckled, because they did not recognize him!

Alert editors and producers of television panel shows realized some time ago that there was no use asking a leader like Mr. Wilkins about the Negro revolt because he did not know. He was so out of touch with the real world of Negroes that the Lumumba demonstration in the United Nations building caught him completely unawares. For a generation neither elder spokesmen like Mr. Wilkins nor his organization had taken a public stand on any *international* issue, especially one that might conflict with the policies of the United States government. Now, here were young Negroes demonstrating in the United Nations building, of all places, because a black man had been murdered in an African country thousands of miles away. Wilkins could not explain it, and the more sophisticated Dr. Ralph Bunche, from the rarefied atmosphere of the United Nations Secretariat under the late Mr. Hammarskjold, felt constrained to apologize for the rude behavior of his fellow Negroes. Many people, including conservative Negroes, were confused. Of the white journalists only James Reston of the *New York Times* got part of the message. He wrote that something must be seriously wrong in the Negro community when Negroes could stage such a demonstration. It remained for James Baldwin to place the incident into proper focus a few days later in the *New York Times Magazine* ("A Negro Assays the Negro Mood") in words strong enough to express the emotions of the most militant, associating himself fully with the objectives of the demonstrators. And it was another young writer, Lorraine Hansberry, in the same pages, who delivered a richly-deserved slap in the face to Dr. Bunche for his "apology" by apologizing to Mrs. Pauline Lumumba for the nefarious activities of "our Dr. Bunche" in the Congo.

A popular artist who is also a radical polemicist is not without precedent. The most successful novelist of the nineteenth century was Charles Dickens, who day in and day out flailed the society that rewarded him with wealth and fame. Emile Zola, in his writing and as a public man, never ceased his crusading. Richard Wright was certainly no apologist for American society; he was, in fact, a Communist when "Native Son," his major contribution to American letters, was published. And only yesterday Miss Hansberry's "Raisin in the Sun," a burning indictment of American racism (whether or not the "weepy old ladies" who saw it realized it), was a smash hit on Broadway and a major motion picture.

These examples prove nothing except that it is no mark against Dickens, Zola, Wright, Hansberry or Baldwin if they happen to achieve—not only because of their high level of craftsmanship, but because of peculiarities of time and circumstance—the popular success desired by all of us who work with the pen.

Baldwin's critics are on even more shaky ground when they writhe at his attempts to explore homosexuality in his fiction. Like any good, patriotic American, I believe that all boys should like girls and all girls should like boys. But scores and perhaps hundreds of investigations conducted over the last twenty-five years have revealed that a disquieting number of Americans have more than a passing familiarity with the homosexual experience. I am not qualified to say just how accurate these investigations are, but anyone who insists on believing that the reports of sexual inversion in our society are greatly exaggerated today would best be advised to avoid all of our public parks and public toilets, especially at night.

We are a nation of Puritanical hypocrites. Unable to push a button and make homesexuality disappear, we choose to surrender the subject to the pornographer and confine our knowledge of it to the titillation derived from backroom gossip. In this we resemble the Victorians who, while producing approximately ten children per family unit sought to outlaw from literature and polite conversation the unclean subject of heterosexuality. And just as they failed to exorcise their devil by refusing to face him, so shall we. I, for one, should like to know more about the subject. If Baldwin thinks he can help shed light on it, then he ought to try. We may quarrel with the author about the *way* he treats homosexuality, but the *choice* of subjects is strictly his.

James Baldwin has quite literally been raising hell since he returned from a long European exile in the middle 1950's. To understand the impact he has had it is necessary to survey briefly the literary scene to which he returned, with special reference to writing by and about Negroes. American literature generally seemed stagnant. The big guns of the twenties and thirties were either dead or had ceased to write about

anything that mattered. In "The Old Man and the
Sea," Hemingway was over the hill, having written his
last great novel. In "East of Eden" Steinbeck had written one of those solid, good books that had little to
do with our time. Faulkner, bulging with his Nobel
prize, and more widely revered than ever by the literary
cultists, had finally revealed the true artist within by
declaring that if a showdown ever came between the
Federal government and the state of Mississippi, he
personally would shoot down Negroes in the street. Dos
Passos had long since changed his mind about socialism
and was now locked in passionate, almost obscene,
embrace with his former capitalist enemy.

One picaresque novel about race relations (and this
is too narrow a way of describing it) had achieved a
wide popularity and critical success: Ralph Ellison's
"Invisible Man." Richard Wright, who seemed to have
just discovered Dostoevski and Kafka, had attempted
to achieve new dimensions in "The Outsider," and had
failed. As his first novel, John Killens had contributed
"Youngblood," a big book about the South in the
social protest tradition, which received much less attention than it deserved.

Another important factor which must be mentioned
in our glance at the mid-fifties was the general dis-
orientation in the Left-wing movements of the big
cities. For better and for worse, one of the major influences on Negro writing for two decades had emanated
from the Communist Party and the progressive political
movement generally. On the Left the young Negro
writer found a haven and encouragement that existed
nowhere else for *him*. It was the Left that usually
published his first story or produced his first play. The
relationship between the Negro writer and the Left
requires a much more exhaustive analysis than is possible here. In order to keep within the scope of this
article I will suggest only two effects the relationship
had on the Negro writer: first, it broadened his perspective so that he saw his own struggle within the

context of the world struggle for power between socialism and capitalism; but secondly, the Stalinist insistence on doctrinaire novels and plays according to "socialist realist" theory tended to cut the young writer off from other currents in literature which might have enriched his craftsmanship and heightened his art.

By the middle fifties, with the American Left reeling under the attacks of McCarthyism (and the even more devastating effect of Mr. Khrushchev's speech to the Twentieth Congress of the Soviet Communist Party), with most of the writers of the so-called "Negro Renaissance" either dead or silent in the colleges, the young Negro writer found himself without a center in which to learn his craft and chart his direction. To him the social protest tradition, the category into which falls the great bulk of all writing by and about Negroes, apeared to be a worked-out mine. Every fact of his daily life told him that racial oppression had not disappeared, but what more could be said about it, at least in the old art forms? Why, he asked himself, should he expend his creative juices attempting to prove positions that were incontrovertible a hundred years ago? I mean, Mrs. Stowe,[122] in what was certainly the worst-written best seller ever published, had pretty well demonstrated before the Civil War that the black man in America had a rough row to hoe. Frederick Douglass had argued as eloquently for human freedom as anyone had before or has since, and W. E. B. Du Bois had published in 1903 a poignantly beautiful book about the Southern situation, "Souls of Black Folk," which seemed almost to be applicable fifty years later. Toss in another two score works of excellence and several thousand mediocre and just plain bad novels, plays, poems and essays, all expostulating more or less on the same theme, and there is small wonder that the Negro writer felt very much up the creek.

And then came Baldwin. From the Paris of Sartre, Beauvoir and Camus; from the expatriate Paris of Richard Wright, of the progenitors of the concept of

"Negritude," Senghor, Diop and Cesaire, came Baldwin, cutting, slashing and stabbing his way onto the American literary scene. Just over thirty years old, he had a solid first novel under his belt, "Go Tell It on the Mountain," a second one, "In Giovanni's Room," (a little strong on homosexuality for most American stomachs) and a remarkable book of penetrating essays, "Notes of a Native Son." In Europe he had certainly heard of Marx and Engels, imperialism and colonialism, but in his exile he had missed the day-to-day struggles (the Rosenbergs, Willie McGee, the Martinsville Seven) that had helped to shape his Afro-American contemporaries. Perhaps as a consequence, he was remarkably free of clichés, the bane of the creative writers, clichés not only of expression but of ideas. He had absolutely no gods, either of the Left or the Right. He seemed free, as dice-shooters say of the houseman, to call the shots the way he saw them. Naturally he was possessed of an outsized ego. One felt from the intensely personal nature of his work that he believed the earth had been created on the day he was born and that the entire white power structure of the United States had been mobilized with the single purpose of oppressing *him*.

My wife and I returned to the United States in 1958 after a four year absence in the Caribbean. I had kept in touch with several of the writers, but in my files I can now find no hint that any of them ever mentioned James Baldwin to me in their letters. Back home in New York, I was surprised to learn that, except for actress-playwright Alice Childress, the writers of my acquaintance not only did not know Baldwin but, in the British snob sense of the expression, did not care to know him. In the minds of most of them, Baldwin was an "arty" upstart and the colored darling of the avant-garde magazines (*Partisan Review, Paris Review*) who would soon be exposed for the dilettante phony he was.

Early in 1959 the American Society of African Culture (AMSAC) called a Negro writers conference.

Baldwin, who finds it difficult to decline any invitation, was conscripted to appear as one of two guest speakers on the panel of which I was chairman. As I remember it, the topic of my panel had to do with the role of protest literature in modern Negro writing. Baldwin, we assumed, was supposed to defend the art-for-art's-sake approach, a task, considering the attitude of the writers attending our meeting, roughly comparable to being assigned the defense of Christians in ancient Rome. Although two panels were in session at the same time, most of the writers showed up at my panel, presumably to give Baldwin a piece of their collective mind. He solved the problem neatly by simply not showing up.

A month or so later I made a naive attempt to arrange a match between Baldwin and several writers I knew. I spoke to him over the telephone and invited him out to our flat in East Elmhurst, Queens, N.Y. Perhaps because he felt guilty about not having attended his "lynching party" at the conference, he accepted the invitation. It was a long distance by subway train, but he arrived ("Hi, I'm James Baldwin"), a man of medium height and slender build, with protuberant eyes popping out of a dark brown Harlem face. One can't help thinking about Baldwin's face. I have never seen any face like it which was not the product of one of our American slums. Looking at it I could understand why the word "terror" so often crops up in his descriptions of his childhood. His face has nothing to do with genetics; it could only have been chiseled by the city, in the muck and shadows of tenements, where children learn early that disaster can strike at any time from any quarter, from the cop on the beat, the gang around the corner, or from one's own bitter and disillusioned parents. Baldwin's is the face of the little street scrapper, sweeping the horizon with his radar antenna (those eyes) ever alert for a sign of danger.

Baldwin is one of the most loquacious men I know— he can, in fact, talk rings around anyone I have ever met except Malcolm X—but that evening he sat in stiff, eager silence, wanting to like and be liked, holding in check that ready wit of his. I believe the others wanted to like him too. They had appreciated some of his work, and there was nothing petty or spiteful about them. But somehow the evening just would not come off. As soon as was decently possible nearly all of the writers left except Baldwin. Then, like a prisoner released, he opened his shirt collar, relaxed visibly and began to talk a-mile-a-minute, with rampaging insight and brilliant flashes of humor, about everything under the sun. Our conversation did not end until eight o'clock the next morning when Baldwin took a taxicab back to Manhattan.

People who cannot make up their minds about Baldwin are likely to develop certain symptoms of schizophrenia. On Monday they are enthusiastic about something he has written in a magazine, and on Tuesday they quite literally hate him for something he is supposed to have said on television. I remember the glee with which two writers, previously neutral about Baldwin, greeted me at a lawn party in Long Island.

"Now your precious Baldwin has done it," they shouted. "Now he has really torn his drawers."

In the course of a long article for *Holiday* magazine, one of the most perceptive ever written about Harlem, Baldwin had "torn his drawers" by stating that some of the occupants of the Riverton housing project urinated in the hallways as a form of protest against discrimination. Baldwin, inexcusably, had his facts wrong. But what was of even greater interest was the basis on which he was attacked by outraged Harlem newspapers the following week. How dare he write such a thing about Riverton, where distinguished Negro judges, doctors and other professional people lived? Surely his intention had been to slander Harlem. One columnist hinted darkly, and somewhat in contradiction to the thesis of an impeccable community which he was defending, that the author would be well advised to remain downtown with his dilettante friends or, better, to return to Paris, as he would no longer be safe in the Harlem streets.

Now, anyone who has ever lived there knows that Harlem is a community of many problems and desperate misery. It is, in fact, a much more anguishing environment than even Baldwin has described—and if one doubts this let him walk through the crowded corridors of any public school in Harlem and talk to the children, or let him make a tour of the hundreds of bar-rooms in the district, nearly all of which are owned by outsiders, and observe the hopelessness, the anguish and the pointlessness in the lives of the customers. The appalling thing about Harlem is not merely its physical face of poverty: there are much worse slums in the world, much poorer people and entire countries with hardly any schools at all. But what ought to frighten the hell out of any sensitive person is that Harlem exists in the middle of New York City, the shining jewel of American accomplishment, testament to the American dream; exists as a cage without visible bars, in which are trapped scores of thousands of youngsters growing up in a world which has already made it clear it does not want them, boys and girls on whose faces one sees either despair or a dangerous desperation before they are fourteen years old. *Harlem is the ugly, ultimate symbol of the nation's failure*. Baldwin saw all this and wrote it in the *Holiday* article, but the Negro editors and some of Baldwin's fellow writers were only moved to indignation because of a fancied slander on Harlem's professional class!

The misunderstanding between Baldwin and other young black writers, with whom one might think he would have much in common, is yawningly apparent in Sylvester Leaks' letter. Baldwin is taken to task for a long list of sins, including having written that as a Harlem boy he had to effect a truce with reality, that he hated and feared white people and despised black people because they had not produced a Rembrandt.

The reference to Rembrandt is hardly worth a comment. There are approximately 155 million white Americans in a nation that is more than 160 years old, and they have never produced a Rembrandt, a Beethoven or a da Vinci either. All this proves is that supreme geniuses appear infrequently and flower only in the proper environment. If Beethoven had been born the son of a poor white sharecropper in Mississippi fifty years ago, we would never have heard of him. I know of no instance where a racialist, who claimed superiority on the basis of his supposed descent from geniuses, has ever *himself* created a single work of art or invented anything that advanced human civilization. Leaks also asserts that the black man's resistance to oppression is never found in Baldwin's work.

Augusta Strong, in a penetrating article (*Freedom-ways*, Spring 1962) wrote: "I hope that Baldwin is being as *wisely read* as he has been *widely* published in some of the leading publications."

One wonders if Baldwin is being wisely read by those who should be closest to him.

I know Sylvester Leaks to be a militant writer, of great personal courage, sincerely dedicated to the cause of black freedom. (He has, indeed, the admirable and very unliterary quality of knowing when the time comes for a writer to lay down his pen, stop talking and wade in with his fists.) Certainly he knows that the black youngster who does not effect some sort of truce with reality will simply not be allowed to survive.

I remember as a child being sent to spend my summer vacation with relatives in the small South Carolina town where I was born. One afternoon while passing through a white section with an older male cousin we were attacked by two white children, a boy and a girl, throwing cotton bolls. I was eleven years old and already I hated white people. My values were those of the slums of Washington, D.C. I fell upon both the boy and the girl, knocked them to the ground and tried to kick them to death. Then, with my cousin pulling me after him, we fled across town to the colored section and my grandmother's house, where I proudly blurted out the story of my triumph. But by administering justice to my white attackers I had endangered the entire Negro community. One of my uncles bestowed upon me a memorable whipping; that night, my tail still burning, I was smuggled aboard a northbound train. The truce I had to effect with reality was to surrender my presumption that in South Carolina I was a boy like any other with the right to defend myself in a fight. The reality was that if my grandmother and my uncles had allowed me to hold to that presumption I would simply not have lived to the age of twelve.

The remarkable thing about this story is that it is not at all remarkable, but commonplace. In one way or another, on one level or another, every black adult in the United States today has had to make his truce with the reality of white power.

Still examining Sylvester Leaks' letter, I think it is indeed an odd Negro child who, observing the might of white people, has not at some time wished that he had been born white, and who has not turned back his hatred of the white world upon himself and his own people. In a recent piece for *The New Yorker* ("Letter From a Region of My Mind"), Baldwin wrote:

Negroes in this country . . . are taught, really, to despise themselves from the moment their eyes open on the world. This world is white and they are black. White people hold the power, which means that they are superior to blacks (intrinsically, that is: God decreed it so), and the world has innumerable ways of making this difference known and felt and feared. Long before the Negro child perceives this difference, and even longer before he understands it, he has begun to react to it, he has begun to be controlled by it.

It is difficult to see how anyone can disagree with anything so self-evident. Is it that for centuries we have been so blugeoned by white stereotypes of Negroes that we are afraid to face any truth that does not reflect credit on ourselves? Until the black writer can do this he is not free, cannot do his job without the uncomfortable awareness of two pairs of eyes peeping over his shoulders: his white publishers and his militant fellow Afro-Americans who will damn him loudly if anything he writes seems to lend support to white stereotypes of Negroes. It is a tightrope no creative writer ought to be forced to walk. Baldwin seems to say, as all writers must, "To hell with you both; I will be true to myself." And his work suggests that he knows that in the world we live in today the stereotype is a two-edged sword; Americans, black and white, must either throw off their faith in American mythology (which includes those stereotypes) or the nation itself will be plunged into a series of crises from which it may not survive.

Early in his career Baldwin made a great point of disavowing protest writing. Yet, as Augusta Strong states in her article, "Go Tell It on the Mountain" is a perhaps less explicit, but no less effective, protest against American segregation as anything that can be cited. Indeed, it seems to me that everything Baldwin has written, excluding *that book* ("In Giovanni's Room"), has been in the finest protest tradition. With some chagrin he must observe that the genre which seemed to be dying of its own dead weight in 1955 is now very much alive and kicking, thanks largely to his restoration of the essay as an art form.

In summing up, can one say precisely what has been Baldwin's achievement? I think it has been his ability to capture in beautiful, passionate and persuasive prose the essence of Negro determination to live in the American house as a free man or, failing that, to burn the American house down. I don't think Baldwin is himself yet willing to set the torch to the house. Other militant black intellectuals have, for the most part, broken off their dialogue with white America. As far as possible they address themselves only to their own people urging them to more aggressive levels of struggle. Baldwin, almost alone, still talks to the whites, in love and compassion, offering them a way out, if only they will listen.

James Baldwin

~✦~

A TALK TO HARLEM TEACHERS*

L ET'S BEGIN by saying that we are living through a
very dangerous time.[123] Everyone in this room is in one
way or another aware of that. We are in a revolutionary
situation, no matter how unpopular that word has become in this country. The society in which we live is
desperately menaced, not by Khrushchev, but from
within. So any citizen of this country who figures himself as responsible—and particularly those of you who
deal with the minds and hearts of young people—must
be prepared to "go for broke." Or to put it another
way, you must understand that in the attempt to cor-
rect so many generations of bad faith and cruelty, when
it is operating not only in the classroom but in society,
you will meet the most fantastic, the most brutal, and
the most determined resistance. There is no point in
pretending that this won't happen.

Now, since I am talking to schoolteachers and I am
not a teacher myself, and in some ways am fairly easily
intimidated, I beg you to let me leave that and go back
to what I think to be the entire purpose of education in
the first place. It would seem to me that when a child
is born, if I'm the child's parent, it is my obligation

---

* This article was adapted from a speech given in 1963.

and my high duty to civilize that child. Man is a social animal. He cannot exist without a society. A society, in turn, depends on certain things which everyone within that society takes for granted. Now, the crucial paradox which confronts us here is that the whole process of education occurs within a social framework and is designed to perpetuate the aims of society. Thus, for example, the boys and girls who were born during the era of the Third Reich, when educated to the purposes of the Third Reich, became barbarians. The paradox of education is precisely this—that as one begins to become conscious one begins to examine the society in which he is being educated. The purpose of education, finally, is to create in a person the ability to look at the world for himself, to make his own decisions, to say to himself this is black or this is white, to decide for himself whether there is a God in heaven or not. To ask questions of the universe, and then learn to live with those questions, is the way he achieves his own identity. But no society is really anxious to have that kind of person around. What societies really, ideally, want is a citizenry which will simply obey the rules of society. If a society succeeds in this, that society is about to perish. The obligation of anyone who thinks of himself as responsible is to examine society and try to change it and to fight it—at no matter what risk. This is the only hope society has. This is the only way societies change.

Now, if what I have tried to sketch has any validity, it becomes thoroughly clear, at least to me, that any Negro who is born in this country and undergoes the American educational system runs the risk of becoming schizophrenic. On the one hand he is born in the shadow of the stars and stripes and he is assured it represents a nation which has never lost a war. He pledges allegiance to that flag which guarantees "liberty and justice for all." He is part of a country in which anyone can become President, and so forth. But on the other hand he is also assured by his country and his countrymen

that he has never contributed anything to civilization—
that his past is nothing more than a record of humilia-
tions gladly endured. He is assured by the republic that
he, his father, his mother, and his ancestors were happy,
shiftless, watermelon-eating darkies who loved Mr.
Charlie and Miss Ann,[124] that the value he has as a
black man is proven by one thing only—his devotion
to white people. If you think I am exaggerating, examine the myths which proliferate in this country about
Negroes.

Now all this enters the child's consciousness much
sooner than we as adults would like to think it does. As
adults, we are easily fooled because we are so anxious to
be fooled. But children are very different. Children, not
yet aware that it is dangerous to look too deeply at anything, look at everything, look at each other, and draw
their own conclusions. They don't have the vocabulary
to express what they see, and we, their elders, know how
to intimidate them very easily and very soon. But a
black child, looking at the world around him, though he
cannot know quite what to make of it, is aware that
there is a reason why his mother works so hard, why
his father is always on edge. He is aware that there is
some reason why, if he sits down in the front of the bus,
his father or mother slaps him and drags him to the
back of the bus. He is aware that there is some terrible
weight on his parents' shoulders which menaces him.
And it isn't long—in fact it begins when he is in school
—before he discovers the shape of his oppression.

Let us say that the child is seven years old and I am
his father, and I decide to take him to the zoo, or to
Madison Square Garden, or to the UN Building, or to
any of the tremendous monuments we find all over New
York. We get into a bus and we go from where I live
on 131st Street and Seventh Avenue downtown through
the park and we get into New York City, which is not
Harlem. Now, where the boy lives—even if it is a housing project—is in an undesirable neighborhood. If he
lives in one of those housing projects of which every-

one in New York is so proud, he has at the front door, if not closer, the pimps, the whores, the junkies—in a word, the danger of life in the ghetto.

And the child knows this, though he doesn't know why.

I still remember my first sight of New York. It was really another city when I was born—where I was born. We looked down over the Park Avenue streetcar tracks. It was Park Avenue, but I didn't know what Park Avenue meant *downtown*. The Park Avenue I grew up on, which is still standing, is dark and dirty. No one would dream of opening a Tiffany's on that Park Avenue, and when you go downtown you discover that you are literally in the white world. It is rich—or at least it looks rich. It is clean—because they collect garbage downtown. There are doormen. People walk about as though they owned where they were—and indeed they do. And it's a great shock. It's very hard to relate yourself to this. You don't know what it means. You know —you know instinctively—that none of this is for you. You know this before you are told. And who is it for and who is paying for it? And why isn't it for you?

Later on when you become a grocery boy or messenger and you try to enter one of those buildings a man says, "Go to the back door." Still later, if you happen by some odd chance to have a friend in one of those buildings, the man says, "Where's your package?" Now this by no means is the core of the matter. What I'm trying to get at is that by this time the Negro child has had, effectively, almost all the doors of opportunity slammed in his face, and there are very few things he can do about it. He can more or less accept it with an absolutely inarticulate and dangerous rage inside—all the more dangerous because it is never expressed. It is precisely those silent people whom white people see every day of their lives—I mean your porter and your maid, who never say anything more than "Yes, Sir" and "No, Ma'am." They will tell you it's raining if that is what you want to hear, and they will tell you the sun is shining if *that* is what you want to hear. They really hate you—really hate you because in their eyes (and they're right) you stand between them and life. I want to come back to that in a moment. It's the most sinister of the facts, I think, which we now face.

There is something else the Negro child can do, too. Every street boy—and I was a street boy, so I know—looking at the society which has produced him, looking at the standards of that society which are not honored by anybody, looking at your churches and the government and the politicians, understands that this structure is operated for someone else's benefit—not for his. And there's no room in it for him. If he is really cunning, really ruthless, really strong—and many of us are—he becomes a kind of criminal. He becomes a kind of criminal because that's the only way he can live. Harlem and every ghetto in this city—every ghetto in this country—is full of people who live outside the law. They wouldn't dream of calling a policeman. They wouldn't, for a moment, listen to any of those professions of principle of which we are so proud on the Fourth of July. They have turned away from this country forever and totally. They live by their wits and really long to see the day when the entire structure comes down.

The point of all this is that black men were brought here as a source of cheap labor. They were indispensable to the economy. In order to justify the fact that men were treated as though they were animals, the white republic had to brainwash itself into believing that they were, indeed, animals and *deserved* to be treated like animals. Therefore it is almost impossible for any Negro child to discover anything about his actual history. The reason is that this "animal," now that he suspects his own worth, now that he is beginning to believe that he is a man, has begun to attack the entire power structure. This is why America has spent such a long time keeping the Negro in his place. What I am trying to suggest to you is that it was not an accident, it was not an act of God, it was not done by well-meaning people muddling into something which they didn't understand. It was a deliberate policy hammered into place in order to make money from black flesh. And now, in 1963, because we have never faced this fact, we are in intolerable trouble.

The Reconstruction, as I read the evidence, was a bargain between the North and South to this effect: "We've liberated them from the land—and delivered them to the bosses." When we left Mississippi to come North we did not come to freedom. We came to the bottom of the labor market, and we are still there. Even the Depression of the 1930's failed to make a dent in Negroes' relationship to white workers in the labor unions. Even today, so brainwashed is this republic that people seriously ask in what they suppose to be good faith, "What does the Negro want?" I've heard a great many asinine questions in my life, but that is perhaps the most asinine and perhaps the most insulting. But the point here is that people who ask that question, thinking that they ask it in good faith, are really the victims of this conspiracy to make Negroes believe they are less than human.

In order for me to live, I decided very early that some mistake had been made somewhere. I was not a "nigger" even though you called me one. But if I was a "nigger" in your eyes, there was something about *you*—there was something *you* needed. I had to realize when I was very young that I was none of those things I was told I was. I was not, for example, happy. I never touched a watermelon for all kinds of reasons. I had been invented by white people, and I knew enough about life by this time to understand that whatever you invent, whatever you project is you! So where we are now is that a whole country of people believe I'm a "nigger," and I *don't*, and the battle's on! Because if I am not what I've been told I am, then it means that *you're* not what you thought *you* were *either!* And that is the crisis.

It is not really a "Negro revolution" that is upsetting

this country. What is upsetting the country is a sense of its own identity. If, for example, one managed to change the curriculum in all the schools so that Negroes learned more about themselves and their real contributions to this culture, you would be liberating not only Negroes, you'd be liberating white people who know nothing about their own history. And the reason is that if you are compelled to lie about one aspect of anybody's history, you must lie about it all. If you have to lie about my real role here, if you have to pretend that I hoed all that cotton just because I loved you, then you have done something to yourself. You are mad.

Now let's go back a minute. I talked earlier about those silent people—the porter and the maid—who, as I said, don't look up at the sky if you ask them if it is raining, but look into your face. My ancestors and I were very well trained. We understood very early that this was not a Christian nation. It didn't matter what you said or how often you went to church. My father and my mother and my grandfather and my grandmother knew that Christians didn't act this way. It was as simple as that. And if that was so there was no point in dealing with white people in terms of their own moral professions, for they were not going to honor them. What one did was to turn away, smiling all the time, and tell white people what they wanted to hear. But people always accuse you of reckless talk when you say this.

All this means that there are in this country tremendous reservoirs of bitterness which have never been able to find an outlet, but many may find an outlet soon. It means that well-meaning white liberals place themselves in great danger when they try to deal with Negroes as though they were missionaries. It means, in brief, that a great price is demanded to liberate all those silent people so that they can breathe for the first time and *tell* you what they think of you. And a price is demanded to liberate all those white children—some of them near forty—who have never grown up, and who never will grow up, because they have no sense of their identity.

What passes for identity in America is a series of myths about one's heroic ancestors. It's astounding to me, for example, that so many people really appear to believe that the country was founded by a band of heroes who wanted to be free. That happens not to be true. What happened was that some people left Europe because they couldn't stay there any longer and had to go some place else to make it. That's all. They were hungry, they were poor, they were convicts. Those who were making it in England, for example, did not get on the *Mayflower*. That's how the country was settled. Not by Gary Cooper. Yet we have a whole race of people, a whole republic, who believe the myths to the point where even today they select political representatives, as far as I can tell, by how closely they resemble Gary Cooper. Now this is dangerously infantile, and it shows in every level of national life. When I was living in Europe, for example, one of the worst revelations to me was the way Americans walked around Europe buying this and buying that and insulting everybody—not even out of malice, just because they didn't know any better. Well, that is the way they have always treated me. They weren't cruel, they just didn't know you were alive. They didn't know you had any feelings.

What I am trying to suggest here is that in the doing of all this for one hundred years or more, it is the American white man who has long since lost his grip on reality. In some peculiar way, having created this myth about Negroes, and the myth about his own history, he created myths about the world so that, for example, he was astounded that some people could prefer Castro, astounded that there are people in the world who don't go into hiding when they hear the word "Communism," astounded that Communism is one of the realities of the twentieth century which we will not overcome by pretending that it does not exist. The political level in this country now, on the part of people who should know better, is abysmal.

The Bible says somewhere that where there is no vision the people perish. I don't think anyone can doubt that in this country today we are menaced—intolerably menaced—by a lack of vision.

It is inconceivable that a sovereign people should continue, as we do so abjectly, to say, "I can't do anything about it. It's the government." The government is the creation of the people. It is responsible to the people. And the people are responsible for it. No American has the right to allow the present government to say, when Negro children are being bombed and hosed and shot and beaten all over the deep South, that there is nothing we can do about it. There must have been a day in this country's life when the bombing of four children in Sunday School would have created a public uproar and endangered the life of a Governor Wallace. It happened here, and there was no public uproar.

I began by saying that one of the paradoxes of education was that precisely at the point when you begin to develop a conscience, you must find yourself at war with your society. It is your responsibility to change society if you think of yourself as an educated person. And on the basis of the evidence—the moral and political evidence—one is compelled to say that this is a backward society. Now if I were a teacher in this school, or any Negro school, and I were dealing with Negro children, who were in my care only a few hours of every day and would then return to their homes and to the streets, children who have an apprehension of their future which with every hour grows grimmer and darker, I would try to teach them—I would try to make them know—that those streets, those houses, those dangers, those agonies by which they are surrounded, are criminal. I would try to make each child know that these things are the results of a criminal conspiracy to destroy him. I would teach him that if he intends to get to be a man, he must at once decide that he is stronger than this conspiracy and that he must never make his peace with it. And that one of his weapons for refusing to make his peace with it and for destroying it depends on what he decides he is worth. I would teach him that there are currently very few standards in this country which are worth a man's respect. That it is up to him to begin to change these standards for the sake of the life and the health of the country. I would suggest to him that the popular culture—as represented, for example, on television and in comic books and in movies—is based on fantasies created by very ill people, and he must be aware that these are fantasies that have nothing to do with reality. I would teach him that the press he reads is not as free as it says it is—and that he can do something about that, too. I would try to make him know that just as American history is longer, larger, more various, more beautiful, and more terrible than anything anyone has ever said about it, so is the world larger, more daring, more beautiful and more terrible, but principally larger—and that it belongs to him. I would teach him that he doesn't have to be bound by the expediencies of any given Administration, any given policy, any given time—that he has the right and the necessity to examine everything. I would try to show him that one has not learned anything about Castro when one says, "He is a Communist." This is a way of *not* learning something about Castro, something about Cuba, something, in fact, about the world. I would suggest to him that he is living, at the moment, in an enormous province. America is not the world and if America is going to become a nation, she must find a way—and this child must help her to find a way—to use the tremendous potential and tremendous energy which this child represents. If this country does not find a way to use that energy, it will be destroyed by that energy.

HARLEM AND JOBS, POLITICS, AND BANK ACCOUNTS

Hope R. Stevens

꙾

ASPECTS OF THE ECONOMIC
STRUCTURE OF THE
HARLEM COMMUNITY

IT IS axiomatic that one who keeps his thoughts to himself preserves his claim to possible wisdom and I should perhaps have been more firm in my resistance when asked to present a layman's view of the current economy of the Harlem Community. However, the prospect of commenting on those aspects of living directly concerned with economics in this area of "de facto" racial segregation, where I have had my being for nearly forty-one years, proved to be too great a temptation. The facts and figures generally associated with economic analysis will not appear since a layman should not play with charts, tables and statistics, the tools of the scientist. But the right to think, each in his own way, interpreting one's observations or impressions within the limit of one's lights, remains a most valuable tool, unaffected by other un-American or unequal social attitudes.

How is the economy of the people of Harlem to be described? We may begin by referring to the capital accumulation evidenced in the segregated community. We talk of the purchasing power of the colored people in New York City and arrive by simple multiplication at figures running into billions of dollars representing their market potential. This is true only if we assume that by and large, the total income of the average black wage earner is spent to meet his needs and satisfy his wants. But in this assumption there is no room for savings, and capital can only be accumulated through retained earnings.

A growing percentage of Afroamericans do practice thrift. This number is responsible for the thousands of savings accounts in banks scattered throughout the metropolitan area. In the main they prefer to save their money with large banks. In the late forties, Walter A. Miller, young West Indian realtor in Harlem, with the encouragement of fellow islanders Dr. Joseph D. Gibson and Dr. Charles A. Petioni, organized a group and secured a charter for the Carver Federal Savings and Loan Association. Shopping for a manager with experience was futile—few colored persons had been exposed to working in banking institutions above the level of porter.

It was decided to employ a young man who for some years had held a subordinate position in the mortgage department of a bank and to allow him to grow with the newly formed institution. Today with continuing community support, the Carver Banking Association has attracted savings accounts almost exclusively from non-whites totalling in excess of $21 million. The young mortgage assistant became president of the institution; branches have been established in Brooklyn and downtown Manhattan.

Contrasted with this is the experience of the only other Savings and Loan Association organized by Afroamericans in the State of New York—The Allied Federal Savings and Loan Association in Jamaica, Long Island. It is located in a comparatively prosperous area of homeowners. After some nine years of operation, Allied has assets of less than $8 million. Various explanations

have been given for Allied's failure to develop more
rapidly but the fact remains that it has not exactly been
taken to the bosom of the Jamaica community.

Harlem lives on credit—its future wages are to a great
extent pledged for the consumer goods purchased in
the present. Afroamericans are great shoppers. Most
Harlem homes are equipped with color television, hi-fi
radios and refrigerators. These, together with the furniture, are usually bought on the credit installment plan
covered by chattel mortgages. Clothing is bought on
credit. The automobiles that line the streets of Harlem
—Cadillacs and Chryslers, Volkswagens and Fords—
are purchased, in most instances, on the credit plan.

This mortgaging of future income to provide the
wants and luxuries of the present, while not confined
to the blacks, has operated to prevent any considerable
capital from being formed. Investment in the stocks
and bonds of the industrial enterprises of the nation is
minimal. There is little or no risk capital available in
the Afroamerican community. Those who have more
than average money are usually reported to have accumulated it in various unorthodox ways. In many instances, they are afraid to have their investments identified. Real estate was and still is the favored asset into
which to convert money.

Most capital controlled by whites is frequently held
by the second, third or fourth generation of the ac-
cumulating family. Afroamericans in Harlem with some
money have generally saved it up over a long period
of time, putting it together in small amounts on the basis
of careful, thrifty practice and self-denial. Or they have
acquired it in games or systems of chance, or through
having managed to be identified with the proper political party in the days when liquor licenses were first issued and were profitable.

Whatever the background or history of the individual,
investment money, which is risk capital, is not in sight
among Afroamericans of substance. There have been a

few instances in which the public has been aroused to invest money, and lost—Marcus Garvey's Black Star Line is one—and the period of recovery from such disappointing experiences is long. Business failures are more frequent in American private enterprise than business successes, and yet the American public continues to invest. And to the extent that risk capital from nonwhite sources is unavailable, integration into the power structure of the economy will necessarily be deferred. The Afroamerican has not yet been permitted to peer over the edge of the plateau on which the financial resources of the nation are constantly rearranged. He does not know what goes on there nor has he any part in influencing the economic shape of things to come. Nor is there any evidence that more than token representation in this area will be realized in the near future.

Mortgage practices in home financing provide an interesting study of the comparative helplessness of minority homeowners or would-be buyers. Housing is and will remain in short supply in New York, according to the experts. First mortgages may be obtained for up to sixty-six percent of the price of the property, leaving thirty-four percent to be provided by a second mortgage or raised as a cash down payment. When the minority home buyer applies for a first mortgage from a lending institution outside of Harlem, it is immediately assumed that no sources are available to him in the local community. He is frequently required to pay an advance "commitment fee" of about three and one-half percent with his application. He is later required to pay a closing fee of about three and one-half percent. If he has been guided by a broker, he is faced with a mortgage brokerage fee of from two to five percent. All of these percentages are computed on and deducted from the face amount of the mortgage and fall into the category of expenses. They do not affect the rate of interest, which is usually seven and one-half to eight and one-half percent annually on the face amount of the loan, as this is reduced by the monthly or quarterly payments of principal provided for in the plan of liquidation. In addition, the purchase price of the house is always inflated where Federal Housing Administration financing is contemplated. The points or percentage discount, usually four percent of the mortgage, are payable by the seller and are passed on to the purchaser through a higher purchase price. In reality the interest rate amounts to nine percent or more annually on the net made available to the purchaser.

The really shameful practice—and one that must be aired—is the second and third mortgage system. In New York State, the law limits interest for the use of money. As long as there is no public outcry, the government supervisory agencies will await the reaction of some judge whose sense of equity and justice will revolt against the system and an explosion will occur. If a serious political issue can be raised, the legislature or congress will step in and perhaps act.

As it stands, a prospective purchaser with limited funds can usually count on securing a first mortgage. By agreeing to pay a highly inflated purchase price, he can usually arrange a second and sometimes a third mortgage with the seller who resells these mortgages to money lenders, taking a commission of from twenty to thirty-five percent in the case of the second, and from twenty-five to forty percent in the case of the third mortgage. The installments on second and third mortgages are quite sizable, as these loans must be repaid quickly, in from three to five years.

The burden of debt is staggering and the pressure of the installments on the homeowner, unbearable. One can only conclude that those who deal in this type of financing look toward the time when the mortgage payments fall in arrears, and the property—including the improvements and substantial investment made by the purchaser—can be confiscated. This is the all too common result for minority purchasers, especially where they have

failed to consult with lawyers in whom they have confidence. Too frequently they are persuaded to "save the
expense of a lawyer" by having the seller's lawyer "make
up the papers."

In this way the Afroamerican family has come to
acquire some experience in realty in New York. The
sacrifices, the exploitation, the wholesale larceny that
have been involved in their efforts to own real property
—the excessively high purchase prices, the bonuses in
mortgage financing—all represent millions and millions
of dollars unjustly syphoned away from the nonwhite
community. Deep wounds of resentment, hostility and
flaming hate have been added to the scars of four centuries of degradation and planned dehumanization.

As with the purchase of real estate, so it is with the
acquisition of merchandise. It is generally known that
automobiles are purchased on the credit installment plan
but what is not fully appreciated is that children's
clothing, women's dresses and coats, men's suits and
shoes, household furniture, radios, television sets,
watches and jewelry are, to a considerable degree, acquired on the hire-purchase system. Under the stimulus
of newspaper advertising and television and radio com-
mercials, people will agree to buy what they want, not
merely what they need. The automobiles that line the
streets of Harlem are chiefly used to drive the owners
a few blocks after work each day, from home to 125th
Street or to visit someone a short distance across town.
The automobile has become important to nonwhites in
the way it is to whites, as a status symbol. The difference lies in the average earnings of the white and
the nonwhite auto purchaser—the latter's earnings are
so much lower than his white counterpart's, and he
must stay in debt much longer to complete the purchase
while many important needs of the family remain un-
filled.

The whole system of credit purchasing is loaded with
abuses. In a community in which the reading level of the
inhabitants is low, a written contract has little signifi-

cance to the purchaser. As a rule, he signs "here" without reading anything. He frequently neglects to demand a copy of the agreement. He seldom preserves receipts or money order stubs. The result is that payments in excess of the amount owed are constantly made and ascend to staggering sums annually for the entire community.

The conditions relating to apartment rentals are too well known to require elaboration. Afroamerican New York residents pay more for less in rented apartments than any other people in our city. Luxury rentals of twenty to twenty-five dollars per week for a single room, with or without private bath and utilities are about average for rooming house accommodations. This is an area in which supply and demand determine price and the orthodox American economy is preserved. To lawyers who frequent the inferior criminal courts where complaints against landlords are processed, it is a matter of constant wonder that the filthy backyards and area ways and the dark, rat-infested tenements in which so many of our working people live, seem to continue unchanged in their condition, year after year. Rumors of understaffed agencies and widespread corruption in the form of payoffs to inspectors continue to circulate with no one ever being willing to come forward with the facts. The control of rentals has undoubtedly operated to protect the tenants, but the failure to achieve reasonable adjustments in the face of rising costs has also made for the constant deterioriation of housing in Harlem and similar areas, bringing to the tenant less value for his rental dollar than ever before.

How does the Harlem dweller eat? In this era of frozen and refrigerated foods, the people of Harlem have comparatively easy access to average food supplies. The nationally known food chains have not neglected to take advantage of the concentrated purchasing power of minority families in New York. The outlets are everywhere. The small shopkeeper is rapidly being eliminated by competition from the chains. He can exist only as an after-hour parasite, charging over thirty cents for a quart of milk at 8 P.M. which the housewife could have purchased for twenty-seven cents at 6:30 P.M. and the same for other staples. He earns the ill favor of his customers and when finally, under the pressure of competition he is eliminated, no one mourns his passing. The small shopkeeper has become a casualty to the economic change that has given the shopping center to the American community.

But on wages of sixty-three to eighty-five dollars per week, how much can the Harlemite in the lower income brackets spend for food? Rent comes first, then food. Balanced diets are expensive. The great irony of the American civilization is here illustrated—excess food production—meats and vegetables in embarrasing surplus—while the cost to the low income consumer of such staples as milk, eggs, flour and meat places them beyond his reach.

Where, then, does the money come from to keep the bars and grills busy with customers, the liquor stores thriving, and the drug pushers active? There is no simple answer to these questions. The suggestion that the people have too much money to spend is naive. The fact is that the money withheld or diverted for liquor is often, though not always, that which should be reserved for the landlord, the furniture salesman or the insurance collector. The proliferation of drug addiction is concomitant with the spread of crime. The drug addict cannot earn enough to meet the cost of his habit. Theft becomes the only means by which he can supply his daily needs. The cost of drug addiction to the Harlem community is becoming ever more burdensome and the end is not in sight. Both city and state officials have been extremely unrealistic in not assessing the proportions of this vice. Yet it must come up for reckoning despite the current tendency to brush all reference to drug traffic under the social and political carpet, and pretend it has disappeared.

It has been asked whether drug or policy rackets could thrive without the permission or protection of the police. Both seem to flourish in Harlem. Clearly, the police are handicapped in law enforcement without the cooperation of the average citizen. The average citizen in Harlem is convinced that the police cannot protect him against organized crime and there is little or no assistance that the police can expect or will receive from the Harlem citizen whether he is a victim or an informed observer. The examples of reprisals against loyal citizens who have aided the police are too many and too vivid not to be remembered and no one wants to be that patriotic.

For many years, there has existed a belief that Harlem provided a ready market for stolen goods. The truth appears to be that the once thriving "hot" market in Harlem has long ceased to have any real meaning. However, there is a class of shrewd peddlers who have learned that carefully selected bargains secured in "close outs" or from warehouses, purchased at wholesale prices, can be much more readily sold under the "hot goods" label through the beauty parlors, nursing homes and restaurants, than they can through normal channels—and, for cash! Sometimes stolen goods also flow along this route, but most of the furtively displayed, once-in-a-lifetime bargains, that so readily appeal to the cupidity of the respectable housewife or career woman, are entirely legitimate offerings.

It has been said, perhaps with a high degree of truth, that the largest business in Harlem is done by the churches. The area ministers allegedly collect more money, net, than men or women in any other enterprise or profession. Questions are being raised with greater insistence as to what the ministers and the churches are giving in return. "Sister Mary" says "amen" much more generously when the minister talks about some "pie here and now," then when he makes unctuous reference to "pie in the sky." The promise of a life in the hereafter with abundance of "milk and honey" recently caused one street corner skeptic to mention the cathartic properties of both these foods when taken in excess.

Some churches have instituted thrift programs by forming and operating credit unions. Others have developed community centers in which various forms of social action for youth and adults are carried forward. But the potential of the churches, through their ministers, for influencing the economic life of the Harlem community is far from being organized or released. Churchmen as a group hardly tend to encourage a diversion of funds from the collection box into other channels. There is a conflict here between the church's attitude toward money and the churchgoers material interests. It is inevitable that a revolt will set in against this general situation—indeed, it may have already begun.

The Muslims preach the doctrine of self-help. They constantly deplore the lack of black ownership of any of the means of production. Their program provides for the organization and operation of Afroamerican restaurants, factories, chain stores, and canneries that will create jobs. They scoff at the efforts of the Urban League and the NAACP to seek jobs in the white man's enterprises.

The logic of their arguments is strong, appealing, effective and persuasive. And the fact is, that except for their demand for a separate state for blacks, their enuciated program and statement have achieved general acceptance by a majority of Afroamericans, who, in Harlem, like those in the West and South, understand more and more clearly the relationship between their economic exploitation and deprivation, and the denial of their rights and liberties. They are finding that the segregated living imposed on them, confers economic advantages—with profits—on whites. Racial discrimination looms as an economic factor in their minds. It is no longer a question of "social equality" but rather one of "economic justice." This is the ship, all else is the sea.

Proportionately, nonwhite New Yorkers feel the weight of the tax burden most heavily because so many fall into the low income brackets. The indirect taxes which contribute to the inflationary high prices of goods and services have their impact. But minority workers are actually called upon to subsidize those who are better off economically by providing services in institutions and in industry at wages that are below the true value of their labor.

The hospital strikes have demonstrated that hospital workers—chiefly Afroamerican and Puerto Rican—were and are furnishing labor at wage levels recognized to be below the poverty level of subsistence. The voluntary hospitals do not hesitate to use such labor at low wages in order to remain competitive in respect to their paying patients. And so it is in those industries and trades where unskilled labor is used. In the semiskilled and skilled crafts which have organized to protect their wage levels, racial discrimination has long been practiced. Afroamericans have not been permitted to work as bricklayers', carpenters', and electricians' helpers over the years and have not become skilled in these trades.

It has often been pointed out to the officials and legislators in the State of New York that the minimum wage is wholly inadequate to meet the needs of any family in New York no matter how small. It is to be noted that the minimum subsistence budget of the Department of Welfare is much higher than the minimum wage. The political and business leaders want to be sure that increases do not drive industry from the state.

It seems clear that this economic theory provides for the existence of a class of workers whose labor would be priced below the subsistence level and that it is now the turn of the Afroamericans and Puerto Ricans in New York to fulfill that role as other national and ethnic groups in past years did, who moved on to more favored brackets. In the light of our economy of abundance, the great wealth that our state and nation have developed, such thinking is unimpressive.

The current economic policy requires that concepts of right and justice be balanced with Machiavellian calculation and sense of timing. It seems clear, however, that it would be wiser to support a minimum wage more in keeping with the needs of decency and self-respect of all of our citizens.

The system of public instruction has long been geared to depress the level of education of Afroamerican children. For many years, educational planners as well as teachers acted as if it didn't matter too much whether pupils in Harlem schools learned or did not learn. Children of minority groups were thought to be biologically inferior anyway—what was the point in expending energy to make them learn when the work that would be available to them would be in unskilled categories where minimum education would be adequate?

Generation after generation of such pupils were processed through Harlem schools, promoted from one grade to the next and turned out as graduates, unprepared, unable to read at the level established by the curriculum and ill-equipped to compete in the world of labor and industry with their white opposite numbers. Protests, agitation and considerable attention have been focused on the problem for many years; but the segregated schools stemming from segregated housing continued to repeat the process. Now at last there appears to be some appreciation on the part of the school authorities of the fact that "where there has been no learning, there has been no teaching." Confronted with the problems of "dropouts," drug addiction among teenagers, the mounting number of pregnancies among girls of school age, and continued street gang activities, the greater New York community is finally taking a

closer look at the schools. The understanding is beginning to get through to more and more parents and
community leaders, that a low reading level will be a
barrier to Johnny's earning capacity in the years ahead
just as it is to his father today.

Statistics show that a disproportionate percentage of
the nonwhite population of Harlem receives assistance
from the Department of Welfare compared with white
families in the city as a whole. There should be nothing
surprising in this fact. The family budget established by
the Department of Welfare is often above the income
of many families that do not and would not accept aid
from that agency.

Chickens will come home to roost. So much time,
energy and money have been invested in these United
States in planned programs to retard the progress of
black citizens, to create barriers in their path, to
humilate and discourage them, that it is to their eternal
credit that there are so few criminals, derelicts and
habitual drunkards. The injustice, denial of due process,
police brutality, gratuitous humiliation, cowardly assault
by many against the few or one, are ways in which the
white majority has sown the wind down through the
years. Can the whirlwind be harnessed? Deflected? Prevented? Only time will tell and time appears to be
running out.

The future? The ferment that has gripped our
country in the area of race relations will continue to
seeth until a healthy change occurs. The young people
of the Harlem communities of the nation will continue
to challenge and defy the customs, practices and
methods that operate to deny them the right to work,
the right to equal pay and equal opportunity. They have
actually accepted the proposition that they are born in
and belong to a democracy—that they are created equal
to all others in this democracy and that they cannot
be deprived of life, liberty and property without due
process of law. They believe that the denial, because
of color, of the opportunity to qualify for a job is

deprivation, without due process, of a property right having economic value. They are determined to play their part to defend and uphold this democracy for their own benefit and the benefit of all, until those who are legally charged with the responsibility to uphold it, come forth to its defense. By the strong irony of fate, the centennial of the Emancipation Proclamation found the grandchildren and great grandchildren of the bondsmen in the forefront of the battle to save the nation and to fulfill the American dream.

The healthy impatience of the Afroamerican in Harlem, the refusal to tolerate bigotry and injustice, the emerging unity of purpose to forge a common front against racialism, are heightened by the knowledge that black, brown and yellow brothers, in all sections of the world, have their eyes focused on this, our homeland. There is one tie that binds them all—their common hatred of racist oppression which, in varying forms, they have all experienced, as the Afroamerican continues to experience, always from the whites. We must expect a tightening of the sinews of opposition as those who are irredentist in their attitudes resort to desperate measures, until sanity arises in this bewildered and floundering land of ours.

Americans of African descent are the only ones who did not ask to be admitted and did not volunteer to come. Their right to stay and to inherit the land is incontestable and they know it.

The achievement of the right to work—a property right at present hampered by racialist exclusionary practices—will remove the primary obstacles to the equality of people, regardless of their race and color. The present purchasing power of the people of Harlem is estimated at several billions of dollars annually— a factor that is proving to be extremely consequential to the industrial and business community.

It would therefore seem to be logical and factual to conclude that there is no special economic theory applicable to the Harlem community. The minority people who were once limited to Harlem for their living space by the social pattern evolved for them by the whites, have, by and large, elected to continue to remain in Harlem now that they are freer to live wherever they are able to purchase or rent homes. This freedom is of course highly relative in that the majority of the non-white population simply cannot afford to move into more desirable housing.

The gap in family income between whites and non-whites is the primary determinant of the social distance that exists and will continue to exist between the two ethnic groups until the gap is narrowed.

Removal of educational inequality in the public school system, whatever the reasons for its existence, will work a major change in the income potential of the Afroamerican family. With better participation in remunerative employment, some significant capital accumulation may be anticipated. This will lead to a more rapid integration of nonwhite persons into business, trade and financial operations.

Penetration of the power structure will mean inclusion in broad policy-making. It will be simpler then, for minority representatives in business and finance to drive home the truths, now mere postulates, to the majority, that it is costly and unprofitable to support a segregated industrial society and that nondiscriminatory patterns of living avoid waste, improve business and increase profits.

Many hopeful signs suggest that the Harlem community can leap forward economically; not the least important of these is that the controllers of business in Harlem are anxious to find ways of changing old images and creating new ones, fresher and more realistic. There are also those in the minority ranks who feel that this is good and are working to see what can be done about it more quickly.

Leonard W. Holt

༄

BIRMINGHAM'S HARLEM

J UST BEFORE the outbreak of the French Revolution,
an advisor is supposed to have informed the King that
civil disorder was imminent: "The people are crying for
bread." The "wise" queen, who knew how to discharge
her responsibilities, is supposed to have made a statement about giving them cake.

Today a lot of folks in Harlem, and in little Harlems
all over America, are rejoicing because the "Messiah"
is proposing legislation which would seek to outlaw
racial discrimination wherever the public is served. For
the black American, this is cake.

Unlike the Frenchmen, who apparently got neither
bread nor cake from the King, Negroes will get cake,
especially in those areas where they are strong enough
to insist that racial discrimination in public service be
abolished, law or no law.

Up on Fourth Avenue and Sixteenth Street, Birmingham's Harlem, and elsewhere in the South, there won't
be much "cake" unless the brothers should happen to
get some *bread*[125] to buy it with.

It's not the fault of the politicians that cake (service
at lunch counters, admission to theatres, removal of

racial signs and the like) is what's being offered to pacify the rumblings of angry black masses. It's cake we have been asking for, primarily. It is not only true that Kennedy was "naive," as James Baldwin said after the widely publicized secret meeting with the Honorable Mr. Robert Kennedy, then Attorney General.

We, too, are sometimes naive.

Recently I made two trips to Birmingham and to its Harlem: one while the massive protest of 4,000 Negroes was in progress, another shortly after.

As grand and glorious and inspiring as the Birmingham Movement was in its totality, the promises of downtown merchants which were accepted as the price for calling off the demonstrations were a slender victory. (We assume, as the Rev. M. L. King and the Rev. F. L. Shuttlesworth assume, that the promises will be fulfilled. There is an attitude, however, among some in Birmingham's Harlem, which says, "I think the same thing of these promises as I do of the promises the white man made to the Indians.")

Summed up, these promises consist of integration of facilities in seven downtown department stores, five clerical jobs and the creation of a bi-racial committee. For this there were 3,330 arrests, there were beatings, dog bites, clubbings, school expulsions and more than a million dollars spent. I consider the promises "cake" at a time that people in Birmingham don't have bread.

Heading home to Norfolk, Virginia, from Birmingham, I stopped in Greensboro, North Carolina, where 2,000 had filled local jails over the integration of two restaurants and two theatres. A like situation existed in other North Carolina cities: Raleigh, Durham and Charlotte. And so it was also in Tallahassee, Florida.

In the same vein as all these "cake" projects was the voluntary, and unsought-after, integration of theatres in Norfolk and drug store lunch counters in Lynchburg, followed by the chambers of commerce of Atlanta, Georgia, and Charlotte, North Carolina, going on record as recommending integration of all public facilities. Meanwhile the Attorney General met with chain theatre owners seeking a similar objective.

How surprising this must seem to the jobless black men in Gary, Indiana, where Negroes make up 48 per cent of those out of work. In all of this negotiating, protesting, jailing and concessioning, minimal or no attention was given to jobs. Nationally, we seem to be obsessed with the concept of the cake of public facilities. And it is cake that the power structure of the South, and the North, is most willing to concede.

The businessmen have noticed, just as we have, that bus integration in Montgomery, Alabama has meant little because ninety per cent of the Negroes still head straight for the back. Counts were probably taken in the "tea rooms" of Richmond's Thalheimer Department Store of how Negroes don't use the facilities that were opened only after a year of arrests, picketing and boycotting. The judge in Lynchburg, Virginia, probably knows the birth dates of all thirteen Negroes who actually use the "other side" of his courtroom—and the justice dispensed is the same as before the United States Supreme Court ruled.

The importance of shifting direction from "cake" to "bread" was dramatized in Birmingham by the folks from Birmingham's Harlem late one Saturday night: the demonstration that finally got some federal action when the troops were moved into a nearby base. This demonstration was violently ugly. Its character was determined by its participants: the dispossessed, unemployed and not-too-impressed-with-nonviolence folks.

Blasts of dynamite at the home of the Rev. A. D. King[126] and the A. G. Gaston Motel set off the demonstrations during hours when the joints were swinging all the way. Thousands of Negroes were in the area.

At the time the blasts crumpled the brick buildings, they shattered the cup of tolerance and survival. Angry black angels shook the nation as shots were fired, knives flashed, bricks hurled and the people tried to destroy everything white. This dispossessed element was leaderless and without direction except for the consuming hatred so prevalent in ghettos.

This demonstration reminded all that the integration movement is often "show-casey" and for the "uppity" folks, as one of those who boasted of being part of the berserk throng put it. Partially the speaker was right. The masses of Negroes are not so much affected by the refusal of downtown stores to permit them to try on clothing in a place like Birmingham, as they are by the fact that they can't afford clothing. In Chicago the 70,000 who lined up for hours to get surplus food because their relief checks were being held up gain little solace from the fact that if they had money they could go to the dining room in the Marshall Field store and sit without jim crow.

The men and women involved in Birmingham's violent protest were for the most part hopelssly unemployable in a day of automation, and, they will gain little in this life—or the next—from the promised integration of five lunch counters and the creation of a biracial committee.

Widespread unemployment is the canker of the working folks of Birmingham. And Negroes are the ones afflicted most by the disease. Birmingham is almost a one-industry town: steel. "First it was foreign-made steel, then automation." Birmingham Negroes are paying with their jobs for both the importation and the automation.

Into this wound, salt is being rubbed by the loss of traditional jobs as truck driving and garbage collecting. As men are laid off from the plants, vacancies in the garbage department are being filled from the ranks of the white unemployed. It is the members of this vast, idle army of unemployable Negroes who may erupt again and again in the Harlem of Birmingham. One can only wonder how different in this respect is the city of

Birmingham from other cities, North and South, where there are more than five lunch counters integrated.

America's leaders appear to be aware of the catalytic effect a "cake" demonstration to integrate lunch counters can have on a "bread" demonstration of black violence. They are rushing to integrate places that most Negroes don't know exist in a lot of Southern cities. Jobs and training opportunities for the thousands of unemployed Negro citizens are still the key issues in our country.

Milton A. Galamison

∾⊱⊰∾

BEDFORD-STUYVESANT—
HARLEM ACROSS THE RIVER

B ROOKLYN'S BEDFORD-STUYVESANT[127] area is a land of
superlatives. Compared with other communities of the
world's largest borough it claims the most residents, the
most teen-agers, the most overcrowding, the most
churches, the greatest religious diversity and the highest
rent per square foot of living space. The area under
discussion also houses the greatest economic need, the
greatest number of public assistance cases, the highest
rate of infant mortality, the highest incidence of tuber-
culosis, a disproportionate crime and delinquency rate
and more exploitation than conceivable in an area so
geographically limited. In countless ways the Bedford-
Stuyvesant area defies statistical norms.

It is the residential area of least desirability on the
totem pole of cultural status-seeking.

Most articles on "The Box," as the area is sometimes
called, are insensitive and unfair. To gratify perverted
public fancy for sensationalism, to confirm prejudices,
writers have consistently projected a distorted image of
an abused but heroic people. They burlesque the broken-
ness and ignore the creativity. They dramatize the
juggled crime statistics and neglect the impressive well-
spring of spiritual and religious life. They catalogue the

shiftless and overlook the teeming thousands who daily crowd the transportation facilities enroute to gainful employment.

While intent that non-resident readers should suffer no pangs of guilt for the plight of "The Box," those who write commentary on Bedford-Stuyvesant forget that no area could be so deprived unless there were forces outside far more evil than the forces within. In short, articles that most seek to defame and incriminate the people of the area have been the most serious indictments of the people not of this area. Efforts to present the Negro as an isolated monstrosity, however literary, do not negate the reality of the political, social, economic and historic context in which the ghetto Negro has been created. They do not absolve guilt. They confirm it.

This is not a community of slum-dwellers. It is more a haven for corrupt, absentee landlords and real estate speculators. This is not a community of shiftless husbands. It is a world of wounded men historically deprived of the right to equal employment. This is not a vast neighborhood of negligent mothers. It is a congregation of homemakers without homes and toilers without rest. Nor are our children justly depicted by delinquency statistics. They are condemned at the outset by an unequal, ethnocentric educational structure which few survive. Feeling with all other human beings the need for success, they seek to gratify this need in less creative endeavors. They have not failed so much as they have been failed. The Bedford-Stuyvesant area is not a front-page anomaly. It is a land of ghettoized human beings: men denied creative work, women denied creative living space and children denied a qualifying education. Few who write about or read of the area could manage half as well under similar circumstances.

The gigantic question mark, then, does not hover over the residents of the area. The basic question is: whose condition is blessed at the expense of this blight? In what community will we find the sinners who destroy the families of men for the sake of their ambition and the minds of children for the gratification of their greed?

As the Bedford-Stuyvesant area is a land of super-latives, it is also a land of dead-end streets. Here Dante might well have posted the sign hung over the threshold of the entrance to his Hell, *Abandon hope all ye who enter here.* The usual routes by which people achieve redemption are few and elusive in this community. Education would be one such avenue, politics another.

There are two school sysfems in New York City. One is for the whites and for the sprinkling of Negroes who manage by design or grace to matriculate. The second school system is for the ghetto children, and the dis-·parity is grotesque. Unlike the conventional school sys-tem, the racial school system functions by a one-word policy called "Ifism." In essence, this policy maintains that the children involved could learn "IF." They could learn if they were not from the South. They could learn if they had a different set of parents. They could learn if they enjoyed higher income homes or if they just weren't on public assistance. They could learn if they didn't come from a broken home or perhaps if the home, even though broken, had a library. These are obviously conditions which the child cannot change. It is also ap-parent that if conditions of this kind are set up as an obstacle to learning, conditions impossible to fulfill, they will preclude both teaching and learning. The supreme and thoroughly possible condition has yet to be stated: that the children might learn if they were properly taught.

Like the community generally, the schools have their share of superlatives: the most over-crowding, the most part-time sessions, the most inexperienced and substi-tute teachers, the most out-of-license instruction, the most nonresident staff members and the most teachers lowest on the salary scale. The curriculum, like the low expectation attitude, is predicated on "Ifism." Since one is never quite sure what the curriculum is, it will suffice to say that it leaves the majority of children woefully unprepared to compete academically and vocationally with aspirants from other communities. The fruit of the system is perceptible on the high school level, where the dropout rate among Negroes is frightening, and in the free institutions of higher learning, such as Brooklyn College, where Negroes, who most need the free education, have long since been squeezed out by the competition and are infinitesimal in number.

Over-idealistic efforts like "Higher Horizons" have not raised standards in the ghetto schools. Innovations such as "Open Enrollment" have not desegregated one school in the black community nor aborted the growth of additional segregated institutions. Indeed, we are manufacturing backward children so rapidly in the ghetto schools no conceivable appropriation of funds could balance the scales.

Meanwhile, two formidable obstacles impede efforts to improve the situation. One is a conviction on the part of some misguided if not dishonest souls that standards can be appreciably raised in the ghetto schools. The second is an illusion on the part of others that, were the standards raised, the educational system would be equal. Those who hold the second view have completely missed the psychological and sociological ramifications of the Supreme Court Decision on Segregated Education. Those who hold the first point of view, who believe that it is possible to lump together thousands of children with below average scholastic foundations and produce standard graduating classes, are hopelessly gullible. Desegregation is the only wholesome answer to this existing educational farce. Any step short of this is speculating with the destiny of little children and the future of a great nation.

One might suppose that the same concentration of Negroes who account for so many segregated learning institutions would also produce a formidable political force. Such, however, is not the case. It should be added to the list of area superlatives that ours is the borough community most without political representation. The 255,000 residents of "The Box," who comprise nearly ten per cent of the borough's population, have no congressional or senatorial representation. Failure to produce leadership in state-wide and national offices is due largely to the ingenious zoning of the political districts. Only a colossal and diabolical depravity could have conceived the gerrymandering of the congressional districts. Political representation, then, which might provide an escape route to freedom, is frustrated by a circuitous scenic railway of shifting district lines.

The perennial failure of the majority of qualified voters in the area to register has become the subject of public scandal. Having never regarded politics as an institution for the investment of optimism, this writer has neither joined in the criticism nor shared the enthusiasm for voter registration. In this matter, however, I bow to those who hold the contrary opinion and aid the efforts toward greater voting strength that my pessimism or their optimism might be sooner confirmed. Apparently, you see, the quantity of political representation does not depend on the length of the voter registration list. For all its scandalous neglect of the franchise, the Bedford-Stuyvesant area has managed to achieve the identical political mediocrity evident in other and more affluent areas.

When the community trumpet is sounded for the promotion of voter registration, all manner of irrepressible questions come to my mind. I wonder if by some peculiar convergence of circumstances we might get a candidate worth voting for. I wonder if the failure of the people to register is due to apathy, cynicism, disillusionment or realism. I see Harlem as an example of advanced political representation and wonder, if this is the state of affairs we have to look forward to, if the end is worth the journey. With every respect for those who disagree, I have never expected political enthusiasm to exist in a culture in which the citizenry appears resignedly doomed to perpetual choices between the lesser of two evils.

Politics is the hall where decency bows to expediency. Here the bell of morality is seldom sounded. If sounded, it is seldom heard. If heard, it is seldom heeded. If this is the avenue to freedom, I, moving doggedly in some other direction, will miss it. The political world is Ibsen's madhouse. "It's here that men are most themselves; themselves and nothing but themselves."

The housing story is almost too commonplace to recount. The community is replete with stately, statuesque brownstones that speak of an era gone by. These three-and four-story dwellings once gave shelter to one white family each and were more than adequate for a middle-class family with servants. The advent of Negroes, from twenty to ninety per cent of the area population between 1930 and 1957, precipitated the exodus of whites and, as the face of the community changed, a number of innovations took place which would determine the course of the future. Not the least significant of these changes occurred in the mortgage policy of the borough banks. Whereas it had been policy to grant mortgages on the value of a property—after all, real estate is real estate—obtaining a mortgage now became contingent on the borrower's character or on the applicant's knowing John Smith, the one Negro among the bank president's acquaintances.

In the course of this frustrating process, real estate combines and lawyers became the accessible middlemen for the procurement cf mortgage loans. Obtaining a legitimate mortgage became a kind of underground enterprise like locating a bookmaker. Practices became increasingly conscienceless and charges boundless. In many instances what might have represented a substantial down-payment was consumed in fees, carrying charges and other baffling transactions. Houses were sold to buyers with the tacit understanding that the exorbitant mortgage payments could not be met without violating fair rent and occupancy laws. The foul deed was done! The blueprints had been drawn for the construction of a ghetto.

The ensuing and inevitable overcrowding, transiency and outrageous rents had their birth in the circumstances outlined. It is common knowledge that, were the fair rent and occupancy laws enforced, countless people would lose their homes.

For the most part the proud, orderly brownstones along the tree-lined streets do not confirm the ugly, press-created image of the area. For the most part the residents are responsible, hard-working home-owners and citizens. It is principally where the absentee speculator has cast his net that the most deteriorated living conditions exist.

Government housing, conceived to provide a solution to the problem, has become more a part of the problem than its answer. It has magnified and multiplied the grievous conditions created by lending institutions and real estate interests. The policy of littering an already-deprived community with low-income housing projects is visionless and contemptible. No housing development constructed with public funds should be restricted to one economic or racial group. Such a practice lends government approval to class stratifications and social distinctions. Housing units should contain apartments for varying income groups. It is one thing for a people to resist living in proximity to those at whom they would thumb their noses. It is another matter entirely when the people's government appropriates public funds to make practicable the acting out of these irreligious and undemocratic attitudes.

The Negro quarter is a place of comparable splendor during the greater part of the week. An average day finds the children safely tucked away in school and the adults pursuing the necessary art of making a living, and there is a magnificent serenity abroad. Like the three bowls of porridge in the vacated home of the three bears, however, there are perceptible signs which tell much about the invisible residents. Countless delivery trucks, bearing national trade names and chauffeured by white drivers, congest the shopping district. They speak of far-flung union halls where this people cannot find employment. Check-cashing establishments crop up here and there bespeaking the tragic anonymity and faceless-ness of the people, an existence that defies the deepest human needs for identity. An incredible number of bars, taverns and retail liquor stores tell the tale of congested living quarters and life lived outside the home.

On week-ends there is a bursting at the seams. The cup of frustration runneth over and some seek visions of a better world through the bottom of an upturned whisky glass. Men and women chained through the long week to the flywheel of futility find a sense of release and power. The image of the area is often unfairly de-fined in terms of this temporary and concentrated escape. By Sunday the storm has spent itself, the pent-up fury has run its course, drifted out to sea, and the com-munity assumes its quiet posture with little evidence of the turbulence.

It should be reported that an effort was made several years ago to limit the rapidly multiplying number of liquor stores in the Negro quarter. To this end a survey was made by two qualified experts and at the expense of eight hundred dollars. The study confirmed our wildest speculations that there existed in the Bedford-Stuyvesant area more than three times the number of liquor establishments found in a comparably-sized com-munity. Armed with this statistical picture I appealed to the area's Neighborhood Council, an echelon group composed of the presidents of the various neighborhood block associations. The response was instant, wrathful indignation and they unanimously agreed on a three-point program. First, they would underwrite the cost of the survey; secondly, they would organize a delegation to Albany to protest the heinous condition; thirdly, they would demand a moratorium on the issuance of new liquor licenses and on the transfer of existing liquor licenses in the community.

The crusade to defend the community against creeping saturation was of short duration. Not many days after the eventful meeting I received a letter from the president of the association. His type is of more importance than his name, his disease more significant than his identity. The letter said in essence that the executive council of the association had found it necessary to invalidate the action of the meeting on the grounds that to prevent the opening of new liquor establishments would be tantamount to creating a monopoly for those businesses already in existence.

I was stunned! The voice was the voice of Jacob, but the hands were the hands of Esau. It was not hard for even a disillusioned clergyman to conclude what had happened here. But then, no people could be kept in this kind of predicament were not their best efforts constantly undermined and betrayed by those in whom they place their trust.

In studying another aspect of the retail liquor store business more recently, we estimated from available facts that more than half a million dollars is gleaned annually from sales commissions alone. Of this startling sum, less than five per cent accrues to Negro salesman. The Dorian Gray portrait of the scarred economic soul of the community becomes ominously clearer.

The same dismal and disproportionate statistics that apply to Negro unemployment throughout the nation apply here. A survey was conducted in the not-too-distant past to determine the number of business establishments in the quarter that did not employ Negro help. There were few such establishments in the district studied, and most of those without representative employees offered satisfactory reasons for the omission. One pharmacy, for example, had the union confirm its effort to locate an available Negro pharmacist. None could be found. Another union supported a local shoemaker's explanation that no skilled Negro was available. A third store consisted of three separate concessions operated by three different families. There was almost no evidence of a flagrant refusal to employ Negroes.

The ministers did become greatly exercised over the failure of neighborhood merchants to support non-profit community agencies such as the YMCA, and to rectify the situation, they organized a Ministers' Movement. The merchants were operating without any sense of responsibility to the area's civic and benevolent causes. They were taking everything out and giving nothing back. The Merchants' Association was practically defunct. Repeated appeals on behalf of the most deserving charitable efforts elicited no response.

In the wake of this apathy the ministers and their people picketed the merchants. The demonstrations brought an instant and enthusiastic response. A series of joint meetings followed during which machinery was set up to prevent continuation of the historic neglect, and, while much remains to be done, there now exists a cooperative effort in a new direction. The ministers, meanwhile, have set their sights on larger, city-wide and national industries; efforts will be made to involve the people in selective buying campaigns wherever discrimination rears its ugly head.

The most blatant violation of fair employment practices was uncovered in the local plant of a prominent dairy company by an aspiring political group. This plant, located deep in the heart of "The Box," employed less than five Negroes among its more than two hundred workers. In fact, the only black face in evidence on the site was a worker with thirty-five years seniority who had been upgraded to the grand responsibility of guiding trailer trucks to the loading platform. With the help of an advertising executive of a Negro magazine, conferences were set up with personnel representatives of the company. Since it had never been their policy to discriminate against Negroes, the request for a new policy was not in order. It was all a big mistake. But they did agree to make a deliberate effort to compensate for the oversight and even to provide on-the-job training for Negroes. Within the past month I received a call from the personnal director asking for some twenty job applicants to function as salesmen on delivery routes.

The people are not idle. The storm is ever-brewing. Any evidence of injustice can precipitate a storm of social action. Those who listen can hear the rumbling beyond the hills.

If "colony" can be acceptably defined as "a territory distant from the people who govern it," the picture we have been painting here is that of domestic colonialism. The delivery trucks and the merchants, the real estate speculators and the rent gougers, the business executives and the bank tellers, the school principals and the ethnomaniacal school teachers, the precinct captains and the wine merchants all come from faraway places. The hospital in which I am born, the apartment in which I live and the cemetery in which I am buried are owned and controlled by commuter circuit riders whose allegiance lies in another world which I cannot visit, not even in my dreams. The masters of my destiny are faceless foreigners who find my community a satisfactory place to make a living but not a very satisfactory place to live. If my people suffer injustice it is because it is impossible to deal justly with those we neither know nor understand.

The Bedford-Stuyvesant section has not been consumed by the fires of nationalism as have some other

communities in our urban centers. There is a degree
of nationalism but it has neither the fervor nor the following evident in other areas. A warm evening might
find at least two speakers holding forth on diametrical
corners of a major intersection. But the listeners are
generally few in number and the pausing passers-by
seldom remain for long and never appear quite convinced. The area has never been a Roman marketplace
where people exercise their idle curiosity to hear and
to do some new thing. Noisy harangues and chattering
public address systems do not seduce the people from
their homes.

There may be several reasons for what seems, on the
surface, a state of lethargy. The reader may add his own
to those suggested. The people appear to be a comparatively conservative people. The issues that have com-
manded community attention have, for the most part,
been so counterfeit, so thoroughly shallow, only the
feeble-minded afforded themselves the luxury of distrac-
tion. The leadership has been so divided, so shamelessly
opportunistic, and the fruits of invested labor so disil-
lusioning, the people have cultivated an instinctive
suspicion of Pied Pipers. The most frequently-heard
music is the monotonous tune of the axe grinder.

There is no intention to imply that the dwellers here,
like elsewhere, are not in search of an identity. There
is a growing pride in race and the towering question
seems to center in what shall be done with this. Extreme
nationalism has dichotomized the Negro movement.
Whereas the major battle was between the forces of
action and the forces of inertia, the current warfare
seems to be between the forces of integration and the
forces of separation. There is, on the one hand, the
proud, emotional, noisy retreat to the cubbyhole where
the Negro is already physically confined, and there is,
on the other hand, the stumbling march toward a unifying, integrated life.

Black nationalism has provided many Negro leaders and politicians, who never lifted a finger on behalf of equal rights in the first instance, with a convenient mask for their cowardice and duplicity. It ought to be said here, lest I forget, that I regard these existing Negro separationist movements as the biggest Uncle Tom movements in the country. Look beneath the castigation of white people and the "Let's you and him fight" kibitzing and you find the black incarnation of Governor Wallace's fondest dreams.

What amazes me is how the same Negro leaders who rant with the separationists and supremacists of the North rave also with the integrationists of the South. I expect it's important to be on every platform.

Even more amazing is the number of Negro leaders in the North who confine their militance to the Southern issues. Safe in New York City, they are as busy as the proverbial queen bee, pardon the Freudian slip, fighting the far-away battle of Alabama while the local human wreckage and civic garbage heap high to the roof-tops. It is as if there were no battle to be fought on Brownsville's Alabama Avenue. Like Dickens' Madame Jellybee, they suffer the kind of social presbyopia that sees so readily the problems at a distance but remains blind to the duties close at hand. Obviously the best way to help the people struggling in the South is not with a bundle of old clothing. Identical struggles must be waged where we are. We have too many heroes by mail who would rather sweep below the Mason-Dixon Line than clean their own doorsteps.

Even as I write there is before me as press release from the New York City Board of Education. It proudly announces that the new superintendent of schools has invited a number of civic organizations to sit with him for the purpose of discussing school desegregation. Conspicuously absent from the organizations listed are the two organizations that have done more than any others to revolutionize the racial policy of the school system: The Brooklyn Congress on Racial Equality and the Parents' Workshop for Equality in New York City Schools. The job of desegregation will be achieved with or without the roundtable discussions and their ensuing studies. But this release dramatizes so well what we have been trying to say here. We are caught in a sick chess game and the black people are the pawns. Wherever the militant Negro fights for an equal slice in America, he is swept under the rug by local whites and climbed on by the opportunists in his own race. The white majority continues to listen only to the Negroes, hand-picked, purchased and paid for, who say what it wants to hear. There is manifest in this an arrogant refusal to listen and an unteachableness that can only lead to destruction.

Charles Dickens raised the question why Midas in his palace should care about Tom all alone in his rat-infested cellar. Then Dickens answered his own question. "There is not an atom of Tom's slime, not a cubic inch of any pestilential gas in which he lives, not one obscenity or degradation about him but shall work its retribution."

We have hope because we live in this kind of universe. We have hope because this greatest darkness must be the darkness before the dawn. We dare hope because, whether or not we read the face of the clock, eternity keeps its own inscrutable timetable. We dare hope because only order can come from this chaos.

Were we to pray we would pray with one voice the prayer of Ezekiel for this Land of Superlatives:

> Come from the four winds,
> O breath,
> And breathe upon these slain.
> That they may live.

John Henrik Clarke

~❧~

THE ALIENATION
OF JAMES BALDWIN

THE NOW FLOURISHING literary talent of James Baldwin had no easy birth, and he did not emerge overnight, as some of his new discoverers would have you believe. For years this talent was in incubation in the ghetto of Harlem, before he went to Europe nearly a decade ago in an attempt to discover the United States and how he and his people relate to it. The book in which that discovery is portrayed, "The Fire Next Time,"[128] is a continuation of his search for place and definition.

The hardships of that search were recently described by Sterling Stuckey, Chairman of the Committee on Negro Culture and History:

> The tragedy of the American Negro is born of the twin evils of the slave experience and varying patterns of segregation, supported by law and custom, that have been nationwide in dimension for a century. The consequences of the Negro's quasi freedom, unfolded against a grim backdrop of two and a half centuries of slavery, have been no less destructive to his spiritual world – his hierarchy of values and his image of himself – than to his every day world of work.

This quasi freedom of the Negro is often more humiliating than slavery and more difficult to fight because it gives the Negro the illusion of freedom while denying him the fact.

Thus the Negro continues his alien status in a country where his people have lived for more than three hundred years. "The Fire Next Time," like most of Baldwin's writings, is about this alienation.

Two essays, one long and one short, make up the book. The short essay, "My Dungeon Shook," originally appeared in *Progressive* magazine. The long essay, "Down at the Cross," originally appeared in the *New Yorker* under the title, "Letter from a Region in My Mind," and the issue in which it came out is now a collector's item.

Baldwin, more than any other writer of our times, has succeeded in restoring the personal essay to its place as a form of creative literature. From his narrow vantage point of personal grievance, he has opened a "window on the world." He plays the role traditionally assigned to thinkers concerned with the improvement of human conditions—that of alarmist. He calls our attention to things in our society that need to be corrected and things that need to be celebrated.

The narrowness of his vantage point is no assurance that he is right or wrong; nor does it negate the importance of what he is saying. The oppressed person is the best authority on his oppression.

Racism in the United States has forced every Negro into a prolonged and pathetic war. He is either at war against his oppression or against the weakness within himself that frustrates his ability to participate in this war effectively. The saddest participants in this war for mental and physical survival and basic human dignity are those Negroes who think that they are removed from it—those who live with the illusion that they have been integrated. The limitation and uniqueness of Baldwin's vantage point is that he is addressing his audience from the war zone.

The first essay, subtitled "Letter to My Nephew on the One Hundredth Anniversary of the Emancipation," is Baldwin's advice to a young relative entering the area of racial conflict on the anniversary of the proclamation that is supposed to have set his people free. The thrust of the author's eloquent anger is deep.

This innocent country set you down in a ghetto in which, in fact, it intended that you should perish. Let me spell out precisely what I mean by that, for the heart of the matter is here, and the root of my dispute with my country. You were born where you were born and faced the future that you faced because you were black and for no other reason. The limits of your ambition were, thus, expected to be set forever. You were born into a society which spelled out with brutal clarity, and in as many ways as possible, that you were a worthless human being. You were not expected to aspire to excellence: you were expected to make peace with mediocrity.

Wherever you have turned, James, in your short time on this earth, you have been told where you could go and what you could do (and how you could do it) and where you could live and whom you could marry. I know your countrymen do not agree with me about this, and I hear them saying, "You exaggerate." They do not know Harlem, and I do. So do you. Take no one's word for anything, including mine — but trust your experience. Know whence you came. If you know whence you came, there is really no limit to where you can go.

This is close to the root of the matter. The Negro was not brought to the United States to be given democracy. When the promise of democracy was made, it was not made to him, and this is the main reason why the growth of democracy in this nation is retarded. Nonetheless, Baldwin advises his nephew not to despair:

You came from sturdy, peasant stock, men who picked cotton and dammed rivers and built railroads, and in the teeth of the most terrifying odds, achieved an unassailable and monumental dignity. You came from a long line of poets, some of the greatest poets since Homer. One of them

*said: "The very time I thought I was lost, my dungeon shook
and my chains fell off." You know, and I know that the
country is celebrating one hundred years of freedom one
hundred years too soon.*

The long essay, "Down at the Cross," is brilliantly
written, though much too long and involved for the
meagerness of its message. In essence, it consists of
Baldwin's reflections on growing up in Harlem and on
how this ghetto upbringing influenced him. Baldwin's
evaluation of the Black Muslims and their leader, Elijah
Muhammad, tells us more about the author than about
his subject. As a guest in the home of Muhammad, he
seems to have vacillated between personal attraction
and ideological estrangement. He speaks of his host as
follows:

*I felt I was back in my father's house – as indeed, in a
way, I was – and I told Elijah that I did not care if white
and black people married and that I had many white friends.
I would have no choice, if it came to it, but to perish with
them, for (I said to myself, but not to Elijah) "I love a few
people and they love me and some of them are white, and
isn't love more important than color?"*

But the people in control of the power structure of
the United States have already answered Baldwin's
question in the negative. This answer is one of the main
reasons for the existence of the Black Muslims, for in
spite of all that can justifiably be said against them,
they have found what most Negroes are still searching
for—a way of reclaiming their dignity as human beings.

Baldwin is a highly regarded intellectual, the most
honored Negro writer since Richard Wright. Yet the
word "struggle," inseparable from the existence of the
Negro people, rarely appears in his work, nor as a
novelist has he yet created a single Negro character
who attains stature in a fight against his condition.
Neither does he show any awareness of the economic

base for oppression. These are serious limitations in a man hailed by many as the spokesman for his people.

There is a tangential aspect of Baldwin that requires brief comment. That is the cult of white followers that has grown up around him. These disciples flock to all his public appearances as to some masochistic ceremony of penance. It is as though they cry out: "Oh, Jimmy, punish us for the sins we have committed against your people." Tears yes, action never. For them Baldwin has become a sponge, soaking up the wastes of their conscience. In fairness to Baldwin, one must say that this cult is not of his making nor is it under his control.

A lot of people are hearing Baldwin's words but missing his message. What the Negro wants is justice, not sympathy; and if justice is not forthcoming, there may well be "the fire next time"—and sooner than we think.

Charles E. Wilson

❧

EDUCATION IN HARLEM—
I. S. 201 IN PERSPECTIVE

W HEN A COLONIZED people cannot recognize or does
not understand the existence, the reality, the mecha-
nisms, and the consequences of its own colonization,
the colonial system is quite secure. Nevertheless, the
colonized make a number of attempts at reform, re-
vitalization, and even rebellion—attempts which are
either doomed from the start or which make a great
deal of noise before returning conditions to the status
quo. Sometimes conditions are—if possible—worsened.
Unwittingly, the colonized invest vast energies in these
efforts to end specific abuses—poverty, poor public
school system, job discrimination, and unequal administration of justice. But since these inequities are *not*
isolated accidents or inadvertent shortcomings of the
social order, as so many maintain, such efforts to bring
about change are largely wasted. For the system may
make concessions in one sector and withhold in another.

Most disheartening is the fact that so few of the
colonized actually learn from their experiences. The
majority are prepared to repeat the same mistakes and
play the same games again and again.

Harlem's colonials have tried for generations to im-

prove the public schools for their children. Their latest
reform attempt—the I.S. 201 Complex Demonstration
District—stands as a monument to the fact that break-
ing the grip of colonialism and bringing about real
change in education is a gargantuan task. It is certainly
beyond the self-seeking opportunism of the urban prim-
itives, beyond the wisdom of the all-knowing Negro
mother figures, beyond the litanies of blackness, beyond
the militance of fashionable revolutionary rhetoric, beyond the programmatic mindlessness, the technological
incompetence and sterile professionalism of nonwhite
Bureaucrats and, certainly, far beyond the fun and
games of the poverticians and Poverty Program graduates.

For what is at issue in the public education struggle
is not merely the replacement of white administrators
by nonwhites, who now refer to themselves as black
but remain staunch bureaucrats. It is the replacement
of unfeeling, unthinking colonialists or neocolonialists
of whatever color by persons who are working toward
the liberation of all human beings. What is at issue is
not merely the replacement of irrelevant curriculum
approaches and traditional teaching methods, but the
replacement of the basic concept of a fixed, centrally
conceived, job- and status-oriented system of learning
which does not correspond to the needs or the cultural
milieu of the individual. What is at issue is not merely
the development of a means of professional accounta-
bility, but the development of a means for local community governance and local community responsibility,
as well as the emergence of systems to make genuine
citizen participation and involvement a reality. Within
the "Negro"–Black–Puerto Rican enclaves, what is at
issue is not merely the removal of the obvious vestiges
of colonialist oppression but the prevention of community creaming[129], the development of a responsive,
responsible system of community representation and
the end of manipulation of the *lumpen proletariat* by
community hustlers. In short what is at issue is the

development of a concept of group relatedness, the formation of a truly humane community and the end of colonialism's inhuman use of human beings.

With so much at stake, it is no wonder that colonialism, its dupes, its allies and its adherents of all colors waged such a clever struggle at I.S. 201 in Harlem. This is not the first time that colonialism has been faced with this kind of problem. Over the years, faced with similar challenges, it has been able to develop a number of different responses. On the one hand, it may offer some kind of token reform: so-called decentralization of school authority may be made to appear like local governance. Such maneuvers are designed to give the appearance of change without the substance.

More imaginatively, colonialism has learned that it can better preserve the status quo by establishing the neocolonial treadmill. By permitting pseudo-nations or pseudo-communities to be "free" or to conceive of themselves as self-determining within ambiguous, ill-defined guidelines for an indefinite trial period, colonialism can then manipulate the internal conflicts, competing petty ambitions, ideological differences and technological backwardness of the colonized in order to produce a resynthesis of the old order.

Within communities like the I.S. 201 area in Harlem and similar places clear across this land there is already an abundance of social, economic, attitudinal, religious and ethnic differences to exploit. Colonialism's second response is therefore a realistic one. The rebellious are funnelled through successive stages of the neo-colonialist process until areas of rebellion become virtual vassal states, with so many energies dissipated in internal conflicts that the areas lose all potential for rebellion. It is not that these trial enclaves fail to produce innovations and significant adaptations in education—or in any substantive area for that matter. For, if we take I.S. 201 as an example, such areas do produce genuine adaptations. There just is not the magical transformation that so many residents of these areas so desperately seek. For often the institutions of these areas are in far too scandalous a state of neglect to attain instant success. And more importantly, the relentless neocolonial juggernaut is just too formidable for rebels who possess neither an ideology, nor a clear-cut set of goals, nor technical expertise—rebels without a long-term strategic approach. Such rebels are led by individuals frequently unencumbered by a sense of history, limited by a grim anti-intellectualism, hobbled by lack of capacity to trust anyone—even themselves—and driven to extremism by underdeveloped egos paired with overdeveloped vocal chords.

Thus the first task for individuals in other communities faced with the need for educational change is to learn and remember the experience of I.S. 201 in Harlem. Second, experienced individuals and communities should make every effort to bypass the two colonial barriers standing in the path of real change. These barriers are the official temporizing that changes nothing but does in fact establish a new layer of protection for the old order (educational decentralization is an example of this kind of barrier) and the many traps of neocolonialism.

And incidentally, the way to neocolonialism is paved with militant speeches, fighting press notices, verbal postures and praiseworthy gestures. In the 201 Complex case, at least, the trip to neocolonialism began at the same time the first steps were taken toward freedom. The slide to neocolonialism is made all the more inevitable by a refusal to go to the people, a failure to invite, even to urge the people to participate, a reluctance to mobilize the people of the community *in their own behalf*. That, then, is the lesson of 201 for black people, for Harlem's people. Neocolonialism's programs, plans and panaceas may slow the most wary revolutionary, but neocolonialism will certainly capture outright those colonized groups who don't recognize or see the traps.

"201"—A Place, A Hope, However Faint

The people of 201 did not set out to fall into the snares of neocolonialism. Those heroic folk had waged a courageous struggle against the so-called expertise of the educational bureaucrats, against the claims of the United Federation of Teachers (UFT) and against the intransigence of the Central Board of Education.

The Struggle between these rebels and the municipal educational establishment was not publicly recognized as an anti-colonial struggle. (In America nothing is ever called by its right name.) The struggle was joined over the question of local community control of education. The community control advocates sought to withdraw certain pivotal functions from the central headquarters of the urban school system. In place of centralized authority they demanded:

1. local control of the budget and budget processes
2. local control of the process and practice of construction and major repair
3. local control of personnel practices
4. local control of the right to purchase or participate in the purchase of books and supplies
5. local control of the right to curriculum reform
6. maintenance of the physical integrity of the district to insure a fair evaluation of the district's functioning.

The case for community control actually lay in each community's classrooms. In these classrooms of the poorer districts until the time of the Demonstration, pitifully little had been done for, or with, the children and parents of that depressed area. After all, weren't the children . . . uneducable?

As in so many black and minority group residential areas throughout the nation, the school facilities of I.S. 201 area were outmoded, inadequate, understaffed, with no health counselors, no classes for visually handicapped children and but one class on the intermediate level for the intellectually gifted serving the 3,900 young people of the community. And of course, over half of the district children were reading two or more years below grade level. Almost 40 per cent of the teachers were permanent substitutes and there were but ten student teachers for the five schools of the district.[130] Under the old order, teachers possessed a truly important privilege—they were able to label children an "uneducable," "disruptive," and "disturbed," even though many of those same teachers possessed only the most tenuous grasp of basic teaching and classroom management skills. More than a location, this section running westward from the Triboro Bridge to 7th Avenue, and bounded by 124th and 132nd Streets, was the scene of a seemingly unending struggle against a system of centrally directed bureaucratic totalitarianism. For the rest of the Harlem community the area became a symbol of the dogged determination of parents and community activists not to submit to the petty, pedagogical tyranny of an unfeeling school system.

It was for this area that the Board of Education proposed its devious and defective experimental scheme for parent participation and community involvement. And it proposed it for this area because the area was already in an active state of revolt against the educational Establishment, because ethnic and ideological differences existed there and could be compounded by the confused opportunism of the poverticians and War on Poverty grads. The Establishment proposed a change in the governance of education for blacks because such a change would almost surely arouse white colonials.[131]

The educational Establishment knew that real change in education is difficult to achieve for the following reasons:

1. the diffuseness and multiplicity of educational goals

2. the lack of an established engineering function and scholarship habits as part of the educational system
3. the lack of evaluation and feedback capacity within the educational system
4. the existence of reticence, suspicion and fear on the part of educators
5. the existence of management and funding problems in most systems.

Related to these factors inhibiting educational change, there is also a hierarchy of levels of change. From the easiest to the hardest to accomplish, these changes range from:

1. substitution—replacement of one insulated element by another, for example, the adoption of a new workbook
2. alteration—minor change which may have unforeseen system-wide repercussions, for example, acquisition of new lab space and equipment
3. variations—shifts in the equilibrium of the client system
4. restructure—fundamental change in the system's structure and relationships
5. value change—change in national character and the production of a new kind of man. This last is certainly the most difficult and most complex.[132]

After surveying these barriers and the various potential levels of change, the educational Establishment could be almost assured that real educational change would be difficult, if not impossible, for a "Demonstration District." And when the notion of change for black people in public education also involved a threat to the professional status and vested interests of those at the top of the ethnic pecking order, the New York City system was certain that resistance would be total.

There were just too many people and groups benefiting from the flow of dollars into a decadent school structure, founded on false and archaic assumptions of teaching and learning, for the advocates of community control ever to cut through the traps and snares of the neocolonialist maze. Especially, if community leaders didn't know the game or underestimated the colonialists' tactics. But the advocates of community control did try to overcome neocolonialism.

The People Tried

The people, the students, the teachers, the Governing Board[133] and the neophyte staff tried and at first, despite numerous snares, some progress was made. Subtle sabotage of the system by the central bureaucracy at more than one level was commonplace. One unsigned memorandum read:

I will leave it to your discretion whether or not to accept the invitation to visit I.S. 201. However, I can give you a hint on what to expect if you accept. You will probably be asked to evaluate libraries and probably compare them with suburban districts or those in more affluent districts in New York and to help seek to provide funds to upgrade these libraries. You may also be prepared to have any report you issue to them used in an attack on the policies of the present Board of Education. This seems to be par for the course lately. . .

By the cleverly placed finger and the quiet insidious whisper, the bureaucratic establishment would try to slow or hinder any effort to improve conditions. And yet some people in the 201 area tried even harder. During the prolonged strike of Fall, 1968, the teachers and the community kept the schools fully operative.

The union also assisted the educational Establishment in its efforts to sidetrack and frustrate 201's community control of schools. For the UFT, through a kind of symbiotic attachment to the Establishment, had a great deal at stake in any experiment to educate the colonized underclasses. The UFT had just begun to savor its own hard-won privileges. Now, reinforced by shortsighted professional solidarity and buoyed by a conviction of expertise, the union provided the most dynamic defenders and even shock troops for the social order.

Collaboration between union and bureaucracy was necessary because the bureaucracy has no real authority of its own, no legitimacy of its own: it is on leading strings to the Mayor, on leading strings to Albany, on leading strings to trade unions. It loves to talk about keeping politics out of schools, but it went hand in hand with the UFT to Albany to fight for legislation effectively maintaining the status quo. If the bureaucracy lacks the authority to lead the Board of Education, it also lacks the authority and connections within the system to dictate policy. Its posture recalls the politics of the dog without the bone. He has no bone but he has no intention of letting any other dog get it, and he'll fight to prevent him doing so.

The news media, those self-appointed guardians of the truth, also afforded verbal cover for both the union and the educational Establishment. By employing the techniques of confrontation coverage and in some instances seeking to discredit academic accomplishments, the media were able to distract public attention from the solid achievements of the 201 complex and focus attention instead on its exotic aspects and its internal struggles and dissentions. The press would of course misdirect attention at the very time when the New York State Legislature was considering final school decentralization legislation.

Sophisticated observers have long given up looking for accurate reports in the press or hoping that reporters would remember, research and probe deeply enough into issues to find the social truth behind social appearances. That knowledgeable people no longer look for accuracy in reporting is a sharp indictment of the media. Some of those who covered the story of the rebellion of community people against their educational masters are even officially headquartered at the Board of Education. From this vantage point at 110 Livingston Street, they maintain their "objectivity!" But many a black man has learned that such objectivity will always be used against him.

The middle-class style, predispositions and inclinations of the media assure both the union and the school system special access to it. While they deny any conspiratorial relationship between themselves and the educational Establishment, the observed behavior of the press suggests yet another example of class collusion without conspiracy which keeps protest-oriented minorities powerless.

Despite such formidable opposition concrete progress was made. One extremely imaginative school medical screening program, manned by community medical aides, indicated that fully 28 per cent of the District's youngsters had educationally significant vision disabilities, while another 4 per cent had significant hearing limitations. Fewer than 20 percent of these youngsters had been identified by the normal school medical screening procedures.[134]

Experimentally, the Schools of the Future's Words-in-Color reading approach and the use of Cuisenaire rods in math instruction provided exciting new instructional programs in a section of the city where there were few new offerings before the Demonstration era. Efforts were also made to compile and publish a Community Information Manual for the 201 area. This manual sought to make immediately available to teachers, counselors and families of school-age youngsters the necessary information about the social, educational, recreational, employment, medical and social service resources of the community. Reasoning that information and access to information were essential to genuine citizen participation, the compilers of the manual sought to give substance to the growing sense of community and provide to the people of the area a sense of the community's assets as a living environment.

Efforts to reorganize in-service teacher training offerings into a more relevant staff development program —as part of the overall development of school personnel services—were part of the District's "total" approach. Hitherto fragmented areas such as guidance and special education, health, social work, psychological service and psychiatric service were all brought together under the Pupil Personnel Service in order to promote more flexible services to the communities. The District's school business management was modernized, updated and used in such a way as to provide new opportunities, new programs and new educational experiences for students, parents and teachers.

Thus, despite the efforts of a formidable array of adversaries and in spite of the numerous roadblocks set up in its path, the 201 District was able to surmount the barriers to change. Local spirit was high. Morale was impressive, and sacrifice was the order of the day. The existence of hostile forces outside the area bent on destroying this fragile dream of freedom, may also have served as a deterrent to some of the more obvious forms of local opportunism. And those "sacred" reading levels edged forward in three of the five schools of the 201 area!

Big Jobs Left Undone

Yet despite demonstrable evidence of improvement and the reckless adventurism of the UFT, the community was still not really mobilized. It was not really politicized. Efforts to involve and to mobilize the people were discouraged. PTAs and PAs (Parent Associations) never grew to the proportions needed to move a popular uprising beyond local rebellion to broad-based popular revolution. And strangely, the rebels who seemed so dismayed by the ultimate failure of the Central Board of Education to delegate powers to them, made no outstanding effort to sway the State Legislators, made no outstanding effort to turn out the people in protest or mobilize them around the schools and education issues. The rebels were on their way to becoming a new local elite.

During the legislative sessions, some community-control advocates offered the notion of a separate Board of Education for Harlem as a serious proposal. This proposal ignored the reality that the lay Board of Education cannot control the kind of bureaucratic systems that presently exist. The proposal ignored the fact that while everyone talks about Harlem as a community, it is in fact several communities made up of half a dozen ethnically different neighborhoods. It is an area with, to put it mildly, a mixture of factions. Highly volatile when brought together, these factions seem at odds with one another more often than they are in agreement. Further, the proposal for an independent Harlem district fails to take into account the major significant finding of the Demonstration's experience, the feasibility of the complex unit, an organizational unit smaller than the customary New York City school district of twenty to thirty schools but bigger than the single school. The reality that this proposal does not face is that unless there is significant training and political reeducation of nonwhite professional bureaucrats, Harlem will remain a colonial outpost, legislation not withstanding.

Yet the offering of this proposal split the forces pressing for change through legislation into two: community control advocates on the one hand and those seeking an Independent Harlem School System on the other. This split assured the passage of legislation dooming both the school experiment and chances for any real local control.

With the passage of the so-called School Decentralization Bill, the recasting of the New York City system to protect present vested interests and organized self-

interest groups (the teachers' union and parochial
school interest) was complete. The power in education
was placed solidly in the hands of the present structure. But more importantly, passage of the legislation
made the lures and snares of self-seeking opportunism
more attractive and more profitable in the rebel camp.
Individual school administrators now raised the banner
of administrative prerogatives (another mask for privilege). Elected members of the local Board ceased to
be representatives of the people who elected and selected them and began to conceive of themselves as
"the people." Since the community control movement
had never fully worked out its political and educational
ideology and had never agreed on a definition of its
goals, the movement became trapped in an unending
stream of verbal militancy. It adopted the habit of sub-
stituting press conferences for pressure, discredited
serious thought or self-criticism as "academic," and
utilized protest tactics for each and every situation.
The doors to neocolonialism were now fully opened.
Only the way to neocolonialism needed to be prepared.

Preparing the Way to Neocolonialism

The people of the 201 community did not plan to
head toward neocolonialism. In fact, many of them believed that they were headed toward a "new day" of
educational change. Everybody saw change coming.
The way to neocolonialism is often misunderstood by
those colonials who do not know or do not recognize
the danger signs. Beginning with the mere slowing of
the forward thrust, neocolonialism, then a barely perceptible jolt, shifts into a backwards motion, at first
slow, followed by a more rapid slide and, finally, a headlong plunge. And that is what took place at the I.S.
201 complex.

Two factors contributed to the slowing of the forward thrust of the complex. One factor derived from
the basic structure of the Demonstration Project it-

self, the other from the basic outlook of the rebellious participants. From the first, the 201 District was an imperfect federation of a part of Central Harlem and a part of East Harlem.[135] As a result, the Project was subject to a double dose of the divisive antagonisms that are part and parcel of low income residential areas. Ethnic conflicts between blacks and Puerto Ricans threatened the unstable coalition from the outset, for the representatives of the two groups occupying the bottom rungs of the civic ladder were and are constantly at odds.

It would have required a rare political genius to maintain this coalition in a state of equilibrium, and these rebels for the most part were just ordinary folks. Although united by the reality of exploitation and by a shared low status, these two urban groups are just too busy trying to get off the bottom rung to achieve long term political cooperation. With neither a class ideology nor a common objective, and separated by language, values, expectations and even by the degree of expertise available to them, the groups were still expected to play that most complex of political games, coalition politics. As a result, there were personal antagonisms and misunderstandings across group lines, culture shock and an undercurrent of friction which occasionally burst forth in torrents of emotion.

Compounding this structural-organizational weakness, the rebels exhibited a marked lack of trust, and that barrier to institution formation, the oppositional mentality. Technocrats were, of course, regarded with suspicion; Puerto Ricans were suspicious of blacks and vice versa; some whites by their mere presence in the rebel camp were objects of mistrust. Substantive changes in the schools were suspect. For example, changes aimed at humanizing the penal structure of the public schools were resisted by some of the victims themselves. To some, technology itself was suspect. Knowledgeable opinions or technical expertise were also suspect. In fact, to many of the untutored rebels, expertise or knowledge were synonomous with whiteness. In such an environment no one was to be fully trusted. This deep-rooted suspicion helped keep many capable people away.

In place of representatives with technical and political competence, the rebels chose individuals of high verbal militancy or persons they thought they could handle. A number of these "unskilled militants" and "trustees" employed elaborate strategies to mask their personal inadequacies. Gifted with well developed oppositional mentalities, for example, they used espionage techniques and roundabout means of communication rather than rely on the telephone network. Not infrequently these same individuals still referred to their ties with one or another of the former colonial ruling cliques. The mental habits of the colonial bureaucracy are difficult for bureaucrats—white and nonwhite—to break. In this climate of suspicion and uncertainty verbal output and posturing were mistaken for capacity.

Slowly it became apparent that some of the very loudest rebels-without-a-cause really only wanted good white schools in black face. This, the possibility that the rebels and the former colonizers may have held the same basic values, was the most disturbing revelation of all. The argument between such rebels and their former oppressors was really not about new education for the colonized but new educational *leaders* for the colonized, and the hustlers in the rebel camp envisioned an endless gravy train.

Predictable too was the petit-bourgeois mentality of the "rebels." Their aspirations, life styles and tastes were not those of self-sacrificing revolutionaries. They preferred the right label, high-status brand names, the expense account circuit. Many of them considered the investment of time their most noble sacrifice to the cause.

All these shortcomings made the rebels easy marks for the adventurism and envy of both black and white *lumpen proletariat,* and even easier targets for the flattery of so-called sympathetic whites. These encouraged rebels to indulge in bravado and big talk, while the nonwhite *lumpen proletariat* surveyed the scene for the special prizes that they wished to abrogate at a future time, meanwhile applauding every show of defiance as "revolutionary."

Having successfully gained a foothold, the rebels in a large measure became transformed into poor carbon copies—rule-ridden, directive-prone, semi-authoritarian, bureaucratic—of the former oppressors. One of the leading rebels boasted that he was a black bureaucrat, as if that was a badge of honor. The rebels wished those whom they led to trust them, but they trusted no one.

There were, of course, interminable debates on all kinds of issues. The local folk began to believe that *they* could make technical policy decisions without recourse to technical information. In most such debates, reason took a back seat to flamboyant rhetoric and to —of all things—*old school traditions*! By turning up the volume of their discontent or by adopting petulant postures, those with personal ambitious to gratify could gain as much consideration as those putting forward sound proposals. Not blessed with foresight or the habit of planning, the rebels were outstanding at handing out blame for their errors . . . after the event. Meanwhile, they avoided consulting their own constituents— the people of the local community.

Not all the rebels, their education employees and community control advocates were so distracted. Some came to see their role as one of service to the community, and acted accordingly. Others showed real concern for problems of youth and education and the development of new goals, new structures, methods and techniques within the community. But such people were easily outlipped and outmaneuvered by the sharpies. The committed and skilled were either removed, moved along of their own volition, or were buried in a welter of unsubstantiated rumors and the ever-filled sack of dirty names.

Paving the Way With Green

The way to neocolonialism was, of course, paved with green. Paved with money from another one of those all-purpose community tinkering proposals—the Community Education Center proposal. Like the Poverty Programs and the Model Cities proposals, the CEC may have the same effect—disorganization—on disadvantaged communities.

Wisely (or should one say shrewdly?) the 201 community avoided the first hurdle of this proposal by resisting the tendency to fragment community power inherent in the Program's basic guidelines. These guidelines had mandated the formation of a CEC advisory board. In the 201 community especially, the formation of such a board would have institutionalized conflicting educational governing groups within a single community, one of the groups enjoying prominence, the other possessing resources for jobs, special projects and services. Having successfully vaulted this first hurdle, the Poverty Program mentality of some of the rebels took over and assured that they would fall before the second obstacle—fall victim, that is, to poor programming (at high salaries). For CEC's millions whetted the appetites of the rebels and prompted nepotism. The prospect of government dollars flowing in from CEC prompted the resurrection of every debunked poverty scheme developed in the past ten years for East and Central Harlem. Most of these proposals tended to increase the cash flow to local merchants and even to local realtors for storefront facilities. Can you imagine ghetto rebels subsidizing ghetto merchants and slumlords?

The need for display prompted the use of funds to equip offices and purchase facilities. And there was that not-so-subtle encouragement of "Black Capitalism" from many in the program. Of course, the capitalism referred to here was their own capitalism. When confronted by technocrats who would not be a party to this kind of programming the lay community leadership[136] chose a new cadre of poverticians[137] to operate the CEC program.

The charade was now in full swing. For that is what happens when a program poorly conceived, poorly structured, and poorly led takes over, exacerbating existing conflicts and fostering "every man for himself—God for us all" type of ambition. Of course, the local community sees the "game" and wants in on the goodies . . . and local community members find ways in. Thus the rebels were now transformed into counter-rebels beating back some challengers and buying off others and always ducking questions.

The downward spiral to neocolonialism was now accelerating. Totally absorbed in "the game" to the virtual exclusion of all else, the counter-rebels sought to maintain their gains by a series of alliances (liaisons, public relations maneuvers, and public displays). Joining them in the efforts were bureaucrats of uncertain skills and less certain tenure. The bureaucrats now played both ends against the middle. The latter group saw such unions useful as a form of two-fold insurance.

Surveying this through its agents, by this time in the front ranks of the "rebels," the educational Establishment makes no effort to stop the charade, which it allows to go on under what amounts to a sword of Damocles. Why let the sword fall anyway? The District has traveled the full route:

1. rebellion—the retreat of the Establishment
2. early efforts—group morale high
3. counter-rebellion—self-seeking opportunism prompts internal conflict
4. more opportunism and disenchantment
5. neocolonialism—the choice of reabsorbing or letting the enclaves remain free.

Colonialism Has Succeeded Again

This time it uses nonwhites to maintain the colonial order. It is nonwhites who will hold one another in check and few of the nonwhites know the game. In the words of an Ashanti proverb, "By the time the fool has learned the game, the players have dispersed."

Games People Play

The 201 story is not unlike the Poverty-programs story, not unlike the Model Cities story, not unlike all the reform efforts. It is a story of social tinkering without social intent. It is a story of Games People Play. The games of the winners and games of the losers.

For the Establishment it is the story of a route to domestic educational neocolonialism. A route employing ambitious nonwhites with white value structures to do the job for the power order. It is a story of how to keep people enslaved without chaining them to the wall. It is also a story of how local leadership is mentally or financially co-opted, of how those being led are seduced, of how community power and responsibility are destroyed under the heading of "community development," of how the onlookers are deliberately confused in the name of successful maintenance of the status quo.

But the 201 Complex story is more than the Establishment's story. It is an example in microcosm of the games nonwhites play or try to play. *Word games* (overblown rhetoric), *money games* (big salaries for small contributions), *career games* (promotion to prominence without capacity), *technical games* (technology is a white thing so let's not use it), *job games* (write a proposal to fund some hair-brained scheme). It is not surprising that the power order allows such games to be played or that the Establishment rewards those among the poor and nonwhite who play. Nor should it be surprising that the rebels, soon to be counter-rebels, are so much like the "BOO-GE-WASEES." For the game should be played, wittingly or unwittingly, in such a way that the long-term colonial interests of the Establishment are served.

The style, attitudes and behavior of these rebels and so many like them are deeply revealing. Their refusal to go to the people, their failure to mobilize and involve the community, their suspicion, their lack of technical know-how demonstrate that they themselves fear the people they claim to speak for. Their interest lies in using the notion of "the community" to meet their own fantasy needs for power and prestige. Their fear stems from the fact that if the mass truly awakens and the quality of life is significantly improved and blackened, they (the rebels) will all be out of jobs. As such the rebels' behavior is more characteristic of the *lumpen proletariat* and the power narcissists. It is indicative of the disorganized state of the movement today that the *lumpen proletariat* wields so much influence.

This behavior is not unlike the behavior of yesteryear's nonwhite bourgeois leadership, now displaced by the antics and rhetoric of present day community rebels.[138] Not too strangely, the personal aspirations and tastes of the rebels mark them as BOO-GE-WASEES. Their verbal tirades, the name calling (bourgies) reserved for their class competitors in the colonial pecking order, are merely tokens of envy. The rebels in this case and similar situations exploit the sincerity, earnestness and insecurity of people with skills. Those without skills are only too happy to go along, for disagreement is made to seem tantamount to disloyalty. But because these rebels and their allies substitute a revolutionary rhetoric for a revolutionary morality the result is a new nonwhite operational system of exploitation, a system covertly manipulated by whites.

Conceived without an ideology, the 201 Complex rebellion was unable to counter the educational Establishment's ability to conversion, subversion, and diversion of its efforts at change. The rebels failed to realize that successful efforts against colonialism occur when intellectuals and the skilled join hands with the people —not when the people chop the heads from the intellectuals and the skilled. Participation and involvement of community people should be recognized as difficult, subject to all kinds of harassments and burdens.

That the people of I.S. 201 Complex accomplished so much in the early period is to their undying credit. That some later succumbed to the blandishments of colonialism is no reason to discard the concept of the community. But there is a real need for developing a means of rewarding and recognizing those who do serve the best interest of the community, those who remain in contact with that community and continue the process of politically educating the people. Similarly, there has to be a way to punish or get rid of those who either cannot or will not act on behalf of all the dispossessed. Otherwise, nonwhites and blacks will continue to fight one another.

Since education reflects the values of a society the emerging black community should expect to see these very same games in many other areas—education, urban planning, housing, recreation and politics. They have already been seen in poverty and Model City areas. Games of colonialism, games of exploitation, games of social and racial sado-masochism.

If other communities can remember 201 in terms of its early bright hope then *all is not lost.* . . . If other communities do not forget the lessons of neocolonialism at some future date, some local engagements *may be won.* . . .

If people of other communities never forget that neither slavery, white colonialism nor neocolonialism can succeed without the cooperation of some of the nonwhites, then the *first link in the slave chain will have been broken.*

John Henrik Clarke

~❧~

FOUR MEN OF HARLEM—
THE MOVERS AND THE SHAKERS

1. A. PHILIP RANDOLPH

LONG BEFORE the civil rights and Black Power explosions, A. Philip Randolph had earned the right to be called the leader who can lead. Harlem was his base of operations.

For nearly fifty years, A. Philip Randolph has been a leader in the fight for full citizenship rights for black Americans. He is today the elder statesman of Afro-American labor leaders. His credentials now read: father of the historic (1963) March on Washington; President, Negro American Labor Council; lone "Negro" member of the Executive Council of AFL-CIO; International President of the Brotherhood of Sleeping Car Porters.

He proposed the first civil rights "March on Washington" in 1940-41, which resulted in President Roosevelt's famous Executive Order 8802 creating the President's Fair Employment Practice Committee.

He was born in 1889 in a rural town near Jacksonville, Florida, at a time when the Deep South was perfecting the combination of "Negro" disfranchisement and violence which would keep white supremacy unbroken for the next sixty years. After finishing high school, he left the South to continue his education.

In New York City he took some night courses at the College of the City of New York. Being an avid reader, he made very good use of the public library and stated, in later years, that most of his education was obtained by reading "serious books."

In 1917, Randolph began to attract public notice. With Chandler Owen, he launched a monthly magazine, *The Messenger*. This was a strange partnership. Owen was brilliant, witty, versatile, often likened to H. L. Mencken. Randolph was earnest, plodding, and absolutely unswerving. The editors blazoned from the masthead of their publication: "The Only Radical Negro Magazine in America." In an early issue Randolph declared, "We do not accept the doctrine of the old, reactionary 'Negroes' that the 'Negro' is satisfied to be himself, because of our recognition that the principle of social equality is the only sure guarantee of social justice."

Randolph got into his first big trouble by protesting against World War One. He refused to serve and went about the country making speeches against America's joining the war, against "Negroes" fighting in it.

"I was fundamentally and morally opposed to the war," he has said. "I am a pacifist so far as national wars are concerned. I criticized in *The Messenger* and in public speeches the hypocrisy of the slogan 'making the world safe for democracy' when 'Negroes' were lynched, jim-crowed, disfranchised and segregated in America."

In 1918, while making one of his public protests in Cleveland, Ohio, he was arrested by the Department of Justice and thrown into jail. Although he was released in a few days, "patriots" began to denounce him. One paper branded him "the most dangerous Negro in America."

The persecution simply drove him to fight harder. He stanchly held his stand as a pacifist and—much worse to his respectable friends—a Socialist. During and following the war, he ran for Secretary of State for New York, for the New York Assembly, and for Congress, all on the Socialist ticket. His ability to rouse a following, even in that early day, was shown when in 1917 over 25 per cent of the "Negroes" in New York City voted the Socialist ticket.

In 1925 the Pullman porter worked about seventy hours a week at an $18 wage—or 25 cents an hour. Tips brought his gross monthly income to about $100, from which he bought his uniform, shoe polish and dining-car meals—and so used up approximately one third of his earnings. Sometimes he'd wait all day at the Pullman office—at no pay—for an assignment. All this was set down in a "labor contract" negotiated with the company by a union formed and financed by the employer.

In constant fear of idleness and hunger, the porters were afraid to organize. Randolph began visiting them secretly in their homes, holding meetings in railroad yards. In three years he painfully put together locals with a total of 5,000 members.

Nine years of organizing rolled by. It was 1934, a Depression year, and the Brotherhood of Sleeping Car Porters still had no contract and no improved conditions. The porters' treasury was bare. Randolph's wife, a graduate of Howard University, had lost her job as a social worker. There was nothing with which to feed the family—Randolph, his wife, his mother and sister.

It was a dark hour. And now was added temptation. The late Fiorello H. La Guardia, then mayor of New York, offered Randolph a $12,000-a-year job on the city payroll.

"You'll never organize the porters," La Guardia said.

How could La Guardia understand that the fight to organize the porters was more than a union drive alone? If Randolph could hold out, he would show that a black American could achieve a goal under the most adverse conditions. The whole black community was involved. Randolph borrowed subway fare to go down to City Hall to say "No" to La Guardia.

Three years later he won a National Labor Relations Board employee election and with it a contract from Pullman. It called for a 40-hour week, a base salary of $100 a month, and machinery for settling grievances. To black Americans, the Brotherhood with its initial 18,000 members was a more significant organization than the United Automobile Workers with its then 400,000 members.

Success began to come. Porters flocked into the union. Churches and newspapers swung in behind the movement. The 1934 amendments to the Railway Labor Act, outlawing company unions and guaranteeing collective bargaining, gave the chance for victory. The porters and maids put up half a million dollars from their pitiful earnings to make the final push. After a whirlwind campaign in 1935, by a vote of 5,931 to 1,422, the workers chose the Brotherhood to speak for them in collective bargaining. And in 1937 in Chicago, the Pullman Company signed a second contract with the Brotherhood.

A mass meeting was held by Harlem porters to welcome Randolph back from his Chicago victory. He came bearing, gifts; $2 million in pay increases, a cut in porters' monthly mileage from 11,000 to 7,000 miles; shorter working time—240 hours a month instead of the old unending shifts. These were striking changes in work conditions.

Victory was no more a brake on Randolph's efforts than failure had been. He went right on working— dogged and plodding as ever. Since the Brotherhood was a member of the American Federation of Labor, he worked at conventions, at mass meetings, in committees and private talks to get the Federation to wipe out racial bars in all its unions. He pointed out that "labor had paid dearly for its own lack of democracy, for capital kept labor weakened for decades by the use of masses of unorganized and 'unaccepted' workers, first newly arrived immigrants and then the 'Negro' millions who swarmed up from the South to the industrial centers." He declared, "Labor can never fully win until it opens its doors freely and equally to all workers."

It took the Depression and the social revolution of the New Deal to unionize America. Pullman was forced by law to recognize any unions chosen by its employees, and owing to Randolph's tireless work, the porters once more overwhelmingly chose the Brotherhood. In 1937, twelve years to the day after he had begun, the Pullman Car Company signed its first agreement with A. Philip Randolph of the Sleeping Car Porters. Never before had a white employer signed an agreement with a black labor leader.

When the National Negro Congress was organized in the mid-nineteen-thirties, A. Philip Randolph became its President. This militant organization was a forerunner of present-day civil rights groups such as the Congress of Racial Equality (CORE) and the Student Non-Violent Coordinating Committee (SNCC).

In September 1940, Randolph visited the White House and asked that jim crow be taken out of the Army. President Roosevelt did not seem to know what to do. So Randolph left the White House not knowing what to do.

In the winter of 1940, the idea of marching thousands of blacks on Washington had spread everywhere. The march was to take place July 1, 1941. Randolph remembered what he had known as a boy. Black people have power, great power. The problem is to hitch it up to act in a great big way. "March," he said, "for jobs and to get rid of jim crow in the Army." He stayed on the streets—Seventh Avenue, Lenox Avenue and Eighth Avenue. He went into beauty shops, pool rooms, bars, stores and restaurants. He spoke on street corners and in movies.

In April, the President wrote letters asking all war plants to hire black workers. The people in Washington were worried about where the thousands of blacks would eat and sleep if they marched on the city. Randolph said that they expected to march into the hotels and restaurants.

He went to visit the President who greeted him warmly.

"Hello Phil," the President said. Then he began to tell stories and crack jokes.

Randolph stopped him. "Mr. President, time is passing. We want to talk about the problem of jobs for 'Negroes'. They are tired of being turned away at the gates because they are colored. They can't live like this. What are you going to do about it?"

"You're quite right, Phil," the President answered. "I am going to do something about it. You call off your march and I will do something. If you bring that many Negroes to Washington, there will be trouble. Somebody might get killed."

Randolph refused to call off the march unless the President would agree in writing that black Americans could have good jobs in war plants and in the government. But the President would not agree to do this— at this time.

He told Randolph on the telephone next day that he would have a group of people "to see that Negroes were given better jobs." He called the group the F.E.P.C. which meant Fair Employment Practice Committee. Then Randolph talked on the radio to all Afro-Americans. He told them not to march at that time, but to remain as watchdogs to see if the President's order was carried out.

The President's order said nothing about jim crow in the army. In 1948, Randolph held a meeting in Madison Square Garden. About 25,000 Afro-Americans came. They carried signs against going into the Army because of its jim crow. They said they would be better off in the jails. In March, 1948, Randolph and a committee of Afro-Americans went to see President Truman at the White House. Randolph declared that blacks were sick and tired of the government asking them to fight in the Army when they were treated so badly at home. They just would not go into the Army if it meant going into a jim-crow Army.

President Truman did not like this at all. But Randolph did not care. He returned to his soap-box speeches and told all the young men not to sign up for a jim-crow Army. He even stood in front of the White House and sold buttons which said, "Don't Join A Jim-Crow Army." A man named Grant Reynolds helped him.

At last, on July 26, 1948, President Truman decided to write an order which did away with jim crow in the Army.

Randolph was the only black Vice-President of the AFL-CIO. He was the President of the Brotherhood of Sleeping Car Porters, the National President of the Negro American Labor Council. He marched more than 30,000 young people in Washington in 1958-1959 to show that they really wanted white and "Negro" children to go to the same school. Randolph has been asked to visit the White House and discuss the problems of his people by more Presidents than any other Afro-American.

The March on Washington, August 28, 1963, was his twenty-one-year-old dream come true. He believed that as long as one person is not free, no persons are free, and he saw the March as a new beginning for freedom and for a better life for everybody. The planning and execution of this massive march was the high-water mark in his long and eventful career.

By this time, the itinerant preacher's son had been invited to the White House by four United States Presidents. Back in 1925, he had accompanied the militant black leader, W. Monroe Trotter, to an interview with Calvin Coolidge to protest against lynching. And on June 23, 1958, he was spokesman for a delegation of civil rights leaders who met with President Eisenhower. Two more Presidential visits—with Kennedy and Johnson—were to follow, but under radically different circumstances.

For late in 1962, in the midst of an upsurging civil rights revolution, A. Philip Randolph called black leaders together to map out plans for a new March on Washington. This time there would be no cancellation, despite political pressures. Randolph had become convinced that a dramatic display of mass action was essential if the nation was to make progress towards full civil rights. Trade unions, liberals, and religious groups lent unprecedented support to the plan, and on August 28, 1963, more than a quarter million Americans, black and white, descended on the Capitol in a demand for jobs and freedom.

As father and director of the March, the largest demonstration in the history of the country, Randolph had forged an extraordinary unity between the black community and its white allies, and in the process renewed his unsought position as "Dean of the Black Leaders."

2. FATHER DIVINE

Of the many religious Messiahs who came to public attention from the black urban ghetto, Father Divine had the longest, the most consistent, and in many ways the most mysterious career. This career reached its height and declined in Harlem.

He was a player in a great human drama that affected the lives of millions of people, black and white. He was the product of his times, and there is no way to understand him without some understanding of the interplay of forces, the human deprivation and social dislocations that produced the atmosphere in which he thrived. He gave hope to the hopeless, and he fed the hungry and restored their sense of worth and belonging.

No matter what he was to the rest of the world, to the people who found new life and lived again, stimulated by his presence and credo, he was real, he was father, he was God.

Father Divine and his movement did not emerge overnight. He was the beneficiary of a special atmosphere, time and situation that he did not create but that was essential for his emergence. His success with a large number of black and white people has deep historical roots, roots that are deep in Europe and even deeper in Africa. The white man's approach to religion has failed among a large number of white people. The Western black man's approach to religion—a colorful stepchild of the white man's approach—has failed among a large number of black people because of this religion's inability to touch the blacks' innermost psychic being.

Father Divine's movement had its greatest development in Harlem, the world's most famous ethnic ghetto. To understand this movement, it is necessary to understand Harlem and why other men and movements have flourished there.

When Father Divine arrived and began to set up his "Heavens" or "Kingdoms" around 1933, one era was ending and another was beginning. The period of the Harlem Renaissance was over, and it was followed by a national Depression. Father Divine moved into a vacuum left by the decline of the Garvey movement, and the passing of the first of the colorful cult leaders in Harlem, George Wilson Becton.

Both of these leaders gave large numbers of black people a sense of themselves, their identity, and their value as human beings for the first time. Marcus Garvey gave them a sense of nationhood, made them cooperative owners of a shipping line and cooperative

owners within their own communities. The decline
of his movement left a multitude of people stunned
and suspicious of other leaders and their promises.

In his book *Harlem, Negro Metropolis,* the Jamaican
poet and novelist Claude McKay gives the following
picture of Harlem on the eve of the emergence of
Father Divine:

*The church leaders of the community had gone a long
way toward letting the people take extreme license in
spiritual matters. No matter what their personal feelings,
they knew that they had to cater to the emotional needs
of their congregations. In spite of this catering, the regular
churches were not adequate outlets for the burning religious
energy of the black masses. The presence of a great Depression, when economic questions had to be answered as well
as religious ones, made this situation more acute. Cults were
multiplying in Harlem. Some of the New Messengers had
only a small following, a banjo and a tambourine. The side-
walks of Harlem were their churches.*

Among the cult leaders Becton was the star, and
Father Divine was, figuratively, waiting in the wings.

Claude McKay had this to say about Becton in the
same book:

*George Wilson Becton was the first of the great cult lead-
ers to excite the imagination and stir the enthusiasm of the
entire Harlem community. He was the supreme Godsman. He
started his career in Harlem just when the high tide of its
carnival was receding. That was in the beginning of the
nineteen-thirties. Harlem was the wild playground of New
York. A territory abandoned to big lawbreakers, it was the
"widest open" spot when Prohibition was in force and was
the headquarters of the great gangsters trafficking in bootleg
booze and narcotics. At night, its speakeasies drew together
around the same bar the sophisticates and aristocrats of
New York, the hoodlums and the criminals. Like gypsies
summoned for the divertissement of distinguished guests,
"Negro" performers provided rare entertainment. The spirit
of the times was reflected in the state of hectic ferment
among "Negroes."*

Becton invaded the notorious realm of freebooters with

his twelve young disciples and a splendid orchestra. Becton was tall, handsome and college-educated. Harlem cultists before his time were all illiterates. But Becton spoke the language of the educated "Negroes," although he knew how to reach the hearts of the common people. He styled his mission "The World's Gospel Feast." His meetings were not the loose corybantic revels of Father Divine's Kingdoms! They were patterns of order and grace. The congregation waited in hushed silence which was broken by soft strains of music. Pages in fine robes led the singing. The orchestra plunged the congregation into joyful swaying, as they sang gospel hymns to the titillating music of the dance hall. And Becton's commanding presence dominated the scene. Women, responsive to his agile movements and his well-modulated, persuasive voice, swayed like reed.

Becton's "the consecrated dime" ceremony diverted tens of thousands of dimes from the numbers racketeers to the church collections. Though it is hard to prove, this ceremony may have been the cause of his untimely death when his fame was at its peak.

One night in Philadelphia—May 21, 1933, to be precise—he was kidnapped by two white men and literally "taken for a ride" in his own car. When the car was found, Becton's body was punctured with bullets. He never became coherent enough to give any description of his abductors, or why they wanted him dead. Four days later he died in extreme agony.

The death of George Wilson Becton left the field of Harlem wide open for Father Divine to conquer. He now became the main attraction among Harlem cult leaders. The glorious domain of his Kingdoms of Peace was expanding. It was the beginning of his triumphant years in Harlem.

In the fall of 1933, the people of New York City were in the throes of a three-way election battle to decide who would be Mayor of this city. Only one of the contesting candidates saw fit to seek the support of Father Divine and his followers. On November 4th of that year, Father Divine was holding a vespers-banquet in the Rockland Palace. To the surprise of all, in walked the candidate, Fiorello La Guardia. "I came here tonight to ask Father Divine's advice and counsel," he said. "Peace be with you all."

This incredible event, the arrival of a white candidate at a Divine gathering, in the role of petitioner, was an early launching point of Father Divine's influence. Thereafter, candidates of every caliber sought his endorsement. Though he was never overtly political, he did encourage his followers to register and vote for their own benefit and that of their community. The political structure recognized the potential strength of this voting bloc to such an extent that it even waived the stipulation that people use their given names as they registered to vote, and allowed Father Divine's followers to use such names as "Mother's Delight," "Brother of the Good Faith," and "Sister Who Stood by the Way."

Father Divine based his entire spiritual concept on the soaring belief that race should not be a factor in human relations. He refused to acknowledge the concept of race, and permitted no form of racial distinction to exist in his kingdoms. To this day, very few people are aware that he believed in a society based on the fundamental principle of the brotherhood of man and created such a society among his followers.

He gave stimulation and status to people who had nothing by involving them in the human family to the point where their humanity mattered. His people had few previous allegiances. Father Divine was, for them, the bringer of light to the universe and all praises were due to him!

His followers developed skills, worked in the movement and were sought after as domestics and workers because of their high principles of honesty and cleanliness. By 1935, the mystery around Father Divine had deepened and his followers had multiplied. In an article, "There Goes God . . . The Story of Father Divine and His Angels" by Claude McKay, published in *The Nation*, February 6, 1935, we get the following picture of Father Divine during the formative years of his power.

In his sumptuous living quarters, African in the gay con-glomeration of colors, Father Divine in a large easy chair appeared like a slumping puppet abandoned after a marion-ette show. He seemed to have shrunk even smaller than his five foot four, which is not unimpressive when he is acting. He pointed to a seat near him, and said he thought he had said enough at his meetings to give me an idea of his work and mission. I told him that I was interested mainly in his ideas about social problems and interracial relations and would like a special pronouncement from him as a Negro leader and pacifist. Father Divine replied: "I have no color conception of myself. If I were representing race or creed or color or nation, I would be limited in my conception of the universal. I could not be as I am, omnipotent."

I said that I accepted his saying that he was above race and color, but because he happened to have been born brown and was classified in the colored group, the world was more interested in him as a Negro. And I asked him what was his plan for the realization of peace and understanding be-tween the masses and the classes. Father Divine said: "I am representative of the universal through the cooperation of mind and spirit in which is reality. I cannot deviate from that fundamental. The masses and the classes must tran-scend the average law and accept me. And governments in time will come to recognize my law."

I drew his attention to an editorial in the Daily Worker *referring to the demonstration against war and fascism, in which the Communists had paraded in company with Father Divine at the head of thousands of his people carrying banners bearing the Divine slogans. The editorial was an explanation to critical readers of the necessity of cooperat-ing with Father Divine and his followers "carrying such strange and foolish placards." Father Divine said that he was always willing to cooperate in his own way with the Communists or any group that was fighting for international peace and emancipation of people throughout the world against any form of segregation and racial discrimination. But what the Communists were trying to do he was actually doing, by bringing people of different races and nations to live together and work in peace under his will. He had*

*come to free every nation, every language, every tongue,
and every people. He did not need the Communists or any
other organization, but they needed him. For he had all
the wisdom and understanding and health and wealth. And
he alone could give emancipation and liberty, for he was
the victor. I thanked Father Divine for the interview, and
he dismissed me with the gift of a pamphlet.*

The finances of Father Divine and his Kingdoms remain a mystery to this day. The followers who were always willing to testify to the divinity and glory of the
Messiah grew strangely silent when questions were
asked about how the Kingdoms were maintained.

To most Divinites, 1936 was a year of great joy in
the Righteous Government. Trouble came to the Kingdoms following that year. It came thick and fast over
two issues that were not supposed to be in dispute in
the Kingdoms . . . money and sex. About noon on
April 20, 1937, two white men entered Headquarters
Kingdom at 20 West 115th Street, while Father Divine
was giving one of his messages of inspiration to the
angels. One of the white men was a process server.
This intruder was badly beaten and driven from the
Kingdom. Later that day, a police search failed to find
Father Divine in New York. An order was issued for
his arrest, charging felonious assault. Three of his angels were held on the same charge. Three days later
Father Divine was discovered in one of his Kingdoms
in Connecticut and brought back to New York. In Los
Angeles, the same week, John Wuest Hunt, a wealthy
white disciple whose cult name was "Saint John the
Revelation," was arrested under the Mann Act for the
seduction of a young follower named "Miss Delight
Jewel." The most serious and least expected trouble
came when "Faithful Mary," the star angel of the movement, defected. 1937 was indeed a year of tribulation
for Father Divine and his followers.

Incredibly, 1938 found the movement recovering and
Father Divine once more in triumph. The wayward

angel "Faithful Mary" returned to the good graces of the Kingdom. Father Divine and his followers acquired the Krum Elbow estate and became the neighbors of President Roosevelt in Hyde Park. This event was accorded national attention.

In the years between 1938 and 1946, when the Divine Movement began to show signs of decline, Father Divine gave thousands of drifting people a sense of security they had never before envisioned. His movement is essential to an understanding of the spiritual condition of black America between the decline of the Garvey movement and the rise of the Nation of Islam (Black Muslims) and the civil rights movement.

3. ADAM CLAYTON POWELL, JR.

In order to explain the rise and fall of Adam Clayton Powell's political fortunes in Harlem, two entirely different personalities will have to look at Mr. Powell from different vantage points and with different points of view. I think what is needed is a child and a very wise old man. The child is needed to explain what is presently obvious, figuratively and politically speaking. Adam Clayton Powell, the aging emperor of Harlem politics, has no clothes. The wise old man is needed to explain to the child and to the rest of us that there was a time, and not so long ago, when the said emperor had clothes and they were beautiful.

The career of Adam Powell has run the gamut of extremes, the extremes have produced contradictions and the contradictions have produced an enigma that has made the Adam Powell mystique more difficult to explain. Before our eyes this man has literally thrown away a thirty-year-old political career that was the longest, and could have been the most effective, in black America. His defeat, June 17, 1970, in the New York

City primary elections by a comparatively unknown
Harlem politician, Charles B. Rangel, was largely due
to the fact that this veteran of political wars did not
get out onto the streets of Harlem, as Rangel did, and
fight for the privilege of representing the Harlem community in Congress. So his more than twenty years in
the House seemed to have been coming to an end. If
we are to understand the end of his long political career, if indeed it is the end, we will have to look at
the beginning. More than anything else, Powell is a
product of all that is good and bad in the Harlem community.

The atmosphere and conditions that shaped Adam
Clayton Powell's political career existed in Harlem before he was born. To fully understand his political
emergence, we must pay some attention to the talented
and effective Harlem politicians who came before him.
These politicians, collectively, were the first to show the
people of Harlem how to force governmental agencies
to respond to their needs. The more farsighted members of this group learned that to have any impact on
government it is necessary to know not only what is
attainable, but also how and through whom to attain
it. This involved knowledge both of formal political institutions, and of the groups and individuals who actually or might potentially determine and influence what
occurs within the political structure. For Harlem this
meant the discovery of its political self and how to
make the most effective use of it.

While A. Clayton Powell was growing up in Harlem,
the politics of the community was growing up with him.
Harlem became a black community early in this century. From the beginning, politics was a form of community activity, and after 1900 this fact received public recognition. Able spokesmen arose at all levels of
municipal politics and demanded greater representation for the community. Before this time the black
Americans' almost religious devotion to the Republi-

can party had hampered their effectiveness in the politics of New York City. The Republican Party took the Harlem vote for granted and did not feel compelled to cater to it. At this time the Democratic Party had not decided to make a serious bid for the Harlem vote. The activity of Harlem's first major politicians changed this situation and made both parties start wooing the Harlem voter.

Despite the lack of interest shown by several New York Governors in making Harlem a Congressional District, Harlem politicians continued to put up candidates for the House of Representatives. Thus, with A. Clayton Powell not yet on the scene, the way was being cleared for him to become Harlem's first Congressman.

His political career is closely linked with the history and development of the Abyssinian Baptist Church in Harlem, founded by his father. Adam Clayton Powell, Sr., was a religious politician who used his church to project social action programs for community improvement. Powell, Sr., saw no conflict between this activity and his role as the spiritual leader of the largest Baptist congregation in the United States. This church was Adam Clayton Powell, Jr.'s training ground. His father was his first teacher.

In 1930 Adam Powell, Jr., had left Colgate University and was doing graduate work at Columbia University in addition to helping his father manage his large church. At this time a group of doctors who had been banned from Harlem Hospital "because they were Negroes" asked Powell, Jr., for assistance. This was Powell, Jr.'s first major experience of social protest and his first projection of himself in relation to the grievances of the Harlem community.

After seven years as assistant pastor to his father, he was appointed pastor himself when his father retired in 1937. He now assumed his full stature as a community leader. He had followers and well-wishers far beyond the church and the Harlem community. He joined the "Jobs-for-Negroes Movement" and gave it new directions. In 1938, with the Reverend William Lloyd Imes, then pastor of St. James Presbyterian Church, and A. Philip Randolph, he formed the Greater New York Coordinating Committee for the Employment of Negroes.

A young black Cuban, Arnold Johnson (who is still active in community affairs in Harlem), was Secretary of the Coordinating Committee. Other members of the groups were James W. Ford, "Negro" Vice Presidential candidate of the Communist Party; Captain A. L. King, the Garveyite; Ira Kemp and Arthur Reed, founders of the Harlem Labor Union; and Mrs. Elizabeth Ross Haynes. The Committee's first major target was the stores on 125th Street. For years, the owners of these stores had been reluctant to hire "Negro" help. The Committee's weekly picket lines and the "Don't Buy Where You Can't Work" chanting of the pickets struck terror in the hearts of the store owners. The Harlem Labor Union was born and grew during this period.

Adam Powell's political career had its incubation period in the Coordinating Committee for "Negro" Employment. In his book *Marching Blacks* he gives the following description of the Committee and his relationship to it:

From the time the Greater New York Coordinating Committee held its first meeting at my office until the present —the Abyssinian Baptist Church has been the great foundation upon which many people's movements were built. Office space has always been afforded free. Money was ready to underwrite expenses. Eleven thousand people were available to start things moving. The Coordinating Committee was shunned in the beginning by quite a few of the so-called big Negroes. One great intellectual giant, however, stood by my side. Our co-chairman was the Reverend Dr. William Lloyd Imes, minister of St. James, the nation's largest Negro Presbyterian church, President of the Alumni

Association of the Union Theological Seminary, and now President of Knoxville College in Tennessee. William Lloyd Imes brought to the Coordinating Committee that which I did not possess. I was young and he was mature. I was a radical and so was he, but his radicalism was tempered with thoughtfulness. I was impetuous and impatient: likewise Imes, but he paused to reason. A great man, one of the greatest of the great, with the mind of a scholar, the soul of a saint, the heart of a brother, the tongue of a prophet, the hand of a militant—may his tribe increase.

In 1941 Powell mounted a united front campaign for his election to the City Council of New York. This successful campaign made him the first Afro-American to hold that office. Now he had a larger arena in which to operate. This only sharpened his appetite for a higher political office. The long fight to make Harlem a Congressional District was nearer to being won.

When the New York State Legislature passed a re-apportionment bill creating a Congressional District in the heart of Harlem, Powell started to bid for the job of Congressman at once. He had already built the community machinery that would make this possible. He was then the publisher of a newspaper, *The People's Voice*, and was now reaching a national audience. (At this time he had four jobs: he was City Councilman, Baptist pastor, newspaper editor and leader of the People's Committee, a militant Harlem protest group.)

The Harlem riot of March, 1943, made the people of the community aware of the need for more political action. Adam Powell had already announced his intention to run for Congress. He had also announced that he would support Benjamin Davis for his seat in the City Council. Then in 1944, during the Governorship of Thomas E. Dewey, the legislation that officially made Harlem a Congressional District was signed. Adam Clayton Powell had no difficulty in being elected Harlem's first Congressman.

As the elections of 1946 approached, Powell was

eager to keep his mandate intact by once again getting the endorsement of the three major political parties, though he was popular enough to win an election in Harlem without the support of these parties. This is the basis of his political strength. Nevertheless he had alienated a lot of people during his first term in office, including some of his own political camp.

This campaign was long, interesting and hard-fought. During the campaign, a large number of people in Harlem seriously questioned Adam Clayton Powell for the first time. It was a healthy and educational sight to see someone stand up to the Reverend Powell, examine him, and demand that he explain and defend his record in Congress and his total relationship to the Harlem community.

On election day, Powell polled 32,573 votes (22,641 Democratic and 9,932 American Labor Party) to 19,-514 for Grant Reynolds. Compared with later campaigns, Reynolds had made the most impressive showing against the Reverend Powell. This showing was not good enough to keep the Reverend Powell from saying, "My easy victory indicates the solid support of the people in Harlem. . . . Thousands of dollars poured into Harlem could not buy the Negro vote. We have served notice on cheap politicians to stay out of Harlem."

While Mr. Powell was making a record in national politics, the political structure of the Harlem community had started to crack in many places. Benjamin J. Davis, who had been elected to the New York City Council to fill the seat vacated by Mr. Powell, was in real trouble in spite of his popularity in the community. Before his last term had expired, Davis was barred from the City Council because he had been convicted under the Smith Act. In 1951, the Supreme Court upheld the Smith Act and Ben Davis and a number of his fellow Communists were sent to jail. With Adam Powell mostly in Washington and Ben Davis in jail, most of Harlem's day-to-day political housekeeping now went undone. A period of political deterioration had started.

MARCH ON WASHINGTON

Photographs by Paul Breslow

HARLEM STREET SCENE

Photographs by John Taylor

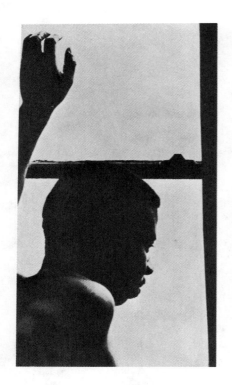

HARLEM AROUND THE TOWN

Photographs by Alvin Simon

Mr. Powell's political star continued to rise nationally and internationally. In 1955 he was an unofficial observer at the Bandung Conference of twenty-nine former colonial nations of Africa and Asia. In 1956 Mr. Powell attempted, unsuccessfully, to spark enthusiasm for his candidacy for Mayor of New York City.

After the election of Earl Brown as City Councilman and Hulan Jack as Borough President, Harlem's political fortunes seemed to be on the rise. But this was not true. Very few demands were being made on the elected representatives. The people were losing confidence in politicians as a breed—although Mr. Powell was dutifully re-elected every two years. When he had an opponent, the community rarely remembered his or her name. He was sent back to Washington to "bless out the white folks in Congress." And so long as he blessed them out loud and strong, very few people cared to find out whether he was right or wrong. There was a lot of talk about his activities, but very little genuine discussion and examination. In the meantime, the political deterioration of the community continued, seemingly unnoticed.

Harlem as a Congressional District had not yet reached its full potential.

After the March on Washington Congressman Powell broke off relations with his long-time friend, J. Raymond Jones. This happened at a time when the two political figures were competing over a community project idea that was to become HARYOU-ACT.

The early years of Adam Clayton Powell represented a political renaissance in Harlem. He might have become one of the most powerful politicians in the history of the United States. He was lucky enough to have a constituency that made him less dependent on the two major political parties. In my opinion he never made the most of this political advantage. Yet his record in Congress is one of the most remarkable that any legislator can boast of in this century. In 1966, Adam Clayton Powell celebrated his twenty-first year in the House of Representatives, and his fifth year as Chairman of the House Committee on Education and Labor. He had successfully guided to passage forty-nine major laws from his Committee. He has never had a bill from his Committee defeated once it reached the House of Representatives. In these five years, some of the most important legislation in the history of the country and the United States Congress was passed.

For the last ten years, Powell has been losing his once-complete control over the political life of the Harlem community. When he was deprived of his seat in Congress, the people of this community twice voted to send him back. This was a sentimental gesture, a show of appreciation for the services of the past years. His defeat in the primary elections of 1970 marked the end of Harlem's patience with him, and the beginning of his sad and public decline.

4. MALCOLM X

The man best known as Malcolm X lived three distinct and interrelated lives under the names Malcolm Little, Malcolm X, and El-Hajj Malik El-Shabazz. Any honest attempt to understand the total man must begin with some understanding of his significant components. The racist society that produced and killed Malcolm X is responsible for what he was and for destroying what he could have been. He had the greatest leadership potential of any person to emerge directly from the black proletariat in this century. In another time and under different circumstances he might have been a king, and a good one. He might have made a nation, and he might have destroyed one.

The seed of his ultimate development was planted many times and in many places, but that seed had its greatest growth in Harlem. And from Harlem, the place of his greatest development, he went on to become a figure of world importance.

In his introduction to the Malcolm X autobiography, M. S. Handler has said, "No man of our time aroused fear and hatred in the white man as did Malcolm, because in him the white man sensed an implacable foe who could not be had for any price—a man unreservedly committed to the cause of liberating the black man in American society rather than integrating the black man into that society."

The bold act of refusing integration is a challenge to a society that never intended to integrate the black American. Malcolm X put American society on the defensive by questioning its intentions toward his people, and by proving those intentions to be false. This is an act of manhood, and it is the basis for most of the trouble that Malcolm had in this country in his lifetime.

It has been said, incorrectly, that *The Autobiography of Malcolm X* is a book about the nature of religious conversion. The book is more precisely about a man in search of a definition of himself and his relationship to his people, his country and the world. Malcolm X knew, before he could explain it to himself and others, that he was living in a society that was engaged in the systematized destruction of his people's self-respect. His first memories are about his father and his attempts to maintain himself and his family while bigoted white policemen, Ku Klux Klansmen and Black Legionnaires were determined to teach him to stay in "his place." The father of Malcolm X was killed while fighting against the restricted position that has been assigned to his people in this country. Malcolm X took up the same fight and was killed for the same reason.

Every major event in Malcolm's life brought him into conflict with the society that still thrives on the oppression of his people. His mother was born as a result of her mother being raped by a white man in the West Indies. When he was four, the house where he and his family lived was burned down by members of the Ku Klux Klan. When he was six, his father met a violent death that his family always believed was a lynching. After the death of his father, who was a follower of the black nationalist Marcus Garvey, his family was broken up and for a number of years he lived in state institutions and boarding homes. When he finally went to school he made good marks but lost interest and was a dropout by the age of fifteen. He went to live with his sister in Boston, and went to work at the kinds of jobs available to "Negro" youths—mainly jobs not wanted by white people, such as shoe-shine boy, soda jerk, hotel busboy, member of a dining-car crew on trains traveling to New York, and waiter in a Harlem night club. From these jobs he found his way into the underworld and thought, at the time, that his position in life was advancing. In the jungle of the underworld, where the fiercest survive by fleecing the weak and defenseless, he became a master manipulator, skilled in gambling, the selling of drugs, burglary and hustling. A friend who had helped him get his first job gave him the rationale for his actions. "The main thing you have to remember," he was told, "is that everything in the world is a hustle."

Malcolm returned to Boston, where he was later arrested for burglary and sentenced to ten years in prison. The year was 1946 and he was not quite twenty-one years old. Prison was another school for Malcolm. He now had time to think and plan. Out of this thinking he underwent a conversion that literally transformed his whole life. By letters and visits from his family, he was introduced to the Black Muslim Movement (which officially calls itself The Lost-Found Nation of Islam).

He tested himself in the discipline of his newly-chosen religion by refusing to eat pork. The event startled his fellow inmates, who had nicknamed him Satan. He describes the occasion in this manner:

It was the funniest thing—the reaction, and the way that it spread. In prison, where so little breaks the monotonous routine, the smallest thing causes a commotion of talk. It was being mentioned all over the cell block by night that Satan didn't eat pork.

It made me very proud, in some odd way. One of the universal images of the Negro, in prison and out, was that he couldn't do without pork. It made me feel good to see that my not eating it had especially startled the white convicts.

Later I would learn, when I had read and studied Islam a good deal, that, unconsciously, my first pre-Islamic submission had been manifested. I had experienced, for the first time, the Muslim teaching, "If you take one step toward Allah—Allah will take two steps toward you" . . . My brothers and sisters in Detroit and Chicago had all become converted to what they were being taught was the "natural religion for the black man."

His description of his self-education in prison is an indictment of the American educational system and a tribute to his own perseverance in obtaining an education after being poorly prepared in the public school.

While in prison he devised his own way of teaching himself, and learned how to speak and debate effectively so that he could participate in and defend the movement after his release from prison. He started by copying words from the dictionary that might be helpful to him, beginning with "A." He went through to "Z," and then he writes, "for the first time, I could pick up a book and actually understand what the book was saying."

This aspect of his story calls attention to the tremendous reservoirs of talent, and even genius, locked up among the masses in the black ghettos. It also indicates what can be accomplished when the talent of this oppressed group is respected and given hope and purpose.

Within a few years Malcolm was to become a debater with a national reputation. He took on politicians, college professors, journalists, and anyone black or white who had the nerve to meet him. He was respected by some and feared by others.

Malcolm was released from prison in 1952, when he was twenty-seven years old. For a few weeks he took a job with his oldest brother Wilfred as a furniture salesman in Detroit. He went to Chicago before the end of that year to hear and meet the leader of the Nation of Islam—Elijah Muhammad. He was accepted into the movement and given the name Malcolm X. He went back to Detroit and was made assistant minister of the Detroit Mosque. From this point on his rise in the movement and in the eyes of the public was rapid.

At the end of 1953 he went to Chicago to live and train with the leader of the Nation of Islam. After organizing a mosque in Philadelphia, he was sent to head the movement in Harlem in 1954, before he was thirty years old. In a few years he was able to transform the Black Muslim Movement into a national organization and himself into one of the country's best-known personalities. As public spokesman and defender of the movement he literally put it on the map. This was the beginning of his trouble with his leader, Elijah Muhammad. When the public thought of the Black Muslim Movement, they thought first of Malcolm X.

Malcolm X had appeal far beyond the movement. He was one of the most frequent speakers on the nation's campuses and the object of admiration of thousands of militant youth. In his pamphlet, "Malcolm X —The Man and His Ideas," George Breitman gives the following description of Malcolm's appeal as a speaker:

His speaking style was unique—plain, direct like an arrow, devoid of flowery trimming. He used metaphors and figures of speech that were lean and simple, rooted in the ordinary, daily experience of his audiences. He knew what the masses thought and how they felt, their strengths and their weaknesses. He reached right into their minds and hearts without wasting a word; and he never tried to flatter them. Despite an extraordinary ability to move and arouse his listeners, his main appeal was to reason, not emotion. . . I want only to convey the idea that rarely has there been a man in America better able to communicate ideas to the most oppressed people; and that was not just a matter of technique, which can be learned and applied in any situation by almost anybody, but that it was a rare case of a man in closest communication with the oppressed, able to speak to them, because he identified himself with them, an authentic expression of their yearning for freedom, a true product of their growth in the same way that Lenin was a product of the Russian people.

At the Grass Roots Conference in Detroit in November, 1963, Malcolm X made his last important speech as a Muslim. In this speech he took a revolutionary position in the civil rights struggle—speaking mainly for himself and not for the leader he always referred to as The Honorable Elijah Muhammad. This speech showed clearly that Malcolm X had outgrown the narrow stage of the Black Muslim Movement.

He devotes a chapter in his book to the growth of his disenchantment and his eventual suspension from the Black Muslim Movement. He says:

I had helped Mr. Muhammad and his ministers to revolutionize the American black man's thinking, opening his eyes until he would never again look in the same fearful way at the white man . . . If I harboured any personal disappointment whatsoever, it was that privately I was convinced that our Nation of Islam could be an even greater force in the American black man's overall struggle if we engaged in more action. By that I mean I thought privately that we should have amended, or relaxed, our general nonengagement policy. I felt that wherever black people committed themselves, in the Little Rocks and the Birminghams and other places, militantly disciplined Muslims should also be there—for all the world to see, and respect and discuss.

The expected split with Elijah Muhammad finally came over a matter that seemed rather trivial. The occasion for the split was a remark by Malcolm after the death of President Kennedy in November, 1963. He had said, in effect, that the President took no action of consequence when black Americans were being killed, and his death was like "chickens coming home to roost."

During the last phase of his life, Malcolm X established Muslim Mosque, Inc., and a nonreligious organization, The Organization of Afro-American Unity, patterned after the Organization of African Unity. He attempted to internationalize the civil rights fight by taking it to the United Nations. In several trips to Africa and one to Mecca, he sought the counsel and support of African and Asian heads of state.

In the Epilogue to the book Alex Haley has written a concise account of the last days of Malcolm X. The book, revealing as it is, reads like the first draft of what could have been the most exciting autobiography of our time. It is unfortunate that Malcolm X did not live long enough to do the necessary editing and pruning that this book needed. We have no way of knowing what liberties, if any, Alex Haley took while editing the manuscript after the assassination of Malcolm X on Sunday, February 21, 1965.

That a man who had inhabited the "lower depth" of life could rise in triumph as a reproach to its ills, and become an uncompromising champion of his people, is in itself a remarkable feat. Malcolm X went beyond this feat. Though he came from the American ghetto and directed his message to the people in the American ghetto first of all, he also became, in his brief lifetime, a figure of world importance. He died on the threshold of his potential. "The Autobiography of Malcolm X," written hurriedly near the end of his life, is a clear indication of what this potential could have become.

HARLEM AND THE POETS

Langston Hughes

❧

JUKE BOX LOVE SONG

I could take the Harlem night
And wrap around you,
Take the neon lights and make a crown,
Take the Lenox Avenue buses,
Taxis, subways,
And for your love song tone their rumble down.
Take Harlem's heartbeat,
Make a drumbeat,
Put it on a record, let it whirl,
And while we listen to it play,
Dance with you till day—
Dance with you, my sweet brown Harlem girl.

MADAM'S PAST HISTORY

My name is Johnson
Madam Alberta K.
The Madam stands for business.
I'm smart that way.

I had a
HAIR-DRESSING PARLOR
Before
The depression put
The prices lower.

Then I had a
BARBECUE STAND
Till I got mixed up
With a no-good man.

Cause I had a insurance
The WPA
Said, We can't use you
Wealthy that way.

I said,
DON'T WORRY 'BOUT ME!
Just like the song,
You WPA folks take care of yourself—
And I'll get along.

I do cooking,
Day's work, too!
Alberta K. Johnson—
Madam to you.

MADAM AND HER MADAM

I worked for a woman,
She wasn't mean—
But she had a twelve-room
House to clean.

Had to get breakfast,
Dinner, and supper, too—
Then take care of her children
When I got through.

Wash, iron, and scrub,
Walk the dog around—
It was too much,
Nearly broke me down.

I said, Madam,
Can it be
You trying to make a
Pack-horse out of me?

She opened her mouth.
She cried, Oh, no!
You know, Alberta,
I love you so!

I said, Madam,
That may be true—
But I'll be dogged
If I love you!

NIGHT FUNERAL IN HARLEM

Night funeral
In Harlem:

Where did they get
Them two fine cars?

Insurance man, he did not pay—
His insurance lapsed the other day—
Yet they got a satin box
For his head to lay.

Night funeral
In Harlem:

Who was it sent
That wreath of flowers?

Them flowers came
From that poor boy's friends—
They'll want flowers, too,
When they meet their ends.

     Night funeral
     In Harlem:

     Who preached that
     Black boy to his grave?

Old preacher-man
Preached that boy away—
Charged Five Dollars
His Girl friend had to pay.

     Night funeral in Harlem.

When it was all over
And the lid shut on his head
And the organ had done played
And the last prayers been said
And six pallbearers
Carried him out for dead
And off down Lenox Avenue
That long black hearse done sped,

     The street light
     At his corner
     Shined just like a tear—

That boy that they was mournin'
Was so dear, so dear
To them folks that brought the flowers,
To that girl who paid the preacher-man—
It was all their tears that made

     That poor boy's
     Funeral grand.

     Night funeral
     In Harlem.

HARLEM NIGHT SONG

Come,
Let us roam the night together
Singing.

I love you.

Across
The Harlem roof-tops
Moon is shining.
Night sky is blue.
Stars are great drops
Of golden dew.

Down the street
A band is playing.

I love you.

Come,
Let us roam the night together
Singing.

MY PEOPLE

The night is beautiful,
So the faces of my people.

The stars are beautiful,
So the eyes of my people.

Beautiful, also, is the sun.
Beautiful, also, are the souls of my people.

KU KLUX

They took me out
To some lonesome place.
They said, "Do you believe
In the great white race?"

I said, "Mister,
To tell you the truth,
I'd believe in anything
If you'd just turn me loose."

The white man said, "Boy,
Can it be
You're a-standin' there
A-sassin' me?"

They hit me in the head
And knocked me down.
And then they kicked me
On the ground.

A klansman said, "Nigger,
Look me in the face—
And tell me you believe in
The great white race."

I, TOO

I, too, sing America.

I am the darker brother.
They send me to eat in the kitchen
When company comes,
But I laugh,
And eat well,
And grow strong.

Tomorrow,
I'll be at the table
When company comes.
Nobody'll dare
Say to me,
"Eat in the kitchen,"
Then.

Besides,
They'll see how beautiful I am
And be ashamed—

I, too, am America.

Countee Cullen

YET DO I MARVEL

I doubt not God is good, well-meaning, kind;
And did He stoop to quibble could tell why
The little buried mole continues blind,
Why flesh that mirrors Him must some day die,
Make plain the reason tortured Tantalus
Is baited by the fickle fruit, declare
If merely brute caprice dooms Sisyphus
To struggle up a never-ending stair.
Inscrutable His ways are, and immune
To catechism by a mind too strewn
With petty cares to slightly understand
What awful brain compels His awful hand.
Yet do I marvel at this curious thing:
To make a poet black, and bid him sing!

INCIDENT

Once riding in old Baltimore,
   Heart-filled, head-filled with glee,
I saw a Baltimorean
   Keep looking straight at me.

Now I was eight and very small,
   And he was no whit bigger,
And so I smiled, but he poked out
   His tongue, and called me, "Nigger."

I saw the whole of Baltimore
   From May until December;
Of all the things that happened there
   That's all that I remember.

Claude McKay

THE HARLEM DANCER

Applauding youths laughed with young prostitutes
And watched her perfect, half-clothed body sway;
Her voice was like the sound of blended flutes
Blown by black players upon a picnic day.
She sang and danced on gracefully and calm,
The light gauze hanging loose about her form;
To me she seemed a proudly-swaying palm
Grown lovelier for passing through a storm.
Upon her swarthy neck black shiny curls
Luxuriant fell; and tossing coins in praise,
The wine-flushed, bold-eyed boys, and even the girls,
Devoured her shape with eager, passionate gaze;
But looking at her falsely-smiling face,
I knew her self was not in that strange place.

HARLEM SHADOWS

I hear the halting footsteps of a lass
    In Negro Harlem when the night lets fall
Its veil. I see the shapes of girls who pass
    To bend and barter at desire's call.
Ah, little dark girls who in slippered feet
Go prowling through the night from street to street!

Through the long night until the silver break
    Of day the little gray feet know no rest;
Through the lone night until the last snow-flake
    Has dropped from heaven upon the earth's
        white breast,
The dusky, half-clad girls of tired feet
Are trudging, thinly shod, from street to street.

Ah, stern harsh world, that in the wretched way
    Of poverty, dishonor and disgrace,
Has pushed the timid little feet of clay,
    The sacred brown feet of my fallen race!
Ah, heart of me, the weary, weary feet
In Harlem wandering from street to street.

IF WE MUST DIE

If we must die, let it not be like hogs
Hunted and penned in an inglorious spot,
While round us bark the mad and hungry dogs,
Making their mock at our accursed lot.
If we must die, O let us nobly die,
So that our precious blood may not be shed
In vain; then even the monsters we defy
Shall be constrained to honor us though dead!
O kinsmen! we must meet the common foe!
Though far outnumbered let us show us brave,
And for their thousand blows deal one deathblow!
What though before us lies the open grave?
Like men we'll face the murderous cowardly pack,
Pressed to the wall, dying, but fighting back!

Ricardo Weeks

SUGAR HILL PREACHER

I am a preacher,
And I'm doing all right.
I am a sinner
Though I preach at night.

I live on Sugar Hill
And my home's up to par.
If luck holds out
I'll soon have a car.

I eat fairly well
From day to day.
I'm never hungry
That I can say.

I am a preacher,
But first I'm a man
Struggling to live
And get what I can.

HARLEM JUNK MAN

All mornin' an' evenin'
Been pushin' ma wagon,
With nothin' inside it.
A-shovin' an' hopin'
To find me some cardboard,
Some rags an' some paper
To make me some dough.

An' still I'm a-shovin'
Without any luck—
Jus' an empty ol' wagon
With a few sheets o' paper.
Need a coat fo' the baby,
An' some things fo' ma woman,
Fo' she's 'specting' another,
Mos' any day now.

Been shovin' ma wagon
All mornin' an' evenin'—
Lawd, don't yo' see me a-shovin'?

BILLY THE KID IN HARLEM

Billy the kid was a colored lad,
The type that neighbors stamp as bad.
His big bad habit was spending time
In hovels and dens of sin and crime.

His ma and pa did all they could,
But he was so bad he couldn't be good.
Many a day when he left for school,
Instead they found him shooting pool.

"Billy," his poor old ma would say,
"Why must you behave this way?
Can't you try being good for me,
And stay out of bad company?"

But Billy was wild. He wouldn't hear.
The neighbors said he just didn't care.
He went right on hanging roun'
With the toughest bunch of boys in town.

One night, while ma and pa were asleep,
Bad news awoke them and made them weep.
It seemed that Billy, the night before,
Had taken a life while robbing a store.

A nine-state alarm was then sent out,
For Billy had fled and was hiding out,
Nobody could find him—not even his boys,
Nor even Marie, who shared his joys.

But some weeks later on Sugar Hill,
Billy was spotted in a bar and grill.
And before he could wipe the sweat from his face,
P.D. cars had surrounded the place.

Revolvers in hand the law stormed in,
Billy drew his amid the din.
"You ain't gonna take me!" he cried in fear.
"I'll kill the first copper who dares come near!"

But before he could fire, they filled him with lead,
And Billy, the kid, pitched forward dead.
Now this goes to show you that CRIME DOESN'T
    PAY!
So all you bad boys better live the right way.

BLACK JOHN HENRY[139]

Black John Henry
Stood like a God
On 133rd
While his people cheered
And wondered.

Black John Henry
Sang in a resonant voice
That the great, dark face of Harlem
Would be soon washed clean.

He sang about
Streamlined houses,
Playgrounds, parks
And clean streets.

He stood like a God
'Neath the weary sun
And laughed
While the grasping landlords
Looked on and frowned.

Black John Henry
Looked like a pyramid
On 133rd
While he passed his hand
Among the crowd.

He sang about a new Harlem,
A great, new metropolis,
A new America—
Black John Henry
On 133rd!

John Henrik Clarke

BABYLON IS NOT DEAD

No, Babylon is not dead,
I saw Babylon yesterday,
In the grinning face of a redcap
In Pennsylvania Station.
And later in the movements
Of a dark girl's body, in a cabaret.
And only last night, I saw Babylon
Preaching against race hatred
From a stepladder on Lenox Avenue.
No Babylon is not dead;
I heard Babylon when a dark girl sang:
"I'm so glad my troubles won't last always."
Babylon is in the oppressed races
Rising from under the yoke of oppression.
Perhaps Babylon did sleep for a while,
But Babylon never died—
This is the day of Babylon's awakening.

SING ME A NEW SONG[140]

Sing me a new song, young black singer,
Sing me a song with some thunder in it,
And a challenge that will
Drive fear into the hearts of those people
Who think that God has given them
The right to call you their slave.

Sing me a song of strong men growing stronger
And bold youth facing the sun and marching.
Sing me a song of an angry sharecropper,
Who is not satisfied with his meager share
Of the products that he squeezed from the earth
While watering the earth with his sweat and tears.

Sing me a song of two hundred million Africans
Revising the spirit of Chaka, Moshesh and Menelik,
And shouting to the world:
"This is my land and I shall be free upon it!"
Put some reason in my song and some madness too.

Let the reason be the kind of reason
Frederick Douglass had,
When he was fighting against slavery in America.
Let the madness be the kind of madness
Henri Christophe had when
He was driving Napoleon's army from Haitian soil.

Sing me a song with some hunger in it, and a
    challenge too.
Let the hunger be the kind of hunger
Nat Turner and Denmark Vesey had
When they rose from bondage and inspired
Ten thousand black hands to reach for freedom.

Let the challenge be the kind of challenge
Crispus Attucks had
While dying for American Independence.

Don't put "I ain't gonna study war no more"
in my song.
Sing me a song of a people hungry for freedom,
Who will study war until they are free!

I'M FROM ALABAMA

I'm from Alabama—red clay still
On m' feet,
I gitta gal 'n Alabama, who lives
On de Chinaberry rout;
Yeh, I'm from Alabama
An' dat's nothing t' brag about.
Done sent fer m' gal 'n Alabama,
So she kin marry me;
Gonna brang dat gal 't Harlem
An' how happee we gonna be.
Gonna build her a house on Sugar Hill,
Where day's never feelin' low;
Yeh, 'm from Alabama,
But I ain't goin' back no more.

LOVE

Who is justice? I would like to know,
Whosoever she is, I could love her so
I could love her, though my race
So seldom looks upon her face.

A QUESTION TO THE WARRIORS

If you are the noble and brave
Who have great harvest to reap,
Why do you cowardly fling death at night
While babies sleep?

SHOCK-PROOF

With strong nations buckling at the knees,
And zealots claiming victories,
I would not be shocked if the stars
Flew away like a swarm of bees,
And if the grass long green
Should suddenly turn pink before my eyes,
I would not be surprised.

THE CITY'S CONQUEST

The city has conquered me
Though it causes me pain,
I love its bewitching spell
That's rampant in my veins.
No matter how hungrily I long
For laughing seas,
And quiet rural charms,
I will not relinquish the city's might
To roam over wooded lands,
And sleep through silent nights.

Sterling A. Brown

THE BALLAD OF JOE MEEK

I

You cain't never tell
How far a frog will jump,
When you jes' see him planted
On his big broad rump.

    Nor what a monkey's thinking
      By the working of his jaws—
    You jes' cain't figger;
      And I knows, because

Had me a buddy,
    Soft as pie,
Joe Meek they called him
    And they didn't lie.

    The good book say
      "Turn the other cheek,"
    But that warn't no turning
      To my boy Joe Meek.

He turned up all parts,
    And baigged you to spank,
Pulled down his breeches,
    And supplied the plank.

        The worm that didn't turn
            Was a rattlesnake to Joe:
        Wasn't scary—jes' meek, suh,
            Was made up so.

II

It was late in August
    What dey calls dog days,
Made even beetle hounds
    Git bulldog ways.

        Would make a pet bunny
            Chase a bad bloodhound,
        Make a new-born baby
            Slap his grandpa down.

The air it was muggy
    And heavy with heat,
The people all sizzled
    Like frying meat.

        The icehouse was heaven
            The pavements was hell
        Even Joe didn't feel
            So agreeable.

Strolling down Claiborne
    In the wrong end of town
Joe saw two policemen
    Knock a po' gal down.

He didn't know her at all,
   Never saw her befo'
But that didn't make no difference,
   To my ole boy Joe.

Walks up to the cops,
   And, very polite,
Ast them ef they thought
   They had done *just right*.

      One cracked him with his billy
         Above the left eye,
      One slugged him with his pistol
         And let him lie.

III

When he woke up, and knew
   What the cops had done,
Went to a hockshop,
   Got hisself a gun.

      Felt mo' out of sorts
         Than ever befo',
      So he went on a rampage
         My ole boy Joe.

Shot his way to the station house.
   Rushed right in,
Wasn't nothing but space
   Where the cops had been.

      They called the reserves,
         And the national guard,
      Joe was in a cell
         Overlooking the yard.

The machine guns sputtered,
   Didn't faze Joe at all—
But evvytime *he* fired
   A cop would fall.

The tear-gas made him laugh
When they let it fly,
Laughing gas made him hang
His head an' cry.

He threw the hand grenades back
With a outshoot drop,
An' evvytime he threw
They was one less cop.

The Chief of Police said
"What kinda *man* is this?"
And held up his shirt
For a armistice.

"Stop gunning, black boy,
And we'll let you go."
"I thank you very kindly,"
Said my ole boy Joe.

"We promise you safety
If you'll leave us be—"
Joe said: "That's agreeable
Sir, by me. . . ."

IV

The sun had gone down
The air it was cool,
Joe stepped out on the pavement
A fighting fool.

Had walked from the jail
About half a square,
When a cop behind a post
Let him have it fair.

Put a bullet in his left side
  And one in his thigh,
But Joe didn't lose
  His shootin' eye.

    Drew a cool bead
      On the cop's broad head;
    "I returns you yo' favor"
      And the cop fell dead.

The next to last words
  He was heard to speak,
Was just what you would look for
  From my boy Joe Meek.

    Spoke real polite
      To the folks standing by:
    "Would you please do me one kindness,
      Fo' I die?"

"Won't be here much longer
  To bother you so,
Would you bring me a drink of water,
  Fo' I go?"

    The very last words
      He was heard to say,
    Showed a different Joe talking
      In a different way.

"Ef my bullets weren't gone,
  An' my strength all spent—
I'd send the chief something
  With a compliment."

    "And we'd race to hell,
      And I'd best him there,
    Like I would of done here
      Ef he'd played me fair."

V

So you cain't never tell
How fas' a dog can run,
When you see him a-sleeping
In the sun.

AN OLD WOMAN REMEMBERS[141]

Her eyes were gentle; her voice was for soft singing
In the stiff-backed pew, or on the porch when evening
Comes slowly over Atlanta. But she remembered.
She said: "After they cleaned out the saloons and the
dives,
The drunks and the loafers, they thought that they had
better
Clean out the rest of us. And it was awful.
They snatched men off of streetcars, beat up women.
Some of our men fought back, and killed too. Still
It wasn't their habit. And then the orders came
For the milishy, and the mob went home,
And dressed up in their soldiers' uniforms,
And rushed back shooting just as wild as ever.
Some leaders told us to keep faith in the law,
In the governor; some did not keep that faith,
Some never had it: he was white too, and the time
Was near election, and the rebs were mad.
He wasn't stopping hornets with his head bare.
The white folks at the big houses, some of them
Kept all their servants home under protection
But that was all the trouble they could stand.
And some were put out when their cooks and yard-
boys
Were thrown from cars and beaten, and came late or
not at all.
And the police they helped the mob, and the milishy
They helped the police. And it got worse and worse.

"They broke into groceries, drug-stores, barber shops,
It made no difference whether white or black.
They beat a lame bootblack until he died,
They cut an old man open with jack-knives
The newspapers named us black brutes and mad dogs,
So they used a gun butt on the president
Of our seminary where a lot of folks
Had sat up praying prayers the whole night through.

"And then," she said, "our folks got sick and tired
Of being chased and beaten and shot down.
All of a sudden, one day, they all got sick and tired.
The servants they put down their mops and pans,
And brooms and hoes and rakes and coachman whips,
Bad niggers stopped their drinking Dago red,
Good Negroes figured they had prayed enough.
All came back home—they'd been too long away—
A lot of visitors had been looking for them.

"They sat on their front stoops and in their yards,
Not talking much, but ready; their welcome ready:
Their shotguns oiled and loaded on their knees.

"And then
There wasn't any riot any more."

SOUTHERN COP

Let us forgive Ty Kendricks
The place was Darktown. He was young.
His nerves were jittery. The day was hot.
The Negro ran out of the alley.
And so Ty shot.
Let us understand Ty Kendricks
The Negro must have been dangerous,
Because he ran;
And here was a rookie with a chance
To prove himself man.

Let us condone Ty Kendricks
If we cannot decorate.
When he found what the Negro was running for,
It was all too late;
And all we can say for the Negro is
It was unfortunate.

Let us pity Ty Kendricks
He has been through enough,
Standing there, his big gun smoking,
Rabbit-scared, alone,
Having to hear the wenches wail
And the dying Negro moan.

HARLEM AND THE SHORT STORY

John Henrik Clarke

࿋

REVOLT OF THE ANGELS

THE TWO HARLEM piano movers who had taken the negative side of the argument were quiet now, waiting for the defender of the affirmative to gather his thoughts. He was a big man; seemingly bigger than his two friendly opponents put together. Because of this, it did not seem unfair that he had no one to assist him in imparting his point of view.

For more than an hour the three men had been standing by their large red truck, waiting between assignments. It was their custom on these occasions to test each other's knowledge of the great subjects and issues that influence the destiny of mankind. The fact that their formal knowledge of these subjects was extremely limited did not deter their discussions in the slightest.

The two small men waited and stole quick glances at their large companion. Their faces were aglow with the signs of assured victory. Finally one turned to the other and said: "We've got 'im at las', Leroy. We've taken King Solomon off of his throne. We've made another wise man bite th' dust."

The speaker's dark face looked as if age had been

baked into it. He kept watching the large man who was collecting his thoughts in preparation for stating his side of the argument.

"I knew we'd tame this wise man some day," the other small man said. The note of triumph and mock haughtiness in his voice gave it a distinct play acting tone. "We got 'im up a creek without a paddle," he went on, laughing a little. "Now, Hawkshaw, lemme see you talk your way out of this trap."

"Don't count your eggs before you buy your chickens," the big man said, straightening up as his loosely hanging stomach spilled over the rim of his belt. "Th' thing to be resolved is whether a man who has been a drunkard most of his life can straighten himself out and become a pillar of respectability an' a credit to his community. You fellas have said this cannot be done an' I disagree . . . I know just th' case to prove my point." He exhaled audibly with some of the pompousness of a political orator preparing for a long discourse.

Then he spoke again, slowly, measuring his words very carefully at first.

"During th' last part of th' depression years there was a fella here in Harlem named Luther Jackson who had been drunk so long nobody could remember how he looked when he was sober. Luther wasn't a violent man; he didn't bother nobody unless he wanted some likker and they wouldn't give it to him.

"One day when Luther was near th' end of a three-week stupor, he wandered into one of Father Divine's restaurants and sat down at th' bes' table. He thought th' restaurant was a bar and th' bes' table in th' house meant nothing to him. Now fellas, when I say this was the bes' table in th' house, I mean it was th' bes' table you'd see anywhere. In those days most of Father Divine's restaurants set up a special table for Father just in case he came in an' wanted to dine in style. This special table had snow white linen, th' bes' of silverware, crystal glasses, th' kind you only see in the homes of millionaires, and a fresh bowl of flowers. A picture of Father Divine was in front of th' flowers with a message under it sayin', *Thank you Father*. It was some kind of deadly sin for anybody but Father Divine and his invited guests to set at this table.

"A big fat angel saw Luther at th' table an' strutted out of th' kitchen blowin' like a mad bull.

" 'Peace, brother,' she said real loud, 'This is Father Divine's table, get up an' get out of here.'

" 'I want some likker,' Luther says, 'an' I want some more t' wash it down.'

" 'Peace, brother,' th' angel says, puffin' an' trying to keep her temper from explodin'. 'This is Father Divine's table, get up an' get out of here.'

" 'I won't go till you give me some likker,' Luther says, 'an' I don't care whose table this is.'

"Th' angel threw her hands in th' air and looked at th' ceilin' like she expected something over her head to come down an' help her.

" 'Peace, Father,' she says, 'remove this evil man from your premises.'

" 'I want some likker!' Luther shouted at her an' slammed his hand on th' table, knockin' down some of th' fine silverware. 'A drinkin' man is in th' house. Go away old woman an' send me a bartender.'

"This made th' angel madder than ever. She went back to th' kitchen holdin' her head like she was scared it was goin' t' fly off.

" 'Where's th' bartender in this place?' Luther asked an' stood up lookin' 'round like he was just fixin' to mop up th' place with his madness.

"Th' big angel was standing in th' kitchen door, shoutin', 'Father Divine don't allow no alcohol drinkers in here. No obscenities! No adulteries!'

"Luther slammed his hand on th' table again an' knocked down some more of th' fine silverware. This made th' angel so angry she couldn't speak. She just

stood in th' door of th' kitchen swellin' up like a big
toad frog.

" 'Gimme some likker and let me get outa here,'
Luther says.

"Then th' angel hollered out all of a sudden and
frightened Luther so much he almost jumped over the
table.

" 'Peace Father!' th' angel was sayin'. 'Give me con-
sole, Father, you are wonderful.'

"Father or someone else must have given her con-
sole an' some new strength to go with it, because she
threw a pot at Luther's head like he was a long lost husband who deserted her with a house full of hungry
young 'uns.

"The pot bounced off of Luther's head an' he hollered like a wild bull. 'What's goin' on in this place?'
Luther was sayin'. 'Where's th' bartender?'

" 'Father Divine don't 'low no alcohol drinkers in
here,' th' angel was sayin' again, 'No obscenities! No
adulteries.' Before she finished sayin' this she threw another pot at Luther's head.

"Luther ducked and stood up in a chair as a skillet
missed his head by an inch. Then he stepped into the
middle of th' table. He had knocked down th' flowers
and some of th' fine silverware. Now th' angel was hollerin' like judgment day was at hand. You see, fellas,
Luther was standin' on Father Divine's picture. She
ran out of pots an' began t' throw big spoons an' ladles.

" 'Peace Father, give me strength,' she hollered, 'give
me th' strength to move this satan from your premises.'

"Then she jumped toward Luther like a tiger an'
knocked 'im off th' table with a rollin' pin. As Luther
fell, he turned th' table over. All of th' snow white
table linen was on th' floor. Th' silverware was scattered around th' table and some of it was in Luther's
pockets. Most of th' millionaire crystal glasses were
broken.

"The fat angel kept screamin', 'Peace! Peace! Peace!'

until some more angels joined up with her. They came at Luther with fire in their eyes. They beat him until he got up, then they beat him down again. Still more angels came and joined the war on Luther—black ones, white ones, lean ones, fat ones, an' all th' sizes in between. They kicked him, they scratched him an' spit on him. While all of this was happenin', an angel came up an' started whackin' at Luther with a cleaver.

"Now Luther was screamin' for his life an' tryin' to get to th' door. Th' angels knocked him down again an' he crawled out of th' door hollerin' for a police to save him. He saw a red box on th' side of a building an' opened it, thinkin' it was a police telephone. He pulled down a lever an' let it stay down. Th' angels had followed him into th' streets. Soon, fire trucks started comin' from every direction—patrol wagons from th' riot squads an' th' emergency squads came. Policemen in cars an' on foot came to th' scene like they were being rained down from th' sky. Still th' angry angels kept chargin' at Luther. The commotion tied up traffic for ten blocks.

"It took more than one hundred policemen to rescue Luther from them angry angels. They had hit him every place including under his feet. The policemen had to take him to th' hospital before they could take him to jail. When he was well enough for his trial, th' judge threw th' book at him an' said he was sorry that he did not have a much bigger book. Life in jail changed Luther. He was, indeed, a new man when he came out. He was upright, law abidin' and he refused to drink anything stronger than coffee.

"So, fellas, I give you the case of Luther Jackson as my proof that a man who has been a drunkard most of his life can straighten himself out and become a pillar of respectability an' a credit to his community.

"Now Luther is a foreman of a stevedore group down on th' docks an' he's also an officer in th' union. He sent down south for his wife an' children an' he made a good home for them right here in Harlem. He is a church goin' man too an' a senior deacon. Nowhere in this land would you find a more peaceful an' law abidin' citizen than Luther Jackson. Since th' day of that fracas with those angry angels to this day, he never again touched another drop of likker."

The opposition had conceded defeat long before the fat man finished the story. A rebuttal was unnecessary.

John H. Jones

❧

THE HARLEM RAT

As BATTLE YOUNG strode home along Harlem's Lenox Avenue on an October evening in nineteen-forty-eight, he scarcely noticed the chilly wind or the passersby. He was too absorbed in his own anger.

He swung a lunch pail as he walked, a tall lithe man in Army clothes, thick-soled boots, khaki trench coat and knitted cap. His brown face was strong featured, and his brown eyes mirrored an eternal hurt, frustration or anger. He was a veteran, discharged only a year, after three bitter ones in the Army.

Crossing One Hundred and Thirty-fifth Street and heading north, his mind searched for the easiest way to tell Belle that he had failed again to get an apartment in the new project going up on Fifth Avenue. He thought of how she wanted to get out of those dismal three rooms on One Hundred and Thirty-eighth Street, so that Jean, their two-months-old baby, would have "a decent place to grow up in."

Belle had cried, threatened, pleaded, scolded, ridiculed and tried just about everything else in what she thought was the best method to make him get out and find a place! "Other vets are finding places. Why can't

you?" she would cry out whenever she heard of someone else getting an apartment.

"We're lucky to find this hole." He told her over and
over again, explaining that he wanted to get another
place the same as she did. But she had always been a
demanding woman, he thought, remembering their
school days in Richmond, Virginia. It had been her
strong persuasion after his Army discharge that brought
them to New York.

And then, when the city-owned project started up
giving priority to veterans, Belle had been certain they
would get in. But just this evening he'd stood in line
for an hour, only to have the interviewer tell him,
"You're making too much money, Mr. Young. Your income is about three dollars a week more than the law
calls for." He had argued at first and finally stalked out
in anger. And now he had to face another one of those
terrible arguments with Belle. God! How he hated to
fight with her!

He walked around an unconscious Sneaky Pete
drinker sprawled on the sidewalk at One Hundred and
Thirty-sixth Street, crossed and glanced toward the Harlem Hospital as an ambulance turned east. Well, he
had to go home he thought, walking on in silence,
swinging his lunch pail and staring in through the windows of the bars, the greasy cafés and the candy stores.

At the corner of One Hundred and Thirty-eighth
Street, he turned east, walked past two tenements and
entered the third. On the stoop stood a half dozen teen-
age boys and girls. Climbing two flights of creaky stairs,
he stopped just at the top of the landing, put his key
in the lock, and went in the door.

Belle could see the answer in his grimy face when he
came in, but she asked the question anyway, asked it
hopefully, standing in the middle of the front room.
"What did they say at the project, honey?" Her voice
was soft but clear.

"For Crissakes! Will you let me get outta these dirty

clothes and catch a breath?" he snapped, and then turned away ashamed.

Belle took the pail from his hands, turned on her heel, and walked into the middle room. She was slender, and her skin was a delicate reddish tan. Her brown hair was held up neatly by a hair net. Brown eyes accented a snub nose and soft, full, unpainted lips. She wore a blue and red flowered house dress, and fuzzy blue slippers.

The small room was dimly lit. On an old-fashioned iron bed in the corner a tiny baby slept. This was Jean. Belle smiled anxiously as she peered at the baby. Satisfied that Jean was snug, she turned and inspected the small, round, black oil stove. The flame glowed through the vents in its side.

Belle shivered slightly, turned it up and silently cursed Kelly, the landlord, for not providing heat.

The ceilings were cracked and falling. The dirty gray plaster walls appeared to have once been buff. Ancient chandeliers had become loosened from the ceiling, and from time to time the crumbling electric wire insulation wore through and short-circuited, plunging the apartment into darkness.

Going down a short hall, Belle mashed a roach with her foot as it scurried across the floor heading for the kitchen. She put Battle's pail on the top of a wooden icebox standing in a far corner and went to her stove. After half an hour, Battle came in wearing a tattered, blue terry cloth bathrobe. His stiff, black hair was cropped short, and he carried an evening paper. His face, now clean, wore an annoyed expression as he walked to a cracked, porcelain-topped table, pulled out a rickety chair, and sat down with a sigh. He glanced at the paper's headlines while Belle stirred a pot. Both looked up knowingly as the steam pipe clanged a staccato beat of an overhead tenant calling for heat.

"That damn water is cold again. The day I leave this filthy hole I'm gonna kick that lousy Kelly right in his can!" Battle stormed. "Ain't no need of sayin' anything to the super. Kelly won't give him no coal!"

"Again?" Belle commented with sarcasm. "It's always cold." Then, "What did they say, Honey?" She reached back on the table for Battle's plate.

"I'm making too much," Battle said, looking hopefully as Belle dished up a sizzling pork chop, steaming lima beans, and kale.

"Jesus God!" Belle exclaimed, pushing the plate of food before Battle. "Whadda they mean? You making too much. We can hardly buy bread and meat!"

Battle chewed a mouthful and swallowed. "Well, there's this law against a guy making more than thirty-six dollars getting in city housing projects."

"Did you show 'em your discharge papers and tell 'em about me and Jean?"

"Sure. But that don't mean nothing."

"Well, since we got to stay here why don't you try to make Kelly fix up a few things and paint?" Belle said as she sat down to her own plate of food.

Battle slammed down his fork, and looked Belle straight in the eyes. "Now don't you go nagging at me again. Haven't I cussed and threatened that fat ass bastard ever since we been here? And Brown in I-E was here long before us, and Kelly ain't done anything in his apartment yet!" He picked up the fork, speared a piece of meat and started chewing savagely.

But Belle wasn't satisfied. She pushed the food about her plate without interest, contemplating an appropriate reply. "Well, can't you think of anything else? Can't you go see somebody? Isn't there a law for his kind? Or do you want me to do it?"

Battle had heard this before. She always managed to imply doubts of his ability to do things the way a man should, hitting his weakest spot. "Look," he muttered through a mouthful of food, "Do you want me to kill that bastard, and go to Sing Sing? 'Cause if I get into one more argument with him and he gets smart, I'm gonna hit him with the first thing I get my hands on!"

"Fighting won't get the place painted, but thinking out a few ways to make him do it might help a little!" she blazed. She hesitated a moment. "You never did go back to that tenants' meeting, like Mr. Brown asked you to. You and the rest of these folks ought to listen to Mr. Brown and get together. You can't do nothing by yourselves."

Battle glowered and broke off a bit of white bread. For a few moments they both ate in silence. Noticing that Battle was almost finished with his food, Belle said, "There's no more meat or beans, just kale, but there's some rice pudding from yesterday, and—"

"Goddam sonovabitch, look at that bastard!" Battle sputtered suddenly, staring at the wall against which the table stood. A fat roach sluggishly made its way ceiling-wards, antennae waving.

"Well, knock him off for heavensake, and stop cussing!"

He reached down, pulled off a battered bedroom slipper and unceremoniously smashed the roach. They both looked disgustedly at the mess. Then, as Belle got up and turned towards the icebox, Battle tore a corner from the newspaper he had been reading and wiped the wall.

"I don't want any pudding now," he said just before she stooped to open the box.

"Well, why did you mash him, Mister nice-nasty?" She came back to the table, sat down, and pulled a pack of cigarettes from her dress pocket. Battle pushed his dishes back and continued to read.

Belle lit her cigarette and blew out the first puff. Her mind was busy trying to hit on the best way to mention their housing predicament again. Battle seemed to sense her thoughts, and he glanced at her from the corners of his eyes several times. "Honey—" she began. Battle stiffened physically and mentally, but he turned to the sports page as though he hadn't heard.

This always annoyed Belle. She reached over and snatched the paper from him. "I'm talking to you, man!

If you don't get me and my baby outta this rat trap, I will!"

Battle suppressed a desire to shout back. Instead he just stared at her and then reached patiently for the paper. She jerked it out of his reach. "You can sit there like a knot on a log if you want to!" Belle blazed.

A whimper from the baby in the middle room went unheard by either of them. Battle raised himself half out of the chair, reached over and grabbed Belle's arm, twisting it and pulled the paper loose. She began to scratch at him but stopped abruptly when an agonizing cry came from the baby. She released the paper, jumped up, and ran from the kitchen. The baby still shrieked while Battle shuffled the crumpled pages back into place.

"My God, Battle! Come here! It's a rat!"

As he dashed into the room, Belle held Jean in one arm, and inspected two rows of teeth marks on the baby's right cheek. Blood oozed from each mark.

"He bit her, Battle! Oh God! He bit her!" she wailed as her husband rushed in.

As Battle looked at the tiny blobs of blood smothering anger rose.

"Better go and put some iodine on her," he told Belle.

He spun at a noise under the bed, and stomped viciously as a dirty gray rat the size of a kitten scampered across the room.

Gritting his teeth he looked into the bathroom where Belle painted Jean's bites.

"How late does Kelly stay in his office?" he asked so quietly it alarmed Belle.

"Eight. What you gonna do Battle? Don't get into no trouble!"

"I ain't gonna start no fighting trouble, but I'm gonna make it hot for Kelly."

He went back in the room, opened a closet and pulled on his clothes. He glanced at a clock on a dresser

that said seven thirty p.m. He went back to the bathroom door.

"Then tomorrow I'm gonna go from door to door
and tell everybody in the tenant council what happened."

Belle smiled as he kissed her lightly, and patted
Jean's head.

He left and went to see the landlord.

Loyle Hairston

❧

THE WINDS OF CHANGE

IT WAS MY BIG DAY and I was so hopped up I woke up before the alarm went off. Geez. The house was quiet except for Sis hummin' out in the kitchen. I set my watch by the clock and gauged my time; then laid out my vine, a clean shirt and things on the bed.

After I brushed my kicks, I looked my wig over in the mirror. My stockin' cap slipped off my head when I was sleepin' and the waves in my hair done unstrung and was all tangled up.

"Damn!"

I mean I wouldn't make my *own* funeral without my *wig* bein' in shape. So I went into the livin' room and called Sonny for an appointment; I *had* to have a marcel! He said he could take me on round ten o'clock. Whew! Glancin' at my watch I seen I had plenty of time; so I went back in my room and took out my bongos and worked out a while.

And just when the licks was comin' good, she opens up on me again. I mean if she wasn't my sister—

"Waddell."

At eight o'clock in the *a.m.*! And pa's tryin' to cop a snooze in the next room.

"Waddell!"

I locked my door, bolted it. She's way out in the kitchen but her voice it busts t'rough the walls like a truck. I didn't say nothin'; the name I had for her was burnin' the tip of my tongue—but I didn't say nothin'. I just kept on workin' out on my bongos, tryin' to think about that audition gig I had to make at one o'clock. My big chance to cop a show, a off-Broadway show; my chance to make enough long bread to put her down —and she wanta heat me up and make me blow it—

"Waddell Wilkins!"

"Goddam it, Sis, leave me alone—*please!*"

"Don't you know papa's tryin' to sleep . . . !"

Don't *I* know it; she's blastin' like a H-bomb and askin' me don't *I* know pa's tryin' to sleep. Geez! I mean I couldn't bear it no longer; so I t'rowed my bongos on the bed and went and run some water in the bathtub.

"You takin' a *bath?*" she said as I went in the kitchen where she was washin' dishes. Her hair was undone, curlin' over her forehead from under her 'kerchief; and her slip was showin' t'rough her loose robe.

"I'm gon wash my head."

She dropped her towel in the dishwater and gaped at me like I just said I was gon commit a murder.

"Aw naw! Don't tell me that wavy-wigged-Waddell's gonna wash out his beauty tresses!"

"Lay off me, Sis; goddam it, lay off!"

" 'Lay off me, Sis . . . lay off!' " She mocked back at me. "You slick-headed ditty-bop, if you spent half as much time tryin' to put something *inside* that worthless hat-rack as you did havin' your brains fried—"

"Goddam it, Sis . . . Aw go to hell."

I took a cake of soap from the cabinet and went back to the bathroom.

I mean what'd she know. She think I'm gon make a audition lookin' like a creep. You think they're lookin' for talent in the raw; appearance is half the game. A blockhead knows that. If you aint pressed and got the right spiel, you aint sayin' *nothin'* to the silks; it's the only language they can dig.

". . . If you had any backbone you'd be out lookin' for a job . . ."

A job! What she think I'm knockin' myself out to make this audition gig for—my old age pension? I asked her that!

"Hah! You'll never have to worry about old age pension; at the rate you're goin', you'll starve to death before you're twenty-one."

Dig her; I mean just dig *her.* Like them Nationalists always say: black folks is like crabs in a barrel—try to climb out and they'll snatch you right back ever' time.

"You know what you are, Sis; you're a creep—that's what you are!"

Then she really exploded. I wrapped my towel round my ears and went on in my room and put my old clothes back on, then hung my *vine* on a hanger, figurin' I'd dress when I got finished at the barbershop. Sis was hammerin' away through the walls like she was in a stone fit; until I couldn't take no more.

I blasted her:

"Shut your trap a minute and take a look at this dump you're livin' in. The walls is cracked; the ceilin's busted; the pipes leak; there aint no heat; no hot water mosta the time; no fresh air. The only thing expensive here is your goddam rent. Geez.

"You want me to grow up a sap like pa—knockin' hisself out on a mail-handler gig at the Post Office where the pay is so lousy he's gotta work a part-time gig to keep the finance company from bustin' the door down . . . I mean are you a damn fool, Sis?"

Sometimes I have to ask myself how come ma had to die and leave me saddled with *her.* Geez . . .

I copped a hack to Ray's Barbershoppe. The joint was already hummin' with cats talkin' about "broads," the numbers they *missed*, integration, the silks, and the figure they was gon play *today*. Half of the chairs was full; there was a few squares *actual'* takin' regular haircuts. Five cats was settin' under the dryers in back diggin' the NEWS. I set down and tried to think about the audition; I mean what them gigs was really like and how many cats I had to compete with, and wonderin' how good I really was on the bongos. My man, Sonny, dug me.

"You ready, Baby."

"Yeah," I winked and took the résumé scratch-sheet he mapped out for me: background; how long I been studyin'; where at; workin' experience; and such particulars. It was boss, the way he faked it. After goin' over it I put it back in my pocket, checked the time, and watched Sonny put the finish on the cat he was workin' on. His wig was shinin' like black satin; and Sonny was layin' in the waves with his hands, rollin' a big one in front and workin' the others in, soft and delicate like they growed natural. It was a swingin' job.

When my turn come I told him I wanted one just like he laid on that cat. Sonny rubbed the process in so thick with his rubber gloves, it started stingin' a little t'rough the heavy layer of grease he packed in my scalp.

"Damn, Baby!"

"Cool it, Mamma," Sonny said, combin' the process into my hair. "The secret to this business is to burn it so close to the scalp, it'll look natural all the way to the roots."

When he finished I dug my wig in the mirror.

"That's boss, Baby—the best I ever seen."

"Wow!" The cat in the next chair said. "You been transformed, daddy-o; if you was a shade lighter, you could pass for a silk!"

"The only way you'll ever get your mop to grow

natural again, Mamma," Sonny boasted, "is to have your head *shaved!*"

"Shee-it," I said, t'rowed my man a five-spot and told him to bank the change.

After I put on my vine and they all wished me good-luck, I went over to St. Nick's and took the A-train down to Fifty-ninth Street. It was only twelve o'clock, so I set in a Brass Rail on Eighth Avenue and tightened my nerves with a few slugs of imperial. Then I boated it down to Forty-sixth where the joint was, took a deep breath, and went inside.

They was runnin' off a dance number on the stage; only some cat in shirt sleeves and a cigar stump stuck in his teeth kept interruptin' 'em ever'time they got started. They was all in a sweat and I was tryin' to dig what was happenin' when this little blade-nosed cat switched over and told me to wait outside.

There was a settin' room on the left full of silk broads settin' round a old table, smokin' and yackin' away about nothin'; so I set on a chair against the wall in the corridor. From another part of the building I heard all sorts of drums beatin' and feet stompin' and a sad chorus that couldn't find the beat. They must be *silks*, I thought; and just to ease my nerves I tried to pick up the beat on my bongos. That huddle of old silk broads stopped yackin' and *dug* me, their eyes slidin' over me and stoppin' on my hair where they lit up and they whispred somethin' to one another. I played it cool.

Then this tall one, with green eyes and faded blond hair, eased out of the door with a cigarette in her mouth, lookin' round like she was pickin' out some-body to a cop a light from. She asked one of the grays in the settin' room, lit up, then leaned against the wall by the dressin' room door. And daddy she was *built!* Without lookin' at her face, I knowed she was buzzin' me with her pearls. Not bad at all—for a silk.

And you could tell she thought I was a big-shot entertainer like Harry Belafonte or somebody, from the way she was diggin' me. Geez! I mean, soon's they think you're famous and pullin' down that long bread they're ready to integrate the hell outa you—

"Hi."

I played a freeze; like my thoughts had me up-tight. But she was standin' right in front of me now; and I'm diggin' the way them leotogs was spellin' the truth out to me the way they was huggin' her. I mean I aint no stone.

"Hello," I said, playin' it straight; silks think you can't talk nothin' but slang.

"Excuse me, but aren't you Doug Ward?"

See what I mean. Like I'm psychic, I dig silks.

"No," I said and t'rowed her a sympathetic smile. Then three more, one of 'em a member, bolted out of the dressin' room and sailed over to where we was. Miss Fine said she was sorry and introduced herself to me, then the three others. I nodded to 'em and told 'em my name and dug 'em where they was sayin' the most. I mean they all was stacked; and they was friendly as hell. But this member—daddy, she was a real fox! Her big nut-shaped eyes was so bright it made you squint when you looked straight at 'em; and she musta been playin' the part of a African in the play because she wore her hair short and natural, like Miriam Makeba. But the way her big goldlooped earrings gleamed against her long satin-smooth neck, she looked like a African *Princess*! Without comin' outa my freeze, I dug her the most.

We struck up a conversation, and Colleen—the bold one—was tellin' me that they was all students with the American Ballet outfit when I was called for my gig. I rushed off hopin' I'd get back before they left so I could put the sound on the princess.

When I got inside and seen five cats in the middle of the floor, stripped down to tights, squattin' behind them long-bellied African drums, I got a feelin' in my gut that I didn't like. In nothin' flat, the cat in charge let me know what the feelin' was. They done changed the "locale" to a African settin' and when I told him that I never done no primitive dancin', he told me, with a lotta friggin' double-talk—to blow! I could see Sis's, face, mockin' and laughin' at me, so clear, I walked into the door.

I was gettin' on the elevator when I heard this Colleen's voice. I turned and she give *me* a sympathetic smile like she knowed straight off what happened. She was dressed and said she was waitin' for the others; then she asked me where I was goin'. I shrugged my shoulders, tryin' to pull myself together.

"Want to come with us?"

". . . Ah . . . I mean—where?"

"To the UN. We're—"

"The UN . . .?"

"Oh, come on. It'll take your mind off this. Okay?"

And before I give her an answer, she told me to wait for the girls while she took her car outa the parkin' lot. After I seen the princess, I forgot ever'thing—but *her!* All the way across town I'm tryin' to figure how I'm gon get her alone so I can sound her, and they're busy yackin' about the UN. It floored 'em when I told 'em I aint never been there. So I remembered what the NEWS always said about the joint and told 'em I didn't go because I thought the place was run by the commies. They bust laughin' on me. And that's when I learnt that Oleta, the princess, was a *pure* African; and that her brother was a member of her country's UN delegation. Geez! I mean I coulda hid in the ash tray on the armrest.

Colleen parked the car and we all strolled up the boulevard to the UN. Out in front a long row of flags was wavin' in the bright breeze, showin' off dazzlin' colors in all sorts of patterns; and I couldn't take my eye off that tall buildin' juttin' against the pale blue as we climbed the steps and went across the stone court to the "General Assembly Building."

Inside it was a boss lay-out; streamlined down to the carpets, with a soft, bluish light streamin' in from the glass walls openin' on a side garden-court splashed with green and bright colored flowers. But when I got upstairs and seen all them African cats settin' round the tables on the main floor, I damn near flipped! Some of 'em wore reg'lar blue-serge; some showed off their native styles. Papers was stacked neat on their desks alongside pitchers of water. And they kept leanin' over to one another, talkin' confidential—puttin' the *ig'* on the silks scattered amongs' 'em.

The gallery was buzzin' with "Lumumba," "Tshombe," and all those "Belgian mercenaries" and "Kasavubu" and about some "resolution" the "Afro-Asian" delegations done put to the floor. Oleta pointed her brother out to me settin' with a lotta young cats with smooth black round faces and woolly hair cropped even all over. They all was beamin' like they had Charley's number; and Charley was settin' there fussin' with his notes like he *knowed* it. I mean it was all I could do to keep from jumpin' up on my seat and bust out clappin'. No wonder the NEWS say the joint's run by Reds!

If Sis could see this, she'd flip—for certain, I thought, sittin' there between princess Oleta and Colleen, with my earphones on, and listenin' to this African talkin' in *French*. And it's comin' t'rough my earphones in *English*! *Geez.* I mean—*damn*!

By the time they got done hasslin' over that resolution and blastin' the silks until they buckled, me and Oleta was hittin' it off fine. And she was lookin' foxier by the minute. I copped her address when we got down stairs. Colleen had to pick her ol' lady up down town and said that she didn't have time to drive us back across town. We walked her to her car where she said she was very glad to meet me, shook my hand, wished me luck in show-business, and give me the nicest smile you could get from a "silk broad." I mean it moved me.

"Now don't forget my party Friday night," she said

to her gal friends, while I was makin' some sounds to Oleta. "You too, Oleta."

"Colleen, you know I have a class Friday night."

"Oh, posh with your class—I insist that you be there!"

"Oh, all right, we'll see," Oleta give in with a smile bright as a rose. Colleen got in her car then called me: ". . . Why don't *you* come too, Mr. Wilkins?"

"Well—"

"Here, I'll give you my address. We'd love to have you," she said, winkin' at Oleta as she scribbled her address on the back of a card.

All the way uptown, Princess Oleta and makin' that party Friday night was the only thing on my mind. It was only Monday and by Friday my process'd need retouchin': so I went by Ray's and made an appointment with Sonny for Friday. I was hongry, but after blowin' my audition, I wasn't in no mood for Sis's abuse; so I copped a sandwich, and took in a flick.

Marilyn Monroe was playin' at the Loew's; only soon's I got comfortable I went to sleep and dreamt I was with Oleta by the lake in Central Park, playin' my bongos and she was dancin' for me; and I was watchin' her Fine Brown reflectin' in the water shinin' with golden moonlight. Then she'd come over and stroke my hair; and in the gleamin' pools of her eyes I seen myself holdin' her close; only I was stripped down like a African warrior and my hair was woolly like them cats at the UN. I woke up then. I mean the dream was gettin' outa hand!

All week long there was something about them Africans that was buggin' me. I mean without even tryin' —they was *sayin'* something. I told Sis about 'em before I left for the barbershop.

"You mean they aint brown-nosin' to the white-folks like some of our 'leaders.' "

I cut out then and there. Geez. You ask her a question and she gotta make a speech. After gettin' my

kicks shined and my fingernails honed and polished, I
set down in the barber chair rubbin' the fuzz on my
chin and thinkin' about Oleta and how fine she was in
a way I aint never seen in a girl, member or silk.
Sonny stopped gassin' with some guys in the back and
put the cloth round my neck. I told him to give me a
shave. And he started crankin' the chair back.

"Not my face, daddy—my *head!*"

It shook the cat so, he dropped his clippers. I just
grinned and laid back and shut my eyes wonderin'
where I could cop myself a deuce of African drums. . . .

GLOSSARY

kicks: *shoes*
vine: *suit of clothes*
wig: *hair*
stocking cap: *woman's silk
   stocking pulled over head
   to hold hair in place*
marcel: *straightened* or
   processed hair
gig: *job*
ditty-bop: *young hipster;
   hepcat*
creep: *bum; shabby dress*
silks: *white folk*
dig: *understand*
copped: *got;* or *to get*
cats: *guys*
squares: *unsophisticated
   persons*
digging: *observing*

boss: *great; extraordinary*
dug: *studied*
mop: *hair*
play it cool: *to keep calm*
grays: *white folk*
pearls: *girl's eyes*
bread: *money*
freeze: *very calm*
member: *Negro*
fox: *pretty girl*
ig: *to ignore*
Charley: *white man*
brown-nosing: *compromis-
   ing one's self to curry
   personal favor from
   "superiors."*
blow: *spoil*
cop a snooze: *get some sleep*
copped a hack: *took a taxi*

Alice Childress

~☙~

THE HEALTH CARD

Well Marge, I started an extra job today. . . .
Just wait, girl. Don't laugh yet. Just wait till I tell you.
. . . The woman seems real nice. . . . Well, you know
what I mean. . . . She was pretty nice, anyway. Shows
me this and shows me that, but she was real cautious
about loadin' on too much work the first morning. And
she stopped short when she caught the light in my eye.

Comes the afternoon, I was busy waxin' woodwork
when I notice her hoverin' over me kind of timid-like.
She passed me once and smiled and then she turned
and blushed a little. I put down the wax can and gave
her an inquirin' look. The lady takes a deep breath
and comes up with, "Do you live in Harlem, Mildred?"

Now, you know I expected somethin' more than
that after all the hesitatin'. I had already given her my
address so I didn't quite get the idea behind the question. "Yes, Mrs. Jones," I answered, "that is where I
live."

Well, she backed away and retired to the living room
and I could hear her and the husband just a-buzzin'. A
little later on I was in the kitchen washin' glasses. I
looks up and there she was in the doorway, lookin' kind

of strained around the gills. First she stuttered and then she stammered and after beatin' all around the bush she comes out with, "Do you have a health card, Mildred?"

That let the cat out of the bag. I thought real fast. Honey, my brain was runnin' on wheels. "Yes, Mrs. Jones," I says, "I have a health card." Now Marge, this is a lie. I do not have a health card. "I'll bring it tomorrow," I add real sweet-like.

She beams like a chromium platter and all you could see above her taffeta house coat is smile. "Mildred," she said, "I don't mean any offense, but one must be careful, mustn't one?"

Well, all she got from me was solid agreement. "Sure," I said, "indeed *one* must, and I am glad you are so understandin', 'cause I was just worryin' and studyin' on how I was goin' to ask you for yours, and of course you'll let me see one from your husband and one for each of the three children."

By that time she was the same color as the house-coat, which is green, but I continue on: "Since I have to handle laundry and make beds, you know . . ." She stops me right there and after excusin' herself she scurries from the room and has another conference with hubby.

Inside fifteen minutes she was back. "Mildred, you don't have to bring a health card. I am sure it will be all right."

I looked up real casual kind-of and said, "On second thought, you folks look real clean, too, so . . ." And then she smiled and I smiled and then she smiled again. . . . Oh, stop laughin' so loud, Marge, everybody on this bus is starin'.

Alice Childress

✿

I GO TO A FUNERAL

IF YOU'LL FIX THE COFFEE, I'll just sit down and rest myself a bit because I'm some wore out! . . . I know you told me not to go to the funeral, but you know how people can get so insulted at a time like that! Them things leave me weak and upset, and it ain't because I'm afraid to die. I just can't seem to put my finger on what bothers me, but I guess it's a little bit of everything.

I only go to whatever funerals I have to, but even at that I've gone to quite a few. You know, I had to show up at Mitchell's service today because I'm such good friends with his sister. Well, I can't even go to a stranger's funeral without cryin' and sometimes I get to wonderin' why I have so little control of myself. And I come to the notion that it's because they *want* it like that . . . No, I'm not kiddin'!

I got to the chapel a little early and it was all gloomy-lit with candles flickerin' shadows on the wall and a organ that I couldn't see was givin' out some real weird sad-like tones. . . . No, I said *tones* and I don't mean *tune*! It wasn't no hymn that you'd ever heard before, it was just a sort of sweetish kind of whinin' and groanin'.

Yes, indeed, the place was banked with flowers, all kinds of fancy pillows made out of roses and wreaths built up on big long stands. There was one floral piece that was made out of carnations and it was a clock with the hands pointin' to the hour that Mitchell had died!

You just shoulda seen the flowers! There was sheaves of wheat and sprays of gladiolas and everything was tied with a ribbon-bow made out of net with satin stripes on it. His casket was gray plush and it was lined inside with white satin all crushed up in little bunches like those Christmas boxes that necklaces come in.

I had to sit down real quick because I started to cry and get weak in the knees. I was hurt and mad all over because I know Mitchell wouldn't of liked all that down-in-the-mouth kinda fixin's! Not the way he used to laugh and make jokes all the time. Why, he was one of the most happy-actin' people I ever knew. But I think what really got me was the little silver-paper words that was written across the net ribbons like *Rest in Peace, The Dear Departed* and *We Mourn*. It was a good thing that I had taken two or three handkerchiefs with me because I was a wreck!

Well, the organ kept goin' on as the people came in and last of all the family came walkin' down the aisle. I was surprised that there was so many of them because Mitchell always struck me as bein' kinda lonely-like. Of course, I knew he had his sister, Emma, and his father, but here come about thirty-five people marchin' together. . . . Oh, I suppose they were family in a cousin and aunt kinda way.

They was all dressed in black, and the women wore black veils over their hats and the men had on white shirts with black ties, plus black bands around their coatsleeves. The undertakers filed in behind them and went and sat over to one side near the front. There was a little light somethin' like a readin' lamp attached to the casket and shinin' right in Mitchell's face. The undertaker went over and put it out and then closed the lid, and the organ started goin' on louder than before!

After the family was seated the service started and the minister read his obituary. It was very nice, I guess, but it didn't sound very much like Mitchell. I mean, when the minister said, "The dearly beloved son of . . ." I got to thinkin' how his father wasn't speakin' to him most of the time because Mitchell wanted to open a shoe-repair shop and his father wanted him to be a doctor.

. . . No, I don't remember all of the obituary, just little snatches like ". . . walked the straight and narrow path . . . was an inspiration in his everyday life . . . lived a life of self-denial . . . humble and meek . . ."

. . . No, honey, that wasn't Mitchell at all and if he *did* go through any *denial*, it wasn't *self* because he wanted some of everything there was to have and tried to get it. He just failed, that's all!

. . . Oh, yes, they had singin'! One lady sang and she had a very nice voice, but she made it tremble too much. I guess she did that so it would sound real sad-like. It sure was sad 'cause she had the whole family sobbin' and sniffin' something terrible. She sang something about "Take Me Home" and it was all about wishin' to go to Heaven.

The minister talked about him goin' to his "just reward" and that really made people cry *real* hard. It beats me why his "just reward" would strike folks as bein' so particular sad because I do think he was a good man as far as I know.

But the worst part was when the undertaker opened the casket again, and they asked every one to file up and look at him *one more time*. I smiled to myself a little because I distinctly remember that one of Mitchell's favorite records was Count Basie's "April in Paris," and he used to holler out the part where the Count says, *"one more time!"* . . . And the whole time that I stood on line waitin' my chance to look at him I could kinda hear him hummin' "April in Paris."

Yes, I guess you could say he looked all right, although I don't know why people always ask, "How did he look?" . . . No, I don't mean you in particular, I mean anybody. Marge, do you know what they had done to Mitchell? They had dressed him in a full-dress suit with a white carnation in the buttonhole and he was wearin' white gloves! . . . Sure, they had bought it special because anyone that knew him could tell you that he liked clothes that were easy-like and was especially fond of tan and gray and green and colors like that!

When the last lookin' was over, the service came to the end and the next part was goin' out to the cemetery. I rode in one of the cars that was for his friends, and there was two fellas and a girl ridin' with me. I felt a lot better as I heard them talkin' about him because they were rememberin' nice things he had said and done and talkin' about him easy and free.

My, but there was a long train of black shiny cars lined up near his grave site in the cemetery and when they started unloadin' his flowers, there was hardly enough space to put them. It suddenly struck me that this burial cost a heap of money!

Everyone stood there and cried as they lowered him in the ground, but they weren't cryin' as hard as they did in the chapel. Everyone threw a flower in the grave. I was plannin' to keep a rose to bring home and press in my Bible, but a lady snatched it out of my hand and threw it away. She said, "It's dead-bad-luck to bring flowers from the graveyard." I asked her why and she said, "It means that there will be a death in *your* family!" Girl, it looks like nobody wants to go to their "just reward!"

When we got back in the cars, we headed over to Emma's house for refreshments. . . . Oh, yes, she had all manner of goodies to eat and plenty to drink and everybody seemed a little relieved that the whole funeral business was over. People kept talkin' about how Mitchell had been "put away beautifully," "the family has certainly done handsomely," "this is the way he would have wanted it," "he would have been proud" and things like that.

I saw a lot of people that neither me nor Mitchell had seen in years, but I guess they were all wishin' just like I was that we could have just *one more time* to be better friends to him. But the past is the past.

. . . How did he die? . . . No, he wasn't sick long, he just went like that, real sudden. You know he had been tryin' to get a nice shop location for a long time, but people wouldn't rent it to him because he was colored. . . . Sure, Marge, they do like that with stores just the same as with houses! . . . Yes, indeed, they will bar your way when it comes to tryin' to buy money-makin' property. Why do you think most colored businesses are all crowded into colored neighborhoods?

Sure, we want to sell things everywhere, too! After all, there's plenty of white shopkeepers in Harlem! Anyway, Mitchell couldn't find a good place so he just miseried along in first one little out-of-the-way side street and then another. One time he tried to get some white people to rent a place for him, but that got all bolexed up in legal procedure, and his father wouldn't help him get the money although he had it to lend. So last week Mitchell dropped dead. They said it was a heart attack, but I do believe he died of discouragement.

The reason I feel so bad about the whole thing is that I know he could have had a right smart little shop for what the funeral cost.

So, Marge, if there's anything you're plannin' to do, and ten or fifteen dollars from me would help you, let me know *now* because I do not intend to ever buy you or anybody else any of those carnation clocks or pillows! . . . I'm not sayin' you will go first! If it makes you feel better, we can pretend that I'm goin' first, and you can advance me some dollars on my next summer's vacation. And I want to thank you, too!

Langston Hughes

～❦～

WHO IS SIMPLE?

I CANNOT TRUTHFULLY STATE, as some novelists do at
the beginnings of their books, that these stories are
about "nobody living or dead." The facts are that these
tales are about a great many people—although they
are stories about no specific persons as such. But it is
impossible to live in Harlem and not know at least a
hundred Simples, fifty Joyces, twenty-five Zaritas, a
number of Boyds, and several Cousin Minnies—or reasonable facsimiles thereof.

"Simple Speaks His Mind" had hardly been published when I walked into a Harlem café one night and
the proprietor said, "Listen, I don't know where you
got that character, Jesse B. Semple, but I want you to
meet one of my customers who is *just* like him." He
called to a fellow at the end of the bar. "Watch how he
walks," he said, "exactly like Simple. And I'll bet he
won't be talking to you two minutes before he'll tell
you how long he's been standing on his feet, and how
much his bunions hurt—just like your book begins."

The barman was right. Even as the customer approached, he cried, "Man, my feet hurt! If you want to
see me, why don't you come over here where I am? I
stands on my feet all day."

"And I stand on mine all night," said the barman. Without me saying a word, a conversation began so much like the opening chapter in my book that even I was a bit amazed to see how nearly life can be like fiction—or vice versa.

Simple, as a character, originated during the war. His first words came directly out of the mouth of a young man who lived just down the block from me. One night I ran into him in a neighborhood bar and he said, "Come on back to the booth and meet my girl friend." I did and he treated me to a beer. Not knowing much about the young man, I asked where he worked. He said, "In a war plant."

I said, "What do you make?"

He said, "Cranks."

I said, "What kind of cranks?"

He said, "Oh, man, I don't know what kind of cranks."

I said, "Well, do they crank cars, tanks, buses, planes or what?"

He said, "I don't know what them cranks crank."

Whereupon, his girl friend, a little put out at this ignorance of his job, said, "You've been working there long enough. Looks like by now you ought to know what them cranks crank."

"Aw, woman," he said, "you know white folks don't tell colored folks what cranks crank."

That was the beginning of Simple. I have long since lost track of the fellow who uttered those words. But out of the mystery as to what the cranks of this world crank, to whom they belong and why, there evolved the character in this book, wondering and laughing at the numerous problems of white folks, colored folks, and just folks—including himself. He talks about the wife he used to have, the woman he loves today, and his one-time play-girl, Zarita. Usually over a glass of beer, he tells me his tales, mostly in high humor, but sometimes with a pain in his soul as sharp as the occasional hurt of that bunion on his right foot. Sometimes, as the old blues says, Simple might be "laughing to keep from crying." But even then, he keeps you laughing, too. If there were not a lot of genial souls in Harlem as talkative as Simple, I would never have these tales to write down that are "just like him." He is my ace-boy, Simple. I hope you like him, too.

Langston Hughes

✿

BANQUET IN HONOR

Well, sir, I went to a banquet the other night,"
said Simple, "and I have never seen nothing like it.
The chicken was good, but the best thing of all was
the speech."

"That's unusual," I said. "Banquet speeches are seldom good."

"This one were a killer," said Simple. "In fact, it
almost killed the folks who gave the function."

"Who gave it?"

"Some women's club that a big fat lady what goes
to Joyce's dancing class belongs to. Her name is Mrs.
Sadie Maxwell-Reeves and she lives so high up on
Sugar Hill that people in her neighborhood don't even
have roomers. They keep the whole house for themselves. Well, this Mrs. Maxwell-Reeves sold Joyce a
deuce of Three-Dollar ducats to this banquet her club
was throwing for an old gentleman who is famous
around Harlem for being an intellect for years, also
very smart as well as honest, and a kind of all-around
artist-writer-speaker and what-not. His picture's in the
Amsterdam News this week. I cannot recall his name,
but I never will forget his speech."

"Tell me about it, man, and do not keep me in suspense," I said.

"Well, Joyce says the reason that club gave the banquet is because the poor old soul is so old he is about on his last legs and, although he is great, nobody has paid him much mind in Harlem before. So this club thought instead of having a dance this year they would show some intelligence and honor him. They did. But he bit their hand, although he ate their chicken."

"I beg you, get to the point, please."

"It seems like this old man has always played the race game straight and has never writ no Amos and Andy books nor no songs like 'That's Why Darkies Are Born' nor painted no kinky-headed pictures as long as he has been an artist—for which I give him credit. But it also seems like he did not make any money because the white folks wouldn't buy his stuff and the Negroes didn't pay him no mind because he wasn't already famous.

"Anyhow, they say he will be greater when he's dead than he is alive—and he's mighty near dead now. Poor old soul! The club give that banquet to catch some of his glory before he passes on. He gloried them, all right! In the first place, he ate like a horse. I was setting just the third table from him and I could see. Mrs. Maxwell-Reeves sort of likes Joyce because Joyce helps her with her high kicks, so she give us a good table up near the speaking. She knows Joyce is a fiend for culture, too. Fact, some womens—including Joyce—are about culture like I am about beer—they love it.

"Well, when we got almost through with the dessert, which was ice cream, the toastmistress hit on a cup with a spoon and the program was off. Some great big dame with a high voice and her hands clasped on her bosoms—which were fine—sung 'O Carry Me Homey.' "

" 'O Caro Nome,' " I said.

"Yes," said Simple. "Anyhow, hard as I try, daddy-o,

I really do not like concert singers. They are always singing in some foreign language. I leaned over the table and asked Joyce what the song meant, but she snaps, 'It is not important what it means. Just listen to that high C above X.'

"I listened fluently, but it was Dutch to me.

"I said, 'Joyce, what *is* she saying?'

"Joyce said, 'Please don't show your ignorance here.'

"I said, 'I am trying to hide it. But what in God's name is she singing about?'

"Joyce said, 'It's in Italian. Shsss-ss-s! For my sake, kindly act like you've got some culture, even if you ain't.'

"I said, 'I don't see why culture can't be in English.'

"Joyce said, 'Don't embarrass me. You ought to be ashamed.'

"I said, 'I am not ashamed, neither am I Italian, and I do not understand their language.' We would have had a quarrel right then and there had not that woman got through and set down. Then a man from the Urban League, a lady from the Daughter Elks, and a gentleman librarian all got up and paid tributes to the guest of honor. And he bowed and smiled and frowned and et because he could not eat fast, his teeth being about gone, so he still had a chicken wing in his hand when the program started. Finally came the great moment.

" 'Shsss-ss-s-ssh!' says Joyce.

" 'I ain't said a word,' I said, 'except that *I sure wish I could smoke in here.*'

" 'Hush,' says Joyce, 'this is a cultural event and no smoking is allowed. We are going to hear the guest of honor.'

"You should have seen Mrs. Sadie Maxwell-Reeves. She rose to her full heights. She is built like a pyramid upside down anyhow. But her head was all done fresh and shining with a hair-rocker roached up high in front, and a advertised-in-*Ebony* snood down the back, also a small bunch of green feathers behind her ear and genuine diamonds on her hand. Man, she had bosom-glasses that pulled out and snapped back when she read her notes. But she did not need to read no notes, she were so full of her subject.

"If words was flowers and he was dead, that old man could not have had more bouquets put on him if he'd had a funeral at Delaney's where big shots get laid out. Roses, jonquils, pea-lilies, forget-me-nots, pansies, dogwoods, African daisies, also hydrangeas fell all over his head out of that lady toastmistress's mouth. He were sprayed with the perfume of eloquence. He were welcomed and rewelcomed to that Three-Dollar Banquet and given the red plush carpet. Before that lady got through, I clean forgot I wanted to smoke. I were spellbound, smothered in it myself.

"Then she said, 'It is my pride, friends, my pleasure, nay, my honor—without further words, allow me to present this distinguished guest, our honoreeeee—the Honorable Dr. So-and-So-and-So.' I did not hear his name for the applause.

"Well, sir! That old man got up and he did not smile. It looked like he cast a wicked eye right on me, and he did like a snake charmer to Joyce, because nobody could move our heads. He did not even clear his throat before he said, 'You think you are honoring me, ladies and gentlemen of the Athenyannie Arts Club, when you invited me here tonight? You are *not* honoring me a damn bit! I said, not a bit.'

"You could have heard a pin drop. Mens glued to their seats. Joyce, too.

" 'The way you could have honored me if you had wanted to, ladies and gentlemen, all these years, would have been to buy a piece of my music and play it, or a book of mine and read it, but you didn't. Else you could have booed off the screen a few of them Uncle Toms thereon and told the manager of the Ham-

ilton you'd never come back to see another picture in
his theatre until he put a story of mine in it, or some
other decent hard-working Negro. But you didn't do
no such a thing. You didn't even buy one of my water-
colors. You let me starve until I am mighty nigh blue-
black in the face—and not a one of you from Sugar
Hill to Central Park ever offered me a pig's foot.
Then when the *New York Times* said I was a genius
last month, here you come now giving a banquet for
me when I'm old enough to fall over in my grave—if
I was able to walk to the edge of it—which I'm not.

" 'Now, to tell you the truth, I don't want no damned
banquet. I don't want no honoring where *you* eat as
much as me, and enjoy yourselves more, besides making some money for your treasury. If you want to honor
me, give some young boy or girl who's coming along
trying to create arts and write and compose and sing
and act and paint and dance and make something out
of the beauties of the Negro race—give that child
some help. Buy what they're makin! Support what
they're doing! Put out some cash—but don't come giving me, who's old enough to die and too near blind to
create anything any more anyhow, a great big banquet
that *you* eat up in honor of your *own* stomachs as much
as in honor of me—who's toothless and can't eat.
You hear me, I ain't honored!'

"That's what that old man said, and sat down. You
could have heard a pin drop if ary one had dropped,
but nary one dropped. Well, then Mrs. Maxwell-Reeves
got up and tried to calm the waters. But she made matters worse, and that feather behind her ear was shaking
like a leaf. She pulled at her glasses but she could not
get them on.

"She said, 'Doctor, we know you are a great man,
but, to tell the truth, we have been kinder vague about
just what you have done.'

"The old man said, 'I ain't done nothing but eat at

banquets all my life, and I am great just because I am
honored by you tonight. Is that clear?'

"The lady said, 'That's beautiful and so gracious.
Thanks. It sounds so much like Father Divine.'

"The old man said, 'Father Divine is a genius at saying the unsayable. That is why he is great and because
he also gives free potatoes with his gospel—and potatoes are just as important to the spirit as words. In
fact, more so. I know.'

" 'Do you really think so, Doctor?'

" 'Indeed, or I wouldn't have come here at all tonight. I ate in spite of the occasion. I still need a potato and some meat—not honor.'

" 'We are proud to give you both,' said Mrs. Sadie
Maxwell-Reeves.

" 'Compliments returned,' said the old man. 'The
tickets you sold to this affair on the strength of *my*
name are feeding us all.'

"Mrs. Sadie Maxwell-Reeves came near blushing,
but she couldn't quite make it, being brownskin. I
don't know what I did, but everybody turned and
looked at me.

"I said, 'Joyce, I got to go have a smoke.'

"Joyce said, 'This is so embarrassing! You laughing
out loud! Oh!'

"I said, 'It's the best Six Dollars' worth of banquet I
ever had.' (Because I paid for them tickets although
Joyce bought them.) I said, 'If you ever want to take
me to another banquet in honor, I will go, though I
don't reckon there will be another one this good.'

" 'You have a low sense of humor, Mr. Semple,' said
Joyce, all formal and everything like she does when
she's mad. 'Shut up so I can hear the benediction.'

"Reverend Patterson Smythe prayed. Then it were
over. I beat it on out of there and had my smoke whilst
I was waiting for Joyce, because she looked mad. On
the way home I stopped at the Wonder Bar and had
two drinks, but Joyce would not even come in the back

room. She waited in the cab. She said I were not the least bit cultural. Still and yet, I thought that old man made sense. I told Joyce, just like he said, 'It is more important to eat than to be honored, ain't it?'

"Joyce said, 'Yes, but when you are doing both at the same time, you can at least be polite. I mean not only the Doctor, but *you*. It's an honor to be invited to things like that. And Mrs. Maxwell-Reeves did not invite you there to laugh.'

"I said, 'I didn't know I was laughing.'

" 'Everybody else knew it,' she said when we got to her door. 'You was heard all over the hall. I was embarrassed not only for you, *but for myself*. I would like you to know that I am not built like you. I cannot just drink and forget.'

" 'No matter how many drinks I drink,' I said, 'I will not forget this.' Then I laughed again—which were my error! I did not even get a good-night kiss—Joyce slammed the vestibule door dead in my face. So I went home to my Third Floor Rear—*and laughed some more*. If I wasn't honored, I sure was tickled, and, at least, I ain't stingy like them Sugar-Hillers. They wouldn't buy none of his art when he could still enjoy the benefits. But me, I'd buy that old man a beer *any time*."

Langston Hughes

❧

DEAR DR. BUTTS

"Do you know what has happened to me?" said Simple.

"No."

"I'm out of a job."

"That's tough. How did that come about?"

"Laid off—they're converting again. And right now, just when I am planning to get married this spring, they have to go changing from civilian production to war contracts, installing new machinery. Manager says it might take two months, might take three or four. They'll send us mens notices. If it takes four months, that's up to June, which is no good for my plans. To get married a man needs money. To stay married he needs more money. And where am I? As usual, behind the eight-ball."

"You can find another job meanwhile, no doubt."

"That ain't easy. And if I do, they liable not to pay much. Jobs that pay good money nowadays are scarce as hen's teeth. But Joyce says she do not care. She is going to marry me, come June, anyhow—even if she has to pay for it herself. Joyce says since I paid for the divorce, she can pay for the wedding. But I do not want her to do that."

"Naturally not, but maybe you can curtail your plans somewhat and not have so big a wedding. Wedlock does not require an elaborate ceremony."

"I do not care if we don't have none, just so we get locked. But you know how womens is. Joyce has waited an extra year for her great day. Now here I am broke as a busted bank."

"How're you keeping up with your expenses?"

"I ain't. And I don't drop by Joyce's every night like I did when I was working. I'm embarrassed. Then she didn't have to ask me to eat. Now she does. In fact, she insists. She says, 'You got to eat somewheres. I enjoy your company. Eat with me.' I do, if I'm there when she extends the invitation. But I don't go looking for it. I just sets home and broods, man, and looks at my four walls, which gives me plenty of time to think. And do you know what I been thinking about lately?"

"Finding work, I presume."

"Besides that?"

"No. I don't know what you've been thinking about."

"Negro leaders, and how they're talking about how great democracy is—and me out of a job. Also how there is so many leaders I don't know that white folks know about, because they are always in the white papers. Yet I'm the one they are supposed to be leading. Now, you take that little short leader named Dr. Butts, I do not know him, except in name only. If he ever made a speech in Harlem it were not well advertised. From what I reads, he teaches at a white college in Massachusetts, stays at the Commodore when he's in New York, and ain't lived in Harlem for ten years. Yet he's leading me. He's an article writer, but he does not write in colored papers. But lately the colored papers taken to reprinting parts of what he writes—otherwise I would have never seen it. Anyhow, with all this time on my hands these days, I writ him a letter last night. Here, read it."

Harlem, U.S.A.
One Cold February Day

Dear Dr. Butts,

I seen last week in the colored papers where you have writ an article for The New York Times in which you say America is the greatest country in the world for the Negro race and democracy the greatest kind of government for all, but it would be better if there was equal education for colored folks in the South, and if everybody could vote, and if there were not jim crow in the army, also if the churches was not divided up into white churches and colored churches, and if Negroes did not have to ride on the back seats of buses South of Washington.

Now, all this later part of your article is hanging onto your but. You start off talking about how great American democracy is, then you but it all over the place. In fact, the but end of your see-saw is so far down on the ground I do not believe the other end can ever pull it up. So me myself, I would not write no article for no New York Times if I had to put in so many buts. I reckon maybe you come by it naturally, though, that being your name, dear Dr. Butts.

I hear tell that you are a race leader, but I do not know who you lead because I have not heard tell of you before and I have not laid eyes on you. But if you are leading me, make me know it, because I do not read the New York Times very often, less I happen to pick up a copy blowing around in the subway, so I did not know you were my leader. But since you are my leader, lead on, and see if I will follow behind your but — because there is more behind that but than there is in front of it.

Dr. Butts, I am glad to read that you writ an article in The New York Times, but also sometime I wish you would write one in the colored papers and let me know how to get out from behind all these buts that are staring me in the face. I know America is a great country but — and it is that but that has been keeping me where I is all these years. I can't get over it, I can't get under it, and I can't get around it, so what am I supposed to do? If you are leading me, lemme see. Because we have too many colored leaders now that nobody knows until they get from the white papers to the colored papers and from the colored papers to me who

*has never seen hair nor hide of you. Dear Dr. Butts, are
you hiding from me – and leading me, too?*

*From the way you write, a man would think my race
problem was made out of nothing but* buts. *But this, but
that, and, yes, there is jim crow in Georgia but –.America
admits they bomb folks in Florida –* but *Hitler gassed the
Jews. Mississippi is bad –* but *Russia is worse. Detroit
slums are awful –* but *compared to the slums in India,
Detroit's Paradise Valley is Paradise.*

*Dear Dr. Butts, Hitler is dead. I don't live in Russia.
India is across the Pacific Ocean. And I do not hope to
see Paradise no time soon. I am nowhere near some of
them foreign countries you are talking about being so bad.
I am* here! *And you know as well as I do, Mississippi is
hell. There ain't no* but *in the world can make it out
different. They tell me when Nazis gas you, you die slow.
But when they put a bomb under you like in Florida, you
don't have time to say your prayers. As for Detroit, there
is as much difference between Paradise Valley and
Paradise as there is between heaven and Harlem. I don't
know anything about India, but I been in Washington,
D. C. If you think there ain't slums there, just take your*
but *up Seventh Street late some night, and see if you still
got it by the time you get to Howard University.*

*I should not have to be telling you these things. You are
colored just like me. To put a* but *after all this jim crow
fly-papering around our feet is just like telling a hungry
man,* "But *Mr. Rockefeller has got plenty to eat." It's just
like telling a joker with no overcoat in the winter time,*
"But *you will be hot next summer." The fellow is liable
to haul off and say, "I am hot now!" And bop you over
your head.*

*Are you in your right mind, dear Dr. Butts? Or are you
just writing? Do you really think a new day is dawning?
Do you really think Christians are having a change of
heart? I can see you now taking your pen in hand to write,*
"But *just last year the Southern Denominations of Hell-
Fired Salvation resolved to work toward Brotherhood." In
fact, that is what you already writ. Do you think Brotherhood means* colored *to them Southerners?*

*Do you reckon they will recognize you for a brother,
Dr. Butts, since you done had your picture taken in the*

Grand Ballroom of the Waldorf-Astoria shaking hands at some kind of meeting with five hundred white big-shots and five Negroes, all five of them Negro leaders, *so it said underneath the picture? I did not know any of them Negro leaders by sight, neither by name, but since it says in the white papers that they are leaders, I reckon they are. Anyhow, I take my pen in hand to write you this letter to ask you to make yourself clear to me. When you answer me, do not write no "so-and-so-and-so* but –." *I will not take* but *for an answer. Negroes have been looking at democracy's* but *too long. What we want to know is how to get rid of that* but.

Do you dig me, dear Dr. Butts?

Sincerely very truly,
Jesse B. Semple

Paule Marshall

꘎꙰꙰

SOME GET WASTED

A SHOUT HURLED after him down the rise: "Run,
baby. Run, fool!" and Hezzy knew, the terror snapping
the tendons which strung together his muscles, that he
had been caught in a sneak, was separated from his
People, alone, running with his heart jarring inside his
narrow chest, his stomach a stone weight and his life
riding on each rise and plunge of his legs. While far
behind, advancing like pieces of the night broken off,
were the Crowns. He couldn't dare turn to look,
couldn't place their voices because of the wind in his
ears, but he knew they were Crowns. They had to be.

"Run, baby, run. You running real pretty, but we's
with you all the way. . . ."

And he was running pretty. So that he began to feel
an ease and lightness. His feet skimmed the path while
his arms cut away the air around him. But then he
had learned how to run from the master. Him and the
Little People was always hanging around the block
watching Turner and the Big People practice their running. Turner was always saying, "Dig, you studs, one
thing, don't never let another club catch you in a
sneak. Especially you Little People. Don't never get

too far away from the rest of the guys. In this club
when we go down everybody goes together. When we
split, everybody splits together. But if you should get
caught in a sneak, haul ass out of there. Run, baby.
Your legs is your life then, you can believe that."

Yeah, Turner would dig the way he was running.
He would go round the block tomorrow, all cool like
nothing had happened and say—ignoring Turner but
talking loud enough so's he hear—"Man, dig what happened to me last night after the action in the park.
Them dirty Crowns caught me in a sneak, man. Come
chasing me all over the fuggen place. But I put down
some speed on them babies and burned their eyes."

Even now, their jeers seemed fainter, further away:
"Run, baby . . . like we said, you running pretty. . . ."
The night was pulling them back, making them part
of it again. Man, he could outrun those punks any
time, any place. His heart gave a little joyous leap and
he sprinted cleanly ahead, the pebbles scattering under-
foot.

The day, this night, his flight had begun a week ago.
The Little People had gotten the word that something
was up and had gone over to the Crib where the Noble Knights, their Big People, hung out. The Crib was
the square of bare earth in front of the decaying brownstone where Turner live.

"The jive is on," Turner said as soon as they were
assembled.

And before the words were barely out, Sizzle who
lived only to fight, said, "Like I been telling you, man,
it's about time. Them Crowns been messing all over
us. Pulling sneaks in our turf. Stomping and wasting
our Little People like they did Duke. Slapping around
our broads when they come outta school . . . Man, I
hate them studs. I hate them dirty Crown buggers."

"Man, cool your role," Turner said. Then: "Like I
said, the jive is on. And strong this time. We ain't just

goin' down in their turf and stomp the first Crown we
see and split, like we always do. This is gonna be organized. We already got word to the Crowns and
they're ready. Now dig. Next Monday, Memorial Day,
we look. Over in Prospect Park, on the Hill. Time
the parade ends and it starts getting dark, time the
Crowns show, we lock. Now pick up on the play. . . ."

Hezzy, crowded with his guys on the bottom step of
the stoop listened, his stomach dropping as it did on
the cyclone in Coney Island. Going down with the Big
People at last! Down with the hearts! And on Memorial Day when every club in the city would be gangbusting. The Italian cats in South Brooklyn, them Spanish
studs in East Harlem. And on the Hill—Massacre Hill
they called it—where many a stud had either built his
rep or gotten wasted.

He had heard how three years ago on Easter Sunday
when the Noble Knights clashed with the Crusaders
on the Hill, Turner had gotten the bullet crease on
his forehead and had started his bad rep. Heard how
the cat had gone to church packing his zip that morning and gone down to lock with the Crusaders that
afternoon.

Hezzy looked up over the heads at the bullet crease.
It was like the cat's skin was so tough the bullet had
only been able to graze it. It was like nothing or nobody could waste the cat. You could tell from his
eyes. The iris fixed dead-center in the whites and full
of dark swirls of colors like a marble and cold, baby.
When Turner looked sideways he never shifted his
eyes, but turned his head, slow, like time had to wait
on him. Man, how them simple chicks goofed behind
that look. The stud didn't even have to talk to 'em.
Just looked and they was ready to give him some. . . .

"Dig, we ain't wearing no club jackets neither," Turner was saying. "Cause they ain't no need to let The
Man know who we is. And another thing, it's gonna be
dark out there, so watch whose head you busting."

The unmoving eyes fixed the Crosstown Noble Knights. "You studs down?"

"We down, man."

"You all down?" His chin flicked toward the Little People at the bottom of the stoop.

"Yeah, we down," Hezzy answered.

"We don't want none of you Little People coming up weak," Turner said.

"Man, I ain't saying we ain't got some punks in the Division, but we leaves them studs home when we bopping."

All around the eyes glanced his way, but he kept his gaze on Turner.

"What's your name again, man?" Turner said and there was a tightness in his voice.

"Hezzy, man," and he touched the turned down brim of the soiled sailor hat he always wore where his name was emblazoned in black.

"You supposed to be president of the Little People since Duke got wasted?"

"Ain't no suppose, man. I am the president."

"All right, my man, but cool your role, you dig?"

He was all flushed inside. His head felt like it was twisted behind drinking some wine—and when the meeting was over and he and his little guys were back on their corner, they pooled their coins for a pint of Thunderbird and drank in celebration of how bad and cool he had been in front of the Big People.

Late that night he wandered alone and high through his turf. And all around him the familiar overflow of life streamed out of the sagging houses, the rank hallways, the corner bars, bearing him along like a dark tide. The voices loud against the night sky became his voice. The violence brooding over the crap games and racing with the cars became the vertigo inside his head. It was his world, his way—and that other world beyond suddenly no longer mattered. Rearing back he snatched off his hat, baring his small tough black child's face. "Hezzy," he shouted, his rage and arrogance a wine-tinged spume. "Yeah, that's right, Hezzy. Read about me in the *News* next week, ya dumb squares."

The night before Memorial Day he wet his bed, and in the morning awoke in the warm wet rankness of himself, shaking from a dream he couldn't remember, his eyes encrusted with cold. Quickly pulling on his hat, he shoved his half-brothers from around him.

"Boy, what time you got in here last night?"

He jammed a leg into his trousers.

"You hear me? What time? Always running the streets . . . But you watch, you gonna get yourself all messed up one of these days . . . Just don't act right no more. I mean, you used to would stay round the house sometime and help me out . . . used to would listen sometime . . . and go to school. . . ."

It was the same old slop, in the same old voice that was as slack as her body and as lifeless as her eyes. He always fled it, had to, since something in him always threatened to give in to it. Even more so this morning. For her voice recalled something in his dream. It seemed to reach out in place of her arms to hold him there, to take him, as she had sometimes done when he was small, into her bed. Jumping up, he slammed the door on that voice, cutting it off and almost threw himself down the five flights of stairs. As he hit the street the sun smacked him hard across the face and he saw his Little People waiting for him on the corner.

The parade was half over when Hezzy and his guys following Turner and the Big People some distance ahead reached Bedford Avenue. Old soldiers, remnants of the wars, shuffled along like sleep-walkers, their eyes tearing from the dust and glare. Boy Scouts, white mostly, with clear eyes and smooth fresh faces, marched under the rippling flags to the blare of "America, America, God shed his grace on thee . . ." and the majorettes kicked high their white legs, the flesh under the thighs quivering in the sunlight. Their batons flashed silver. And the crowd surged against the barricades with a roar.

"Man, dig the squares," Hezzy said, the smoke flaring from under the sailor hat.

"They sure out here, ain't they," the boy beside him said.

"Man! You know, I feel sorry for squares, I tell you the truth. They just don't know what's happening. I mean, all they got is this little old jive parade while tonight here we are gonna be locking with the Crowns up on the Hill. . . ."

Later, in Prospect Park, he watched scornfully from behind his oversized sunglasses as the parade disbanded: the old soldiers wheezing and fanning under the trees, the Boy Scouts lowering the heavy flags, the majorettes lolling on the grass, laughing, their blond hair spread out as if to dry. "Yeah," he said, "I feel real sorry for squares."

As always whenever they came to Prospect Park they visited the small amusement area and Hezzy, seeing that they had gotten separated from Turner and the Big People suddenly let out a whoop and clambered aboard the merry-go-round, his four guys behind him. Startling the other children there with their bloodcurdling cries, they furiously goaded their motionless painted mounts, cursing whenever they grabbed for the ring and missed.

"Man," he said laughing as they leaped off together into the trampled grass and dust. "You all is nothing but punks riding some old jive merry-go-round."

"Seems like I seen you on there too, baby."

"How you mean, man? I was just showing you cats how to do the thing."

Later they sneaked through the zoo, and forcing their way close to the railing with their cocked elbows, teased the animals and sounded each other's mother:

"Yoa mother, man."

"Yours, Jim."

Leaning dangerously over the rail, they gently coaxed the seals out of the water. "Come on up, baby, and do your number for the Knights. The Noble Knights of Gates Avenue, baby."

They stood almost respectfully in front of the lion cage. "Lemme tell ya, Jim, that's about a bad stud you see in there," Hezzy said. "You try locking with that cat and get yourself all messed up. . . ."

And all the while they ate, downing frankfurters and pepsis, and when their money was gone, they jostled the Boy Scouts around the stands and stole candy. Full finally, they climbed to a ridge near Massacre Hill and there, beneath a cool fretwork of trees and sun they drank from a pint bottle of wine, folding their small mouths around the mouth of the bottle and taking a long loud suck and then passing it on with a sigh.

The wine coupled with the sun unleashed a wildness in them after a time and they fell upon each other, tussling and rolling all in a heap, savagely kneeing each other and sending the grass and the bits of loosened sod flying up around them. And then just as abruptly they fell apart and lay sprawled and panting under the dome of leaves.

"Man, you seen the new Buick?" one of them said after a long silence. "I sure would like to cop me one of them."

"Cop with what, man? You'll never make enough bread for that."

"Who's talking about buying it, Jim. Ain't no fun behind that, I means to steal me one."

"For what? You can't even drive."

"Don't need to. I just want that number sitting out-side my house looking all pretty. . . ."

Hezzy, silent until then, said, shaking his head in sad and gentle reproof. "That's what I mean about you studs. Always talking about stealing cars and robbing stores like that's something. Man, that slop ain't nothing. Any jive stud out here can steal him a car or rob a store. That don't take no heart. You can't build you no real rep behind that weak slop. You got to be out here busting heads and wasting cats, Jim. That's the only way you build you a rep and move up in a club. . . ."

"Well, we out here, ain't we?" one of them said irritably. "Most of the guys in the division didn't even show this morning."

"Them punks!" he cried and sat up. At the thought of them out on the corner drinking and jiving the chicks, having a good time, safe, the wine curdled in his stomach. For a dangerous second he wanted to be with them. "Let's make it," he shouted, leaping up, and feeling for the section of lead pipe under his jacket. "Let's find Turner and the rest of the guys." And as they plunged down the rise, he looked up and squinting in the sunlight, cried, "Who needs all this sun and slop anyways. Why don't it get dark?"

As if acceding to his wish, the sun veered toward Massacre Hill and paused there for a moment as if gathering its strength for the long descent. Slowly the dusk banked low to the east began to climb—and all over the park the marchers departed. The merry-go-round stood empty. The refreshment stands were boarded up. And the elephants, sensing the night coming on, began trumpeting in the zoo.

They found their Big People in a small wood on the other side of Massacre Hill, the guys practicing the latest dance steps, drinking from a gallon bottle of wine, playfully sparring, cursing—just as if they were in the Crib, although there was an edginess to all they did, a wariness.

Turner, with Sizzle and Big Moose—the baleful Moose who had done in a Crown when he was Hezzy's age, thirteen, and gotten busted, rehabilitated, paroled and was back bopping with the cats—was squatting under a tree, his impassive gaze on the path leading to the Hill.

Hezzy saw the bulge at his pocket. The cat was packing his burn! And suddenly he felt as safe as the guys back on the corner drinking and jiving with the chicks. Everything was cool.

The dusk had begun slowly sifting down through the trees when Sizzle sprang up—and it was seeing a tightly coiled wire spring loose. "Them sneaky Crown bastards," he cried, almost inarticulate with rage. "They ain't gonna show. Just like the last time. Remember?" he shouted down at Turner. "Remember how the pricks sent us word they was coming down and then didn't show. Punked out. Every last one of the bastards. Remember?"

Turner nodded, his eyes still fixed on the path.

And Big Moose said petulantly, "I never did go for bopping in Prospect Park no ways. Give me the streets, baby, so if I got to haul ass I'm running on asphalt. Out here is too spooky with all these jive trees. I won't even know where I'm running—and knowing me I'm subject to run right into The Man and find myself doing one to five for gangbusting again."

"Man," Turner said, laughing, but with his eye still on the path. "There ain't no need to let everybody know you punking out."

"I ain't punking out," Moose said. "It's just too dark out here. How I'm going to know for sure it's a Crown's head I'm busting and not one of our own guys?"

And Hezzy said, his voice as steady, as chiding as Turner's "You'll know, man. Just smell the punk's breath before you smash him. Them cheap Crowns drink that thirty cents a pint slop."

"Who asked you?" Big Moose swung on him.

"Cool, man," Turner caught Moose's arm and turned to Hezzy. He stared at him with eyes filled with the dusk. "Moose, man," he said after a time, his gaze still on Hezzy, "looks like I might have to put you out of the club and move up my man Hezzy here, especially if the stud fights as bad as he talks. I might even have to move over, Jim . . ."

Hezzy returned the dark and steady gaze, the chilling smile—and again he felt high, soaring.

The Crowns came at the very edge of the day. A dozen or more small dark forms loping toward them down the path which led to the hill. They spotted the Noble Knights and the wind brought their cry: "The Crowns, punks. It's the Crowns."

There was a moment's recoil among the Noble Knights and then Turner was on his feet, the others behind him, and their answering shout seemed to jar the trees around them: "The Noble Knights, muh-fuggers! The Noble Knights are down!"—and with Turner in the lead and Sizzle, Big Moose and Hezzy just behind, they charged up the rise from the other side, up into the descending night and as they gained the low crest and met the oncoming Crowns, the darkness reached down and covered them entirely.

The battle was brief as always, lasting no more than two or three minutes, and disorderly. They thrashed and grappled in the dark, cursing, uncertain whom they were hitting. The cries burst like flares: "The Crowns!" "The Noble Knights, baby!" The dull red spurt of a gun lit the darkness and then they were fighting blind again.

In those minutes which seemed like hours a rubber hose smacked up against Hezzy's head, knocking off his hat and blinding him with pain for a second. He did not mind the pain, but the loss of his hat, the wind stinging his exposed head, terrified and then enraged him. He struck out savagely and something solid gave way beneath the lead pipe in his hand—and as it did something within him burst free: a sap which fed his muscles and sent his arm slashing into the surging darkness. Each time someone rushed him shouting, "The Crowns, punk!" he yelled, "The Noble Knights, baby!" and struck, exulting.

The pipe flew from his hand and he drew his shiv, the blade snatching a dull yellow gleam from somewhere and as he held it at the ready, shouting for a Crown, he heard the first whistle then the next, shrill, piercing the heart of the night. For an instant which seemed endless, there was silence on the hill. And it was as if the sound of the whistle had cut off the air in their throats. Their bodies froze in the violent attitudes of the fight—and it was as if they were playing "statues." Knights and Crowns were one suddenly, a stunned, silent, violently cohered mass. Comrades. For the whisper passed among them without regard to friend or foe: "The Man, baby! The Man." Then the darkness exploded into fragments that took on human form and they scattered headlong down the hill.

The ground below was a magnet which drew Hezzy to it and he plunged helpless toward it, bruised and terrified and suddenly alone as the others behind him raced down another path. And then no longer alone as the shout sounded behind him, "There goes one of the punks, I betcha. Let's waste the muh-fugger."

He had been caught in a sneak.

"Run, baby . . . Like we said, you running pretty . . . But we're still with ya. . . ."

And he was, as they said, still running pretty. He was certain of his escape now. The black wall ahead would soon give way, he knew, to a street and neon signs and people and houses with hallways to hide him until he could get back to his turf. Yet a single regret filtered down through the warm night and robbed the flight of its joy. He longed for his hat. Tears of outrage started up. If only he had wasted one of the bastards to make up for his loss. Or shived one of them good. He ran crying for the hat, until overwhelmed by his loss, he wheeled around and for a moment stood cursing them. Then, turning, he ran ahead.

But in that moment they were on him. It was as if they had known all along that he would pause and had held back, saving themselves till that error. Now they

came on swiftly, intent, suddenly silent. The distance
between them narrowed. The sound of their approach
welled out of the night; and out of the silence came a
single taunt: "What's the matter, baby, you ain't running so pretty no more?"

His fear suddenly was a cramp which spread swiftly
to all his muscles. His arms tightened. His shoulders.
The paralysis reached his legs so that his stride was
broken and his feet caught in the ruts of the path. Fear
was a phlegm in his throat choking off his air and a
film over his eyes which made the black wall of trees
ahead of him waver and recede. He stumbled and as
he almost went down, their cry crashed in his ears:
The Noble Knights, punk! The Knights are down!

He turned as if jerked around and over the loud rale
of his breathing he listened, unbelieving, to the echo of
the words. They called again, "The Knights, muh-fugger!" nearer this time, and the voices clearly those of
Turner, Sizzle and Big Moose. And Hezzy's relief was
a weakness in his legs and a warmth flooding his chest.
The smile that everyone always said was so like his
mother's broke amid his tears and he started toward
them, hailing them with the shiv he still held, laughing
as he wept, shouting, "Hey, you bop-crazy studs,
it's . . ."

The gun's report drowned his name. The bullet sent
a bright forked light through him and pain discovered
the secret places of his body. Yet he still staggered toward them, smiling, but stiffly now, holding out the
knife like a gift as they sped by without looking. Even
when they were gone and he was dead, a spoor of blood
slowly trailed them. As if, despite what they had done,
they were still his People. As if, no matter what, he
would always follow them. Overhead the black dome
of the sky cleared and a few stars glinted. Cold tears
in the warm May night.

HARLEM: HER AUTHORS

Harlem: Her Authors

James Baldwin: Mr. Baldwin is one of the most discussed writers to emerge in recent years. He is perhaps best known for his practically singlehanded restoration of the essay as a literary form. His last two books of essays, *Nobody Knows My Name* and *The Fire Next Time,* have established him as one of the major writers of the postwar era. His latest novel is *Tell Me How Long The Train's Been Gone?*

Claude Brown: Mr. Brown is the author of an autobiography that has had international repercussions, *Manchild in the Promised Land.* It is considered to be one of the great sociological documents of our times.

Sterling A. Brown: The dean of black American poets recently left his post as Professor of English at Howard University, Washington, D.C. to retire after thirty years of creative teaching. He is the author of numerous books and essays and has worked on a new, revised edition of the anthology *Negro Caravan* with co-editors Arthur P. Davis and Ulysses G. Lee.

John Henrik Clarke: Mr. Clarke is Associate Editor of *Freedomways* and the editor of *Harlem, U.S.A.* His last three published books are: *William Styron's Nat Turner ... Ten Black Writers Respond; Malcolm X, The Man and His Time*; and *Harlem, Voices from the Soul of Black America.* He is an Associate Professor in the Department of Black and Puerto Rican Studies at Hunter College of the City University of New York, and a visiting professor at the Africana Studies and Research Center at Cornell University, Ithaca, New York.

Kenneth B. Clark: Dr. Clark is Professor of Psychology at City College of New York and has been Research Director of the Northside Center for Child Development since 1946. His book *Prejudice and Your Child* is considered a standard work on the subject of prejudice in children. He is presently director of the Metropolitan Applied Research Center, Inc. His latest book, written in collaboration with Jeannette Hopkins, is titled *A Relevant War Against Poverty*.

Alice Childress: Miss Childress began her professional career as an actress, receiving her dramatic training at the American Negro Theatre School of Drama and Stagecraft. She is a member of the Harlem Writers' Guild. Four of her plays have been produced in New York's off-Broadway theatres, and recently several of her plays have been presented on New York's educational television channels with subsequent nationwide distribution.

Countee Cullen: Mr. Cullen was one of the notable poets to emerge from the period known as the Harlem Literary Renaissance. His first book of poems, *Color*, was published in 1925 and his second book, *Copper Sun*, appeared in 1926. He died in February, 1946.

Ossie Davis: Mr. Davis attended Howard University where two of his professors were Alain Locke and Sterling Brown. For many years he has been a successful actor and playwright. His best known play, *Purlie Victorious*, was produced on Broadway in 1961. He has recently added the directorship of commercially successful films to his roster of credits.

E.U. Essien-Udom: Mr. Essien-Udom is the author of *Black Nationalism: The Search for An Identity in America*. Early in 1964 he returned to Nigeria where he is now head of the department of government studies at the University of Ibadan; he is also editor of the Africana series of reprints published by Frank Cass Ltd., England.

Elton C. Fax: Mr. Fax is a book illustrator and lecturer. He is also author of the book *West African Vignettes* and has recently finished work on *East African Vignettes*.

Milton A. Galamison: Dr. Galamison is pastor of Siloam Presbyterian Church, Brooklyn, and also president of the Parents' Workshop for Equality in the New York City Schools. For a number of years he was a member of New York City's Board of Education and was recently Director of the Center of Urban Affairs at Harvard University.

Loyle Hairston: Mr. Hairston is a member of the Harlem Writers' Guild; he is a novelist, a short-story writer, and has assisted in the compilation of several anthologies.

Lorraine Hansberry: Miss Hansberry wrote the prize-winning play *Raisin in the Sun,* followed by the highly successful *Sign in Sidney Brustein's Window.* Two of her works which have been produced posthumously are *To be Young, Gifted and Black* and *Les Blancs.*

Ollie Harrington: Mr. Harrington is the author of the book *Bootsie and Others* and cartoonist for the *Pittsburgh Courier.* As a cartoonist he is one of the finest commentators on our times. He was at one time Public Relations Director of the NAACP. Although he has been living abroad for the past fifteen years, he keeps in close touch with the American scene.

Eugene C. Holmes: Dr. Holmes is Chairman of the Department of Philosophy at Howard University where he has served for thirty years, twenty of these with Dr. Alain Locke. Under a grant from Howard, he has recently completed *The Life and Times of Alain Locke.*

Leonard W. Holt: Mr. Holt is a graduate of the Howard University Law School. He practiced in Norfolk, Virginia, where he and his partners served as counsel to more than forty school integration and civil rights cases before he moved to his present practice in San Francisco, Califronia. He is the author of two books on the civil rights crisis.

Langston Hughes: Mr. Hughes has been poet laureate of his people for over twenty-five years. He is one of the best known black writers. His first poem to appear in a nationally known publication was *The Negro Speaks of Rivers* which appeared in 1921 in *The Crisis,* then edited by W.E.B. Du Bois. He died in 1967 at the age of sixty-five. Though born in Joplin, Missouri, his home was Harlem, U.S.A. His friends and admirers were from all parts of the world and of all colors, and in his poetry he left an immortal testament to his love for his people and for Harlem.

John H. Jones: Mr. Jones is a playwright and former editor of a progressive newspaper. His articles and book reviews have appeared in many publications in the United States, including the magazine *Freedomways.*

Sylvester Leaks: Mr. Leaks is a newspaperman and novelist who recently completed a memorial play dedicated to Dr. W.E.B. Du Bois and entitled *In These His Words.* He is treasurer of the Harlem Writers Guild, and for many years

366 HARLEM U.S.A.

has been a correspondent for the newspaper *Muhammad Speaks*. He is presently director of a Brooklyn self-help agency.

Paule Marshall: Mrs. Marshall is the author of the novel *Brown Girl, Brownstones* and a book of short stories, *Soul Clap Hands and Sing*. Her most recent novel, which has won a number of awards is *The Chosen Place, the Timeless People*.

Julian Mayfield: Mr. Mayfield is the author of three novels, *The Hit, The Long Night* and *The Grand Parade*. He spent several years in Ghana as editor of official government publications. Since returning to the States he has taught at Cornell University in Ithaca, New York and is presently with the Schweitzer program at New York University. He has recently completed his autobiography.

Claude McKay: Mr. McKay's first book of poems, *Songs of Jamaica* (1912), won him the Mulgrave Silver Medal and wide acclaim, while his first novel, *Home to Harlem* (1928), gained him the Harmon Gold Award and created a literary sensation. One of his poems, *If We Must Die* (1919), has gone around the world and is perhaps the most quoted and reprinted poem of this generation. Mr. McKay died in 1948.

Loften Mitchell: Mr. Mitchell has engaged in research on the history of the Negro in the American theatre for a number of years. Of his many plays *A Land Beyond the River* is the best known. Another play, *Star of the Morning*, is about the life and career of Bert Williams.

Richard B. Moore: Mr. Moore is a lecturer and writer on Afro-American history. He is owner-manager of the Frederick Douglass Book Store in New York and founder of "The Committee to Present the Truth about the Name Negro."

Carlton Moss: Mr. Moss is a writer associated with the production of educational films in Hollywood, California. Among his films are: *The House on Cedar Hill*, a short film on the life of Frederick Douglass, and *George Washington Carver*. Now in production is a short film on the life of Dr. W.E.B. Du Bois.

Gilbert Osofsky: Dr. Osofsky is a Professor of American Social History at the University of Illinois, Chicago. He is author of the book *Harlem, The Making of a Ghetto* and editor of *The Burden of Race.*

Hope R. Stevens: Mr. Stevens, an attorney, has been associated with progressive efforts to improve the Harlem community for over twenty-five years.

Ricardo Weeks: Mr. Weeks was born in Puerto Rico and came to America in 1925. For nearly twenty years his poems and short stories have appeared in newspapers and magazines throughout the U.S.A. He has published two volumes of poetry: *Freedom's Soldier* and *The People's Sonneteer.*

Charles E. Wilson: For a number of years, Mr. Wilson was a feature writer for *The Liberator;* presently he is an instructor in the Department of Urban Politics at Washington Square College campus of New York University in New York City.

HARLEM:
HER ARTISTS AND SCULPTORS

Harlem: Her Artists and Sculptors

Charles White: The paintings by Charles White are reproduced through the courtesy of the artist. The painting which opens this section is a drawing done in Chinese ink in 1964. Its title is "Uhuru" which is Swahili for Freedom. It is privately owned. The second, done in charcoal in 1962, also privately owned, is "Move Up A Little Higher." The third is the artist's famous head of Abraham Lincoln.

Elizabeth Catlett: The three sculptures are reproduced through the courtesy of the artist.

John Biggers: The paintings pictured through the courtesy of the artist and the University of Texas Press, are: "Mother Earth," detail of mural, Evolution of Life, Science Building, Texas Southern University; "Sharecroppers," drawing, 30 x 40 inches; "The Rural School Teacher," detail of a mural, Naples High School, Naples, Texas; "Cradle," drawing 30 x 30 inches, Houston Museum of Fine Arts Collection; "Market Women," Accra, Ghana, drawing, 30 x 36 inches.

Jacob Lawrence: The paintings appear through the courtesy of the artist, The American Federation of Fine Arts and The American Society of African Culture. Photos by Ed. Bagwell. The pictures, painted for a series called "The Migration," trace the story of the Negro movement out of the South into the cities of the North. Those pictured in the book include "The death rate was high," "Bread – they were very poor," "Sometimes they were made to miss a train," "In the North, the Negro had better educational facilities."

Richmond Barthé: The sculptures of Richard Barthé are reproduced through the courtesy of the Harmon Foundation of New York. They include: "Julius," "Rose McClendon," "The Mother" and "Boy With Flute."

NOTES

Notes

SECTION I

1. Sugar Hill: a ten-block area from 145th to 155th Streets between Edgecombe and St. Nicholas Avenues. The apartment houses on Edgecombe Avenue are considered to be officially on "Sugar Hill."
2. Schomburg Library: reference library branch of the New York Public Library, located at 135th Street and Lenox Avenue; houses the Arthur A. Schomburg collection of Negro literature.
3. Delano Village: located at 139th to 142nd Streets between Lenox and Fifth Avenues; Lenox Terrace: located at 132nd Street to 135th Street between Lenox and Fifth Avenues; Morningside Garden Cooperative Apartments: located between Amsterdam Avenue and Broadway, and between 123rd Street and La Salle Avenue; Bowery Savings Bank Apartments: located at 145th Street and St. Nicholas Avenue. All four are Harlem housing developments.
4. Senior Choirs: this means literally what it says. The adult choir singers in most Negro churches are called "The Senior Choir." Usher Boards: a selected number of people in nearly every Negro church who are responsible for the seating of the congregation. This group has other functions within the church, such as fund raising.
5. Statistics on economics from *The Uptown Chamber of Commerce*; on social factors from *Harlem–Upper Manhattan*, a survey by the Protestant Council, City of New York.
6. Smalls, Rockland Palace, Audubon Ballroom, Renaissance, Connie's: popular Harlem dance halls and night spots.
7. Jackie Wilson: singer and recording star. Apollo Theatre: 125th Street between Seventh and Eighth Avenues.
8. This brief sketch on Harlem, A Negro Community, is documented in the Gilbert Osofsky full-length study:

376

Harlem, the Making of A Ghetto: A History of Negro New York, 1900–1920 (Ph.D. dissertation, Columbia University, 1963) and *Race Riot, 1900: A study of Ethnic Violence*, Journal of Negro Education, Vol. XXIII No 1 (Winter 1963) pp 16–24. The word *Negro* has been capitalized where contemporary sources failed to do so.

9. Battle of Harlem Heights: this is a famous battle of the American Revolutionary War, fought on September 16, 1776. The battle is famous mainly because it was a victory for the American side, after a number of defeats. The area in which the battle was fought is now part of the Harlem community.

10. Dr. Alain Leroy Locke (1886–1954): Professor of Philosophy, Howard University, Washington; Phi Beta Kappa (honorary fraternity, membership in which is awarded for outstanding academic attainment) of Harvard University, Massachusetts; Rhodes Scholar at Oxford University, England; also studied at University of Berlin.

11. Dr. Sterling A. Brown: dean of black American poets; Professor of English, Howard University.

12. Dr. Charles S. Johnson (1893–1956): President of Fisk University, Nashville, Tenn. Sociologist, author, Director of Research and Investigation of Urban League and founder of the League's magazine *Opportunity, A Journal of Negro Life*. Held six honorary degrees from leading European and American universities.

13. *The New Negro: Thirty Years Afterward*, Howard University Press, 1955.

14. Dr. William Edward Burghardt Du Bois (1868–1963): social scientist, historian, Doctor of Philosophy, Doctor of Law, Doctor of Literature, Doctor of Historical Science, Doctor of the Humanities; one of the most brilliant academicians in the U.S.A. Founder of *The Crisis*, the NAACP journal, and its editor from 1910 to 1934. A founder of NAACP. His collected writings, *An ABC of Color*, published by Seven Seas Books, cover sixty years of his life as a leader and a fighter for the rights of his people. Awarded the Lenin Peace Prize in 1959. The founder of Pan-Africanism, Dr. Du Bois went to Ghana in 1961 at the invitation of then-President Dr. Kwame Nkrumah. Dr. Du Bois was then ninety-three years old. Until his death on August 27,

1963, Dr. Du Bois was Director of the Secretariat in charge of publishing the first Encyclopedia Africana, sponsored by the Ghana Academy of Sciences.

15. Paul Laurence Dunbar (1872–1906): first Negro-American poet to become nationally known; Frances E. W. Harper, poet and speaker; Martin R. Delaney, Harvard Medical School graduate, Major in the 104th Regiment at Charleston, first Negro field officer to serve in the Civil War; William Wells Brown, first Negro playwright and novelist, and author of an 1864 bestseller. These three were anti-slavery writers and poets in the pre-Civil War era. Charles W. Chestnutt (1858–1932): first Negro short-story writer.

16. William Monroe Trotter (1872–1934): founder and editor of the Boston Negro newspaper, *The Guardian*; co-initiator with Dr. Du Bois of the Niagara Movement, founded in 1905, to agitate for Negro rights.

17. James Weldon Johnson (1871–1938): noted Negro poet and author, and one of the founders of NAACP.

18. Langston Hughes (1902–1967): internationally famous Negro poet, author and playwright.

19. *Litany of Atlanta* is reprinted in *An ABC of Color*, pp 34–37.

20. Booker T. Washington (1856–1915): born in slavery, began work in Virginia salt mines at the age of nine; at fifteen attended the Hampton, Virginia, trades school; became a teacher in a school for rural Negroes in an Alabama village; raised funds to build and found Tuskegee Institute for industrial and agricultural studies in Alabama; founder of the National Negro Business Week; author of *Up From Slavery* (1900). For Du Bois on Booker T. Washington, see *An ABC of Color*, pp 83–84.

21. Caspar Holstein: real-estate operator, first Negro to become a millionaire.

22. James Vardaman, Mississippi; Benjamin R. Tillman, South Carolina: reactionary, anti-Negro U.S. Congressmen. Thomas Nelson Page, Thomas Dixon: white anti-Negro authors.

23. Frederick Douglass (1817–1895): one of the great men in American history; born a slave, taught himself to read and write; escaped to freedom when he was twenty-one years old and became one of the abolitionist leaders as spokesman and polemicist against slavery.

24. Dr. Carter G. Woodson (1875–1950): head of the Department of History, Howard University. First American scholar to devote himself entirely to the study of Africa. Founder of Negro History Week.

25. Locke, *The Negro in American Literature, New World Writing*, New American Library, p 19.

26. *Ibid.*

27. *Negro Caravan*, edited by Sterling A. Brown, Arthur P. Davis and Ulysses Lee, p 16.

28. Jean Toomer (1894–1967): poet and short-story writer. Countee Cullen (1903–1946): poet. Claude McKay (1889–1948): poet who studied agriculture at Tuskegee and Kansas State University.

29. *Fighting Words:* a periodical of the time.

30. *The Crisis:* publication of the NAACP; *Opportunity:* Urban League journal.

31. Prize-winning authors included Rudolph Fisher, Arthur Huff Fauset, John Mattheus, Eugene Gordon, Marita Bonner, Edwin Sheen, Jean Toomer.

32. William Wells Brown and Martin R. Delaney wrote as pleaders for a cause; Frances E. W. Harper wrote propaganda novels. Paul Laurence Dunbar's four novels were conventional; Charles Chestnutt wrote stories of social realism; the Du Bois novels called for a union of the darker nations and criticized weaknesses in the Negroes' struggles for freedom and America's handling of the race problem; James Weldon Johnson, Nella Larsen, Jessie Fauset, Walter White wrote "passing" novels, i.e. novels about Negroes who were able to pass as whites.

33. Notably: Rudolph Fisher (1897–1934); Eric Walrond; Countee Cullen; Claude McKay; and Wallace Thurman (1902–1934).

34. Professor E. Franklin Frazier (1894–1962): Head of the Department of Sociology, Howard University. Author of *The Negro Family* and *Black Bourgeoisie*. Researcher and adviser for UNESCO study on sociology.

35. Richard Wright (1908–1960): one of the ranking authors in the U.S.A., best known for his novel *Native Son*. Ralph Ellison: novelist.

36. *The New Negro, Thirty Years Afterward*, Howard University Press 1955, p 62.

37. For a listing of important and interesting books on the consciousness of Africa among Afro-Americans, see the Richard B. Moore article in *Freedomways*, Summer 1963 issue, pp 316, 317, 330.

38. Hubert H. Harrison: leader of the Liberty League of Afro-Americans.

39. Bethel AME Church: Bethel African Methodist Episcopal Church.

40. UNIA: Universal Negro Improvement Association.

41. Similar organizations are now flourishing in Ghana which has as its national flag a black star centered on a white and orange field.

42. Rockland Palace: center for protest meetings in Harlem, located at Eighth Avenue and 154th Street.

43. Mrs. Jean Blackwell Hutson: curator of the Schomburg Collection, New York Public Library, now on leave of absence to serve as Assistant Librarian at the University of Ghana.

44. Negro History Week, founded by Dr. Carter G. Woodson, is celebrated annually in February to include the birthdays of two who contributed so greatly to Negro freedom: Abraham Lincoln, born February 12, 1809 and Frederick Douglass, born February 14, 1817.

45. Florence Mills (1901–1927): musical comedy star who reached the height of her fame in the show *Blackbirds of 1926*.

46. Bert Williams (1878–1922): famous Negro stage star. Duke Ellington: famous Negro musician. Ethel Waters: actress and singer. Walter White (1896–1955): head of NAACP for many years.

47. Bricktop: internationally known night-club personality.

48. Moe Gale: white theatrical agent for many Negro theatre stars and orchestras. Lew Leslie: white theatrical entrepreneur who staged important Negro musical comedy and night-club shows. Harpers, Knopf: white book-publishing houses. *The Survey Graphic:* publication edited by Alain Locke. The Harmon Foundation: organization to further Negro art and literature.

49. Arna Bontemps: author and poet; Head Librarian at Fisk University, Nashville, Tennessee. His noted novel *Black Thunder* has recently been reissued as a paperback by Seven Seas Books. Nora Holt: official arbiter of Harlem social events. E. Simms Campbell: noted Negro cartoonist. A. Philip Randolph: Executive Board

member of the American Trade Union Organization A.F.L.-C.I.O. Roy Wilkins: Executive Secretary of NAACP. Alta Douglas (1899–1958): former arbiter of Harlem's social set and wife of Aaron Douglas, noted Negro painter. Josephine Baker: Negro-American artist who rose to fame in the musicals *Shuffle Along* and *Blackbirds* and who is a reigning favorite in Paris night clubs. Was awarded the *Légion d'Honneur* for her heroism in the French Resistance during the Nazi occupation of France.

50. For a partial listing of the nationalist movements of Harlem, see the E.U. Essien-Udom article in *Freedomways*, Summer 1963 issue, pp 335 and 336. A discussion of some of these groups is to be found in the John H. Clarke article in *Freedomways*, Fall issue 1961; in the Peter Kihss article, *New York Times*, March 1, 1961 pp 1 and 25 and Robert L. Teague, March 2, 1961 pp 1 and 17; also, E.U. Essien-Udom's *Black Nationalism: A Search for an Identity in America*, University of Chicago Press, 1962.

51. Two books which bring out the role of the Negro in American history are *Black Thunder* by Arna Bontemps, and *And Why Not Every Man?* edited by Dr. Herbert Aptheker—the first being historical fiction and the second historical nonfiction.

52. Elijah Muhammad: head of the Black Muslims.

53. Grays: Harlem slang to describe white people.

54. Root man: the Harlem "witch doctor" and his merchandise.

55. Jesse Owens. First Negro-American sprinter to win an Olympic championship.

56. Shorty: "to latch on to a shorty" is Harlem slang for ordering a half-pint drink of whisky or gin.

57. Bojangles: Bill Robinson (1878–1949), the world-famous Negro dancer. Joe Louis: world heavyweight boxing champion. The Black Eagle: Herbert Fauntleroy Julian, American aviator who fought in Ethiopia. Judge Hubert Delaney: first Negro to become a judge in New York City. Dr. Louis Wright: famous Negro brain surgeon. The Mills Brothers: popular singing quartet. Lester Granger: head of the National Urban League. "Pig Meat" Markham: popular Negro comedian. Broadway Rose: a questionable Harlem character.

58. Conking: application of hot iron to straighten hair.

59. John Hammond: white millionaire who furthered the careers of Harlem musicians and entertainers. Member of the Board of Directors, NAACP. Arthur Winston: white newspaper columnist, authority on skiing. Baron Timmie Rosencranz: Danish baron, international authority on Jazz and a Harlem resident.

60. Hoods: gangsters.

61. Ella Fitzgerald: singing star of radio, television, night clubs; Chic Webb: noted band leader.

62. Roxy and Palace: de luxe white film theatres of the thirties in mid-Manhattan. Alhambra and Regent: Harlem neighborhood film theatres.

63. Pecks: a slang term for Southern whites who came to Harlem from the South.

64. Washington Heights: Upper Manhattan white middle-class neighborhood.

65. Benjamin J. Davis: Negro-American lawyer, former New York City Councilman and noted Communist leader, who died on August 22, 1964.

66. Theresa Hotel: most famous hotel in Harlem, located at 125th Street and Seventh Avenue, where Fidel Castro stayed when he came to New York with the Cuban delegation to the UN after being refused accommodations by the hotels in "white" Manhattan.

67. On the Lower East Side of New York City.

68. The *New York Herald Tribune, The New York Times*, and the *World Telegram and Sun* sought to maintain objective balanced reporting and sometimes printed editorials supporting MFY to answer particularly strident attacks in some of the other newspapers.

SECTION II

69. Barefoot Prophet: famous Harlem character of the thirties. He preached a one-man religion of a kind and attempted to predict the future of the Negro race. He wore no shoes in winter or summer. His long white robes and bushy white hair made him a colorful figure of his day.

70. Kid Chocolate: Cuban-born boxer who moved to Harlem, became champion in his class, and who was a Harlem favorite.

71. Williams and Walker: famous song and dance duo. After the death of George Walker in 1909, Bert

Williams became the first Negro to be starred on
Broadway.

72. Gertrude Jeanette: writer. Esther Rolle: actress, appeared in the 1964 play *The Blacks*. Lynn Hamilton:
actress, appeared in 1963 in Langston Hughes' play
Tambourines to Glory. Louis Gosset: young Negro
actor, most noted for his role in the play *Take a
Giant Step*. Rick Ferrell: Negro actor. Irving Burgie:
Negro song writer and playwright. He wrote the
famous song, "Island in the Sun" for the American
motion picture of the same name.

73. Samuel Allen: Negro poet and writer, most noted for
his interpretation of the concept of "Negritude," a
kind of intellectual black nationalism.

74. Murdock: early American playwright (1795), who
wrote *The Triumph of Love*, one of the first American
plays involving Negro characters.

75. Phoebe Fraunces: the daughter of Samuel Fraunces,
a Negro tavern owner. George Washington often
dined at Fraunces Tavern. This tavern is still in existence in the Wall Street section of Manhattan. Phoebe
Fraunces is reported to have saved the life of George
Washington by calling attention to the fact that the
British were trying to poison him.

76. James Hewlett: was active in the theatre around 1821.
He founded the Africa Company of Negro Actors.
Ira Aldridge made his American debut with this com-
pany.

77. Ira Aldridge (1807–1867): free-born Negro who became a famous Shakespearean actor in the European
theatres.

78. Sam T. Jack, Dion Boucicault, Will Marion Cook,
Paul Laurence Dunbar, Williams and Walker, Ernest
Hogan, Alex Rogers, Jesse Shipp, S. H. Dudley, J.
Rosamond Johnson were some of the producers, play-
wrights, musicians, actors and managers who brought
about the change in the Negro theatre.

79. Mrs. Fiske, Sarah Bernhardt: Minnie Maddern Fiske
(1865–1932), American; Sarah Bernhardt (1845–
1923), French, the two most famous actresses of
their time.

80. Charles Gilpin (1878–1930): dramatic actor selected
by the Drama League of New York as one of the ten
persons who had done the most during 1920 to ad-

vance the art of the American theatre. Mr. Gilpin
was excluded from the dinner at which the awards
were made because he was Negro.

81. *Shuffle Along, Goat Alley* (1921); *Strut Miss Lizzie,
plantation Revue* (1922); *How Come?, The Chip-
woman's Fortune* (1923); *Chocolate Dandies, Dixie
to Broadway* (1924); *Topsy and Eva,* Paul Robeson
in a revival of *The Emperor Jones* (1925)—all became major downtown offerings during the 1920's. The
first Negro-written Broadway drama also appeared in
1925, Garland Anderson's *Appearances.* Other Broadway successes with a Negro, or part Negro theme,
were *Lucky Sambo, My Magnolias, Deep River, In
Abraham's Bosom, Show Boat* and Wallace Thurman's
Harlem. Porgy and *The Green Pastures* were later
productions.

82. *Hot Rhythm, Brown Buddies, Lew Leslie's Blackbirds,
Sweet Chariot, Fast and Furious, Swinging the Blues,
The House of Connelly, Sugar Hill, Savage Rhythm,
Never No More, Bloodstream, Black Souls, Black-
berries of 1932* were among them.

83. Rose McClendon (1895–1936): noted Negro dramatic
actress. Dick Campbell: theatre producer, director
and an important figure in the Harlem Negro theatre.

84. Harold Jackman (1903–1961): celebrated Harlem
figure, of the theatre in particular.

85. The Federal Theatre: the theatre of the Works Progress Administration (the WPA), the government-
financed project during Franklin Delano Roosevelt's
New Deal which gave work to Americans in the
theatre, arts, music, dance as well as in industry and
farming. While it lasted, it produced a national theatre.

86. Orson Welles: famous white actor-playwright-director-
producer. John Houseman: theatre director and associate of Orson Welles in Harlem's Lafayette Theatre.

87. Canada Lee (1907–1952): noted Negro dramatic
actor.

88. Frank Silvera: Negro actor who has been successful
in non-Negro roles on Broadway and in Hollywood.

89. *On Striver's Row* and *Walk Hard* by Abraham Hill;
Natural Man by Theodore Brown; *Garden of Time* by
Owen Dodson were popular successes of the Ameri-
can Negro Theatre.

90. Plays of the time included *Deep Are the Roots, Jeb,*

Strange Fruit, On Whitman Avenue, St. Louis Woman, Carib Song, Lysistrata, Mr. Pebbles and Mr. Hooker, Bal Negre, Beggar's Holiday, Finian's Rainbow, Street Scene, Our Lan' and *Let My People Free.*

91. Ed Cambridge: one of the few Negro directors of plays.

92. Harold Holifield's *Cow in the Apartment* and *J. Toth; The Bancroft Dynasty* by Loften Mitchell and *The Cellar*; Gertrude Jeanette's *This Way Forward* and *Bolt from the Blue*; Julian Mayfield's *The Other Foot*; Ossie Davis' *Alice in Wonder*; Alice Childress' *Just a Little Simple.*

93. This survey is compiled from two articles which Mr. Mitchell prepared for European publications—the *Enciclopedia dello Spettacolo* in Rome, and the *Oxford Companion to the Theatre*, published in London.

94. Maxwell Glanville: Negro actor and director. Jay Brooks: Negro actor and director. Both Glanville and Brooks are founders of small theatre groups in Harlem.

95. D. W. Griffith (1880–1948): David Wark Griffith was born in the South, the son of a Confederate Army officer. Griffith never rid himself of his anti-Negro prejudice.

96. The exception is Lorraine Hansberry who adapted her prize play *Raisin in the Sun*, to the screen.

97. Speech delivered at a Rally to Abolish the House Un-American Activities Committee, held at Manhattan Center, New York.

98. Dr. Otto Nathan: friend of the late Dr. Albert Einstein and curator of Dr. Einstein's private papers. He is an official in the Committee to Abolish the House Un-American Activities Committee.

99. House rent parties: a private party where everyone pays for what he eats and drinks in order that the host may raise sufficient money to pay his rent.

100. "Garvin Bushell and New York Jazz in the 1920's" by Nat Hentoff. *Jazz Review*, February 1959.

101. "Conversations with James P. Johnson" by Tom Davin, *Jazz Review*, June 1959.

102. "It's Really A Twisting World" by Duke Ellington, in an interview with Stanley Dance, *Jazz*, October 1962.

103. John B. "Dizzy" Gillespie: trumpet player and com-

poser; exponent of the "cool" school of jazz. Charles Christopher Parker, Jr. (Charlie the Bird Parker) was born June 29, 1920 in Kansas City, Kansas, and died March 12, 1955 in New York City. Alto and Tenor Saxophone: the Messiah of "cool" jazz. The famous "Birdland," a downtown dance hall, often referred to as the Carnegie Hall of Jazz and center of the jazz movement, was named for Charlie Parker. He is the composer of "Now's the Time," "Yardbird Suite," "Confirmation," "Relaxing at Camarillo," and others. Thelonius Monk: one of the innovators of modern jazz, a pianist-composer. Among his compositions are "Round Midnight," "Blue Monk," "Well, You Needn't," "In Walked Bud," and "Ruby, My Dear." Earl Bud Powell: Jazz pianist, one of the greats of jazz. Lester Willis "Prez" Young (1909–1959): Tenor Saxophone; innovator of "cool" jazz; affectionately called "Prez" by jazz musicians the world over. The name was given him by Billie Holiday. Kenneth Spearman Clarke (Kenny Clarke): drummer; living in Paris since 1956.

104. "The Ellington Style, Its Origins and Early Development" by Gunther Schuller, *Jazz*, edited by Nat Hentoff and Albert McCarthy.

105. *Ibid.*

106. *New Statesman*, article by Francis Newton, October 11, 1958.

107. Bessie Smith (1894–1937): famous blues singer who died in Clarksdale, Mississippi, of injuries sustained in an automobile accident after being refused emergency treatment by a white hospital because she was Negro.

108. "All Too Soon" by Stanley Dance, article in *Jazz Review*, December 1958.

109. Cutting session: term used for a session where the big achievement was to better or "cut" all the other players.

110. "Jelly Roll Morton in New York" by Danny Barker, *Jazz Review*, May 1959.

111. "Little Jazz—The Early Days" by George Hoeffer, *Down Beat*, January 31, 1963.

112. "Ravel" by Vladimir Jankelevitch.

113. "Comments on Classics" by Donal J. Henehan, *Down Beat*, January 17, 1963.

114. *Jazz Review*, 1959.
115. *Freedomways*, Summer, 1963.
116. Madison Avenue: the term refers to the big publicity, propaganda, advertising and promotional concerns which further big business—most of these concerns have their offices on Madison Avenue in the Fifties of Manhattan.
117. Thomas Wolfe (1900–1938): American novelist.
118. *Purlie Victorious:* The title of Ossie Davis' highly successful play.
119. André Gide (1869–1951): French novelist, essayist, critic. Marcel Proust (1871–1922): French novelist.
120. Ole Miss fiasco and Monroe frame-up: "Ole Miss" fiasco refers to the way things are in the State of Mississippi, particularly as they pertain to the Negro. Monroe frame-up refers to the false charge of kidnapping made against Robert Williams, Mae Mallory and three other Negroes who were engaged in a civil rights fight in Monroe, North Carolina. Williams fled to Cuba with his family.
121. Sir Roy Welensky: former Prime Minister of the now-defunct Central African Federation. Henrik Verwoerd: Prime Minister of the Republic of South Africa, who was assassinated in 1966 by a white opponent of his *apartheid* policies.
122. Harriet Beecher Stowe (1811–1896): author of *Uncle Tom's Cabin.*
123. The James Baldwin article is from an extemporaneous talk which he delivered on October 16, 1963 to some 200 New York City schoolteachers who were taking a special in-service course on "The Negro: His Role in the Culture and Life of the United States."
124. Mr. Charlie and Miss Ann: Negro terms for white male and female bosses.

SECTION III

125. Bread: colloquialism for money, which originated in Harlem.
126. Rev. A. D. King: the brother of Martin Luther King.
127. Bedford-Stuyvesant: New York City area located in the borough of Brooklyn. It is the second largest Negro community in America with a population of about 400,000.

128. The *Fire Next Time* by James Baldwin: New York, Dial Press, 1963.

129. "Creaming" is a familar process resulting from most social policies ostensibly designed to assist the poor. The practice serves to maintain the status quo by co-opting potential or actual leaders, leaving most of the class untouched but less of a threat and perhaps even more miserable than before.

130. Four elementary schools and one intermediate school. P.S. 133, 68, 39 and 24, and Arthur A. Schomburg School, Intermediate School, "the windowless wonder."

131. Americans are almost incapable of seeing themselves as imperialists. Laos, Cambodia and Viet Nam notwithstanding, upper-middle and lower-class whites would be offended by the term "colonial" because they have never considered themselves privileged by virtue of skin color. One needs to question only one of those privileges in employment, housing or education to find out how precious that special status is.

132. The rhetoric of the rebellion suggested at least the third level, but the actions of rebels would eventually speak louder than the hot, very black words.

133. Governing Board is the official designation for "local" Board of Education within a Demonstration District.

134. Findings such as these cast doubt on professional educators' estimates of the educability of lower-class youngsters. Doubt about their estimates of black and Spanish-speaking children is already widespread, and these findings suggest that where there is smoke there may indeed be fire.

135. Divide and rule is still an important imperialist strategy, no matter what region or in what era.

136. It is unfortunate that this writer's grasp of English does not permit use of a word other than "lay" to describe the indigenous community leadership. The term "lay" does not adequately describe these ingenious indigenous leaders, nor does it carry the proper warning to their future victims. Perhaps a better term for this group would be "non-credentialed."

137. "Poverticians"—the name given to a group of technically unskilled persons who come to lead so many poverty efforts. They exist because of their fabulous but engaging incompetence, coupled with their color-

ful slogans and supported by an abundance of sharply developed survival skills.

138. See Bennett, Lerone, *The Black Establishment in Negro Mood*, pp 25–45, especially p 37.

139. *Black John Henry*, by Ricardo Weeks: John Henry is the legendary giant in Negro folklore and spiritual, whose strength and courage are equal to all tasks. In this poem the poet takes John Henry to Harlem.

140. *Sing Me A New Song*, by John Henrik Clarke: Nat Turner, Negro slave who led a revolt for freedom in 1831; Denmark Vesey, Negro leader of the slave revolt of 1822.

141. *An Old Woman Remembers*, by Sterling A. Brown: this poem refers to the 1906 Atlanta riots when the whites of that city murdered the black population until Negro resistance stopped white mob violence.

Selected Titles *from A&B Books*

Blackmen say Goodbye to Misery	10.00
Education of the Negro	9.95
Heal Thyself	9.95
Heal Thyself Cookbook	9.95
Vaccines are Dangerous	9.95
Columbus and the African Holocaust	10.00
Columbus Conspiracy	11.95
Dawn Voyage	11.95
Aids the End of Civilization	9.95
Gospel of Barnabas	8.95
African Discovery of America	10.00
Gerald Massey's Lectures	9.95
Historical Jesus and the Mythical Christ	9.95
First Council of Nice	9.95
Arab Invasion of Egypt	14.95
Anacalypsis (set)	40.00
Anacalypsis Vol. 1	25.00
Anacalypsis Vol. 11	20.00
Documents of West Indian History	14.95
History of the People of Trinidad & Tobago	14.95
The Negro in the Caribbean	11.95
British Historian & The West Indies	11.95
Lost Books of the Bible	9.95

Mail to A&B BOOKS 149 LAWRENCE STREET NEW YORK 11201
TEL: (718) 596-3389 · FAX (718) 596-0968
$ 2.00 first book $ 1.00 each additional book. NY & NJ residents add sales tax.
Please find enclosed check/money order for $_____
Name:_____
Address:_____
City:_____ ST_____ Zip_____
Card Type:_____
Card Number:_____ Exp____/____

We accept *VISA MASTERCARD AMERICAN EXPRESS & DISCOVER*